Religious Pluralism in America

WILLIAM R. HUTCHISON

Religious
The Contentious

Pluralism
History of a

in America
Founding Ideal

Yale University Press/New Haven and London

Published with assistance from the Olaus Petri Foundation, Uppsala University, Sweden.

Designed by Nancy Ovedovitz and set in Quadraat type by Tseng Information Systems. Printed in the United States of America by Sheridan Books, Ann Arbor, Michigan.

The Library of Congress has catalogued the hardcover edition as follows:
Hutchison, William R.
Religious pluralism in America : the contentious history of a founding ideal / William R. Hutchison.
   p. cm.
Includes bibliographical references and index.
ISBN 0-300-09813-8 (cloth : alk. paper)
1. United States—Religion.   2. Religious pluralism—United States—History.
I. Title.
BL2525 .H88   2003
291.1′72′0973—dc21   2002151893

A catalogue record for this book is available from the British Library.

The paper in this book meets the guidelines for permanence and durability of the Committee on Production Guidelines for Book Longevity of the Council on Library Resources.

ISBN 0-300-10516-9 (pbk. : alk. paper)

10 9 8 7 6 5 4 3 2

To my students,
whose questions, challenges, and ideas
have shaped this book more than they know

Contents

Preface

This book is a revised version of the fourteen Olaus Petri lectures that I delivered in spring 1996 at Uppsala University in Sweden. Those lectures, in turn, had grown out of Harvard undergraduate and graduate courses that I had been developing over several decades.

Although the lectures in Uppsala were open to the public, most members of the audience were students who, like those enrolled in the earlier courses at Harvard, were concurrently reading and discussing original sources. Both students and other attendees were, in addition, exposed in the lectures themselves to the kinds of evidence and illustration that are best conveyed with the help of slide projectors and tape players. The process of making the lectures into a book has therefore involved a fair amount of "translation"—more than I had anticipated, hence the time lag between lectures and book—from those immediate ways of conveying ideas and moods to the more conventional ones represented here.

I doubt whether any prose, however eloquent or unprosaic, could compete with the nineteenth-century lantern slides for "Ten Nights in a Barroom"; or with recorded utterances of Dwight Moody or James Baldwin; or with the massed voices of several thousand Baptists belting out their confidence that "we're marching upward to Zion." But I thought it best to incorporate as much as possible from the auditory and visual materials—and, of course, from the sources—and also to maintain, stylistically, some of the relative informality of lectures that were in part extemporaneous.

My wife and I were hosted magnificently in this, our second extended stay in Uppsala, and incurred debts to many colleagues in the Theological Institute and the American Studies and other departments; several of these friends deserve special notice and thanks. The late Carl F. Hallencreutz, the dean of the institute, issued the invitation; and his successor, Carl Reinhold Bråkenhielm, managed the unusually fine academic and living arrangements. Professor Alf Tergel and other members of the senior faculty led weekly discussion sections for the undergraduates who signed on for the lectures, and these intrepid colleagues aided in numerous other ways. The doctoral students who met regularly with me provided insights, and valuable elements of comparative perspective, that I know have enriched what I am able to offer in this written version.

My largest indebtedness, because it was built up over the entire 1985–95 decade, is to the Lilly Endowment, which gave generous support—before as well as during those years—to the Harvard program on Religion and American Culture. When this program was first discussed, the main point of the enterprise was to gain historical perspective on what has been—and was especially at that time—widely perceived as a decline in the condition of "mainline Protestantism." From the beginning, however, the study of religious and cultural diversities in American history was part of our assignment. The Endowment and its vice president for religion, the historian Robert W. Lynn, recognized that only about half of our doctoral students in American religious history, whether enrolled in religion, American civilization, or some other degree program, were focused on mainline Protestantism. For that and other good reasons we were given every encouragement to foster and support the work of those whose principal concerns lay elsewhere. And indeed, as it turned out, thirteen of the twenty-seven appointees to our Lilly Research Groups produced studies of such phenomena as Asian religions in America, Native and African Americans, the Baha'i Faith, pentecostalism, and the World's Parliament of Religions—though all of these projects, thanks in part to the kinds of questions raised in the Lilly program, also explored interactions with the white Protestant establishment.

Similarly, the eight conferences that the Endowment enabled us to stage, and the books and other publications that grew out of them (for example, *Between the Times* in 1989 and *Many Are Chosen* in 1994), dealt ex-

tensively with non-Protestant groups and with secular cultural developments. The same was true of the subproject on "lived religion" that, under
the inspiration and guidance of my colleague David Hall, became an important part of our program and that flowered in Hall's edited volume
Lived Religion in America (1997).

My courses, and thus this book, were greatly informed and enriched by
the findings of the Lilly Fellows, but also by the research of others who
participated in the Lilly conferences and seminars. Such contributions,
whether or not I have been able to take proper advantage of them, have
been quite literally incalculable. The same can be said of the Endowment's
aid and support, particularly as provided steadily and tirelessly by Craig
Dykstra, who succeeded Robert Lynn in 1989.

A large number of graduate assistants, many more than I can list here,
have contributed materially to this project; but several deserve special
mention. Richard Seager not only taught and did research for me; he ran
conferences and programs, and he established a collection of more than
two hundred slides to which Maria Erling and Margaret Gillespie later
added. I drew upon these visual resources not only for my Harvard and
Uppsala courses but also for more limited presentations in various parts
of the world. As the lectures gradually became a book, I had help from
Andrew H. Walsh, Maria Erling, Chris Coble, Michael Kress, Amy Moul-
ton, Curtis Evans, Heather Curtis, Chris White, and Kelly Meader.

Colleagues at Harvard and in the historical profession have offered
valuable criticisms. Ann Braude, John Demos, David Hollinger, and the
anonymous readers for several publishers provided helpful reactions to
an early, quite lengthy, prospectus for this book. Philip Barlow, Jonathan
Sarna, and Richard Seager offered suggestions about sections that touch
upon their areas of special competence. Mark Chaves, Mark Noll, Stephen
Prothero, Thomas Tweed, and Grant Wacker read and critiqued the entire
manuscript. My closest colleague, Virginia Hutchison, did the same, and
also deserves special thanks for putting up with the several years of my
preoccupation with this project.

Finally, a word on a very different matter: annotations. In this book I
have used endnotes for source references and other bibliographic information. Any substantive note—and I have tried to keep these to a minimum—appears at the bottom of the appropriate page.

Introduction: Religious Pluralism as a Work in Progress

The terms *diversity* and *pluralism*, as applied to religion and to American society generally, have surged in prominence and common usage over the past several decades. Both terms come into play when we consider Asian religions and others that are relatively new to the American scene, or when we note the increased visibility of black, pentecostal, and other elements in long-established American faiths. *Pluralism*, understood as the acceptance and encouragement of diversity, is a fighting word for participants in contemporary culture wars, and a key concept for those who write about them. Social critics, mainly but not exclusively conservative, worry about a moral pluralism that they think signals a dangerous loss of consensus in the society. And some analysts of American culture, including a few secular ones, have been troubled by the apparent decline of mainline religious institutions that, whatever their defects, are seen as onetime vehicles of social as well as moral cohesion.

Religious historians, in the midst of all this, have worked conscientiously, often feverishly, to chronicle diversities that we and our predecessors ignored or slighted. And those efforts have not merely succeeded; in some respects they have succeeded too well. Since about the mid-1980s we have been exquisitely aware of the new difficulties that face anyone trying to teach or write in broad terms about "American religious history." Is there such a thing?—or only a great agglomeration of subcultural histories? Given the now-recognized integrity of these subcultures, should we stop trying to tell an overall story? If we do try to retell this larger story, can we hope to "fit it all in" and still fashion coherent interpretations—as opposed to mere factual recitations—concerning the role religion has played in American development?

As the historian Stephen Stein pointed out several years ago, "the time-honored concepts [that once provided coherence] are inadequate for the task at hand."[1] Stein at that point was putting it mildly; the most prominent traditional frameworks have gone the way of the dinosaurs. A Protestant triumphalism that, overtly or otherwise, structured a great many accounts before the middle of the twentieth century has vanished (although some believe it has not vanished without a trace). An equally venerable Whig triumphalism—the vision of religious freedom, like the Common Law, broadening down inexorably from precedent to precedent—may be somewhat more open to rehabilitation, but at the least needs what polite historians like to call complication.[2] Other organizing principles—for example, the powerful one that linked religious history to the story of the American frontier experience—still offer insight yet do not suffice.

Some have reacted to this situation by suggesting we try to get along without broad interpretations of any kind for American religious history.[3] But that cure could be worse than the disease. For one thing, historical writings and academic courses that pride themselves on avoiding explicit propositions about American religion are exceedingly likely to harbor implicit ones. For another, as the philosopher William James urged repeatedly, we need organizing propositions, however tentative, if we are to get around intellectually in a messy world of particulars.

In addition, although focused on-the-ground historical work is as important as ever, that does not mean it is more dangerous to pursue general ideas about American religion than to offer interpretations of, say, southern pentecostalism or the religious history of Omaha. If the first of these is a mere construct (there being many American religions), so are the others (there being a number of ways of defining the South, or pentecostalism, or, indeed, Omaha). The main difference, so far as the perils of generalizing are concerned, may well be that it is somewhat easier for historians and their readers to convince themselves that conceptions of the local or the very specific are not historical constructs.

Surely, in line with Mrs. Loman's oft-repeated warning, attention must be paid, extensively, to stories that differ from that of the white Protestant subculture; and these alternative stories must be accorded their own integrity, above all by those of us who fancy ourselves as card-carrying pluralists.* But I believe that the cautious redefining of an overall American experience must proceed, side-by-side with our efforts to define and describe group experiences (including that of an enormously dominant and influential Protestant establishment).† Having cleaned up our act, having also passed through a necessary stage of "add-on" revisionism in which we have devoted separate lectures and chapters to women, minorities,

---

* More than thirty years ago, in a panel on "Questions Catholic Historians Should Be Asking," I suggested that "it is time to urge scholars of Catholicism, along with others whose specialties lie outside the putative mainstream of American religious development, to reinterpret the general history." I added that historians of these traditions need not wait until the houses of Catholic and black and other history writing are in better order. "Did white Anglo-Saxon Protestant historians show any similar reticence about explaining—to God and the rest of us—what America and American religion are all about?" Catholic and other historians should not hesitate about "trying to record what the history of our religion and culture . . . might look like were we to remove those cultural eyeglasses whose prescription—we are now finally realizing—needs so badly to be rewritten" (Catholic Historical Society paper, December 1970; unpublished). Although appeals of that sort are, in my view, still in order, much has happened in recent decades to rewrite the prescription. Studies of "outsiders" have proliferated—indeed, as Martin Marty and his associates discovered, have greatly outnumbered works on the Protestant majority (Marty, "American Religious History in the Eighties," 336–37). And a number of collaborative works have at least launched the project of reinterpreting the overall story from previously neglected vantage points (e.g., Tweed, Retelling; Sarna, Minority Faiths; Hutchison, Between the Times, part IV).

† Another solution to the problem of fitting it all in, one that comes out of justified resentment against past overemphasis on a "mainline Protestant" story, is to leave out most of that story. This kind of reapportionment has been not merely proposed; it has been rather frequently attempted, as surveys of recent course syllabi will confirm. (For what is, collectively, a stunning testimony to this, see the "American Religion Course Outlines" submitted during the 1990s by participants in the Indiana-Purdue Young Scholars Program. Available online at <http://www.iupui.edu/it/raac/home.html>.) The effects of carrying things to this extreme are dubious not just for the purposes of interpretation but equally for those of elementary coverage. In writing about past American politics, one might minimize attention to Federalists, Democrats, and other electorally and culturally dominant political parties, but the result would have to be called a history of, say, third parties in America. Similarly, economic histories that might try to ignore Standard Oil, United Fruit, and other common targets of resentment could scarcely bill themselves as histories of business in America.

and other formerly neglected players, we still need, in Stein's phrasing, "new models for understanding" the overall drama of American religious development.[4]

Quite obviously, we can't fit it all in, but then we never could, even when "all" was mostly a history of white Protestant male experience. And I do think we can reframe the story in ways that will do more justice to a complicated past and offer better historical purchase on dilemmas of the present.

My own attempt at reframing, which I do not propose as the only or even the best way, should be understood, first of all, as focusing on religious diversities. It therefore slights, at least to some extent, differences of race, class, and gender. Although it by no means ignores these and other forms of diversity, it does not—to resort to a current coinage—foreground them. Secondly, my analysis needs to be understood as proceeding from a standard linguistic distinction that is, however, often obscured in everyday speech: the distinction between a fact or condition called diversity and an ideal or impulse for which the best term is pluralism.* Although the meanings of the two terms do overlap, the difference between them goes to the heart of my argument.

In brief, the argument is that whereas diversity happened to American religion in the first half of the nineteenth century, pluralism of the kind people now discuss did not arrive until the second half of the twentieth. I believe that Americans and their public policy are only now coming to terms, however grudgingly or opportunistically, with a radical diversifica-

---

*Webster's Third International is typical in defining pluralism not as diversity itself but as one of the various things people do and think in response to diversity. Thus pluralism signifies "(1) a state of society in which members of diverse ethnic, racial, religious, or social groups maintain an autonomous participation in and development of their traditional culture or special interest within the confines of a common civilization; [and] (2) a concept, doctrine, or policy advocating this state."

Another word of clarification: Pluralism was not coined for this particular usage until the 1920s. Its fundamental meaning—the welcoming or acceptance of diversity—has been around much longer. As in the case of dozens of other terms, such as imperialism (coined in the 1850s) or liberalism (1820s) or racism (1930s), it has been common to use the modern term for earlier manifestations of what it signifies. I am following that practice.

tion that came crashing in upon the young nation almost at the moment of its birth.

These chapters can therefore be seen as, among other things, ruminations on the late Sydney Ahlstrom's enigmatic remark, in the historical text he published in 1972, that the condition we call pluralism had not even existed through most of the national history. With the spirit of 1960s enthusiasm full upon him, Ahlstrom saw a widespread acceptance of diversity emerging at last, in his own time, as "minorities" gained power and their religions gained recognition. But he thought that up to then, despite an embedded mythology to the contrary, and despite the promises offered in America's founding documents, pluralism had at most been "struggling to be born."[5] This was heresy, even if many others by that time—and not just radical others—had been saying much the same thing.

Heresy or not, what can these analysts have meant by such a negative gloss on the traditional success story? Quite obviously, many diversified societies, throughout history, have either lacked pluralist ideals entirely, or have trumpeted such ideals and failed to make good on them. But surely the United States, the champion of religious freedom and scorner of establishments, was famously not that kind of society.

Like most mythologies, national or otherwise, this one was not all wrong. What Ahlstrom intended in his passing remark, and what I, in agreement, have tried to spell out in this book, is not a denial that early Americans did better than most others, past or contemporaneous, in their responses to religious and cultural diversity. They did do better. The nineteenth century in western Europe was an era of gradual decline for formal religious establishments, and of slowly increasing levels of protection for minority faiths. Americans, faced with greater diversities of all kinds than most European or New World societies, but also less trammeled by constitutional constraints, were not entirely deluded in believing that they had moved farther and faster than, say, Englishmen or Germans or Canadians in the direction of full religious freedom.[6]

The historian should be able to deal sympathetically, and I think admiringly, with the affirming responses to diversity that early Americans fought and sometimes died for. Yet neither the legal toleration confirmed in the revolutionary period, nor the deeper social tolerance that made progress in the nineteenth century, nor even the moves toward inclusiveness that advanced markedly after about 1880 fulfilled what many in mid-twentieth-century America thought were the true implications of the nation's original commitments. For good or ill, the definition of what it means to honor diversity had by then expanded well beyond what it had been in 1800. The meaning of such widely accepted concepts as religious freedom and mutual respect had indeed broadened down from one era to the next.

Although one can identify a number of stages, major and minor, in this quietly persistent process of redefinition, three seem especially evident. The first we can call pluralism as toleration; the second, pluralism as inclusion; the third, pluralism as participation.

Through much of the nineteenth century, a positive response to diversity entailed legal toleration and social tolerance—either of which could sometimes be little more than an absence of persecution. According to this definition of acceptance, a deviant person or group should be accorded the right to exist and even to thrive, but in general to do so only as an outsider to the dominant religion and culture.

By the end of the century, increasing numbers of Americans—"insiders" as well as "outsiders"—were viewing that limited kind of acceptance as inadequate, both morally and practically. Yet the resulting "inclusionist" ideology, which clearly was a move forward in any pluralist perspective, rarely granted to the newly included an equal or proportional right to share in the exercise of cultural authority. To put the point more graphically: even the enlightened notion of inclusion, when it was realized at all, could mean that the newly included sat at the back of the bus—and most of the time it did mean that.

Partly for that reason, some social commentators were attempting as early as the opening decades of the twentieth century to demystify and discredit the much touted "melting pot" ideal. They questioned not only whether the melting pot actually worked but also whether it deserved to work. Because it implied the extinction of group identities and the radical reshaping of individual ones, they feared that it operated to suppress differences far more than to respect and utilize them. Critics therefore saw the melting pot version of inclusiveness as an inadequate realization of pluralism even according to standards set by late-eighteenth-century commitments to equality.

But what might come closer to meeting those standards? The emerging answer, which arose as much from day-to-day social experience as from social theory or judicial decisions, emphasized a right of participation. Pluralism as participation implied a mandate for individuals and groups (including, quite importantly, ethnic and racial groups) to share responsibility for the forming and implementing of the society's agenda.

The more blistering indictments of the American mainstream's seeming inability, under any definition, to live up to its stated pluralist ideals tend to turn a hallowed American success story into the chronicling of a persistent American failure. Whether or not we embrace that degree of negativism, it seems in order to ask why early Americans, in particular, did not do a better job of responding to diversity. Secondly, why did we think we had done so well?

One answer to the first question has already been hinted: no society, past or present, has responded to sudden diversification with a rapid or full embrace of newcomers, or with strong enthusiasm for inhabitants of any kind who propose markedly new ideas and social plans. So if American society experienced a century or more of cultural lag—of widespread reluctance to accept "different" people and ideas—after the huge immigrations and territorial acquisitions of the early nineteenth century, such a lag was scarcely exceptional; it was, rather, one more sad example of a too-common propensity in human societies.

Early-nineteenth-century Americans, like people in other times and places, found demographic and social change traumatic not only because of its rapidity but also because of their determination to retain the comforts of a real or imagined past. It was true that, compared with most other civilizations, of whatever period, the new American nation was not long on either history or tradition. Still, the dominant European component in this society had had two centuries in which to develop and imprint a common culture. Despite significant internal differences, this culture had been, as nearly as one can estimate from this distance, well over 95 percent Protestant Christian. Within that Protestant frame it had been overwhelmingly Calvinist and English-speaking.

The resulting two-century head start had helped engender two kinds of resistance to any full-bodied acceptance of diversity. One was an extreme kind—exhibited, for example, in anti-Catholic, anti-immigrant "nativism"—that is fairly well known and has been quite fully chronicled. The other was a milder but highly effective form of resistance that was grounded more in a unitive impulse than in a xenophobic one.

This second form of resistance, the concern for unity and social coherence, produced in the early republic a powerful counterforce that clearly was in tension with the pluralist impulse, yet did not react to new diversities with violence or scurrilous pamphlets or send-'em-back extremism. As embodied, especially, in America's unofficial Protestant establishment, this unitive ideology responded to diversity with less direct forms of resistance, with some genuine concessions, and with promises to "outsiders" that were conditioned on successful assimilation—all of this premised on at least a few plausible assumptions about what it takes to hold a society together. Americans fell short as pluralists mostly because of a desperate, yet perhaps understandable, desire to re-create the considerable homogeneity of the long colonial era.*

The other question is why Americans, then or later, thought they had done so well in dealing with diversities. My answer, not a startling one, is that the mills of ideological and definitional change do grind slowly and that, consequently, the Americans and America watchers of any given era could easily, employing time-honored definitions, refer to the United States as the showcase for religious pluralism.

Thus in the mid-nineteenth century, although some by then were recognizing toleration as an inadequate response to diversity, the vast majority of participants and observers remained perfectly content with the older standard. And Americans could, by that older standard, plausibly advertise their society as the most tolerant in the Western world (which was the only world they knew). Similarly, in a somewhat later era Americans could

---

* Some historians now feel that, if left unexplained, the conventional use of terms like *colonial era* or *colonial history* can give the impression that one is unaware of the Spanish, French, Russian, and other colonial origins of modern America. I use these terms in the usual way, as a kind of shorthand for "the colonies that were to break from England in 1776."

congratulate themselves on the society's inclusiveness even though "inclusion" involved forms of subordination that many were already viewing as patronizing and generally unacceptable.

Although some Americans, even today, remain wedded to earlier definitions of pluralism when they consider such issues at all, most at least acquiesce in the participatory pluralism that has now been written into public policy by way of civil rights and other legislation. There seems to be broad agreement that it is not in order to tolerate persons or groups and then tell them to take back seats, or to invite them to the meeting and allow them no effectual voice. Given this broad (if still contested) modern consensus, it is all too easy to indulge in our own brand of patronizing and sniff at our misguided foreparents who misread the (to us) obvious implications of the Declaration of Independence. While it is always important for historians and others to guard against that kind of self-righteousness, vigilance is especially needed when the treatment of an historical development is so likely to be freighted with the emotions and advocacies of one's own time.

The historian, or anyone thinking historically, can and should offer moral evaluations; any pretension that we are not doing so will probably be self-delusion. But that is very different from sitting in judgment. That we are not equipped to do, either professionally or morally.

Among many who have made this point, the late Herbert Butterfield of Cambridge University put it most constructively and memorably. The role of the historian, Butterfield held, is not that of a judge who passes sentences; it is that of "a reconciling mind that seeks to comprehend."

> Taking things retrospectively and recollecting in tranquility, the historian works over the past to cover the conflicts with understanding, and explains the unlikenesses between men and makes us sensible of their terrible predicaments; until at the finish—when all is as remote as the tale of Troy—we are able at last perhaps to be a little sorry for everybody.[7]

Although Butterfield's ideal is clearly a difficult one to live up to, there are ample reasons, in a case like the one before us, for modesty about current accomplishments, plus a large dollop of understanding about past failures. If "we are all multiculturalists now," as the sociologist Nathan

Glazer affirms, this is only in part a matter of our responding to such recent wake-up calls as the Black Power movement of the 1960s.[8] Indeed, if the analysis in my own book is even half right, Americans today are being dragged—sometimes kicking and screaming, sometimes in a state of calm and genuine persuasion—into the realities not just of today, but of the early nineteenth century. We are playing catch-up. High fives and other forms of mutual congratulation among the votaries of pluralism are not in order.

Which is also to say that the time has not come, if it ever will, for another round of triumphalism—pluralist triumphalism this time—in historical interpretation. Having recognized that religious pluralism over the American centuries has been a work in progress, we must also accept that it still is. Advanced pluralist thinking has gone beyond mere toleration and mere inclusion; yet, quite obviously, intolerance and exclusion persist.

Nor have all good-hearted, tolerant people become convinced that participatory pluralism is the solution for the present or the wave of the future. The perennial, indeed primordial, tension between the One and the Many assumes new forms but does not disappear.[9] The unity-pluralism argument, which was not settled at any Appomattox of our past, is sure to enliven and trouble our future. Insofar as pluralism now stands for equal participation, nativist concerns about what "they" are doing to "our America" will not disappear, and may intensify. More than that: Wherever participation entails a heightened respect for group identity—as it nearly always does—many besides nativists and conservatives will continue to foresee and warn against what they perceive as a balkanization of American society and the enfeeblement of its religious and moral structures.

Beyond all that, the new pluralism will, soon enough, not seem new. We are already seeing proposals for revised conceptions of ethnicity that would (usefully, I think) revise what we mean by group identity.[10] Further revisions and shifts in definition are inevitable, and may well be salutary. Meanwhile, the pattern laid out in this book can perhaps be given consideration as one proposal for a better understanding of "the past until now."

"Here Are No Disputes": Reputation and Realities in the New Republic

In the course of their nearly two centuries of existence, Great Britain's colonies in North America gained wide, increasing, and mostly admiring notice for both diversity and pluralism. This reputation rested largely upon much-advertised demographic and cultural diversities in parts of Pennsylvania and other mid-Atlantic regions, but in the late colonial and early national eras it was common to extend the observation to "the Americans" generally. When an immigrant agronomist and writer named Hector St. John de Crèvecoeur, in the 1780s, used broad strokes of that kind in characterizing the new society and (along with much else) its religious life, few of his critics accused him of exaggeration or of rhetorical flourish.

IMAGINED COMMUNITY: CRÈVECOEUR'S COUNTRY ROAD

This learned, temperamental son of a French country gentleman had arrived in North America in the 1750s. He had served as a soldier in Canada, then had roamed the Middle Colonies as a surveyor and merchant before settling in New York colony in 1770. In 1782 he published the enormously popular *Letters from an American Farmer*, in which the most famous passage, to this day excerpted in most historical and literary anthologies, rhapsodizes about the diversity of the American colonial population. In answer to his own rhetorical question, "What then is the American, this new man?" he asserted that the American was an amalgam: "Here individuals

Crèvecoeur's sketch of his Pine Hill Plantation, Orange County, New York. From Howard C. Rice, *Le Cultivateur Américain* (1933), frontispiece.

of all nations are melted into a new race of men." Crèvecoeur claimed to know a man "whose grandfather was an Englishman, whose wife was Dutch, whose son married a French woman, and whose present four sons now have wives of different nations." His use of the generic "the American" conveyed, in this celebrated passage and elsewhere, that such living embodiments of diversity were common throughout the colonies.[1]

Several pages later, the author expressed astonishment about the way Americans embraced radical diversity as well as frequently exemplifying it. After asking his mostly European readers to accompany him, in their minds, down a country road somewhere (unspecified) in the colonies, he pointed first to the prosperous farm of a Catholic, "who prays to God as he has been taught, and believes in transubstantiation." This hard worker

Crèvecoeur in 1786. After a portrait by Valière. From Gay Wilson Allen and Roger Asselineau, *St. John de Crèvecoeur* (1987), frontispiece.

and family man, Crèvecoeur avowed, was entirely accepted. "His belief, his prayers offend nobody." And many of his neighbors were beneficiaries of the same tolerant attitude—the "good honest plodding German Lutheran," the fiery "seceder" (from the Church of England) with his well-painted house, and the "Low Dutchman" who adhered to a rigid Calvinism but seemed more preoccupied with his "waggon and fat horses." Everyone tolerated and respected everyone else. In fact, Crèvecoeur asserted, these radically differing believers, if their own houses of worship were too far away, might well run into each other at the Quaker meeting-house!

How could such things be true? The colonies had regularly experienced religious strife, and a Roman Catholic observer (even if Crèvecoeur in these years was a less-than-observant Catholic) had to be aware that his coreligionists in nearly all the colonies had been subjected to civil disabilities. His answer, it seems, was that in that real world where farmers or others live their daily lives, such problems had no reality. For them, at least, "persecution, religious pride, the love of contradiction," and other forms of intolerance that "the world commonly calls religion" had been left behind in Europe. If these various householders "are peaceable subjects, and are industrious, what is it to their neighbors how and in what manner they think fit to address their prayers to the Supreme Being?"[2]

Although these claims about diversity and its routine acceptance appeared in an extraordinary piece of reportage, they were otherwise far from unusual. A great many European commentators on the American experiment, because they were engaged in battles back home over church establishments and religious freedom, were preoccupied with those American conditions that most contrasted with those in Great Britain or on the Continent, and were more than ready to cite the American situation as Great Living Ideal or as Horrible Example.

Often that sort of comparative motivation was merely a subtext or hidden agenda; but in some cases it was very much on the surface. William Cobbett was a prominent, very feisty, English reform publicist whose favorite target of contempt was the Church of England and its "greedy, chattering, lying, backbiting, mischief-making clergy." But in his *Year's Residence in the United States of America*, published in 1819, Cobbett extolled the American religious style. Although he was writing this memoir during the very nastiest moments of New England's Unitarian controversy, he insisted that in America "all is harmony and good neighborhood. . . . Here are no disputes about religion; or, if they be, they make no noise."[3]

Others who invoked and lauded the American example did so with less fire but almost as much exaggeration. The Swedish writer Fredrika Bremer testified, after a two-year American tour in the 1850s, that "nowhere on the face of the earth has the Christian consciousness of true human freedom attained to so full a recognisation as in the United States." And Lord Carlisle, a prominent British statesman who visited in the early 1840s, later informed an audience in Leeds about the "nearly complete absence of polemical strife and bitterness" in the religious life of the young nation.[4]

Not all the Europeans who remarked on American religious pluralism were equally enthusiastic. The Swiss churchman and historian Philip Schaff, even after he had migrated to the United States and become a major spokesman for American ways, acknowledged dangers in what Carlisle had called "unbounded freedom of conscience." And a good many others were not sympathetic at all. The English novelist Frances Trollope, who spent three years in the United States in the late 1820s, considered America's pluralistic religious life a sheer disaster. She deplored "the almost endless variety of religious factions" and the fact that, as she saw it, every religious congregation "invests itself with some queer variety of external observance that has the melancholy effect of exposing all religious ceremonies to contempt." It was impossible, Trollope thought, "in witnessing all these unseemly vagaries, not to recognize the advantages of an established church."[5]

Plainly she got that wrong. Many who criticized the disorderly features of American religion thought an establishment of the usual sort would be far worse. Almost no one, however—whether booster, belittler, or something in between—doubted what we might call the Crèvecoeur Proposition: that the American religious scene was extraordinarily diverse, and that the Americans not only tolerated this diversity but welcomed and took immense pride in it.

Some promoters of these pluralist claims extended them beyond the Protestant Christian sector of American society. Crèvecoeur, for one, featured a Catholic believer on his ecumenical country road. Hannah Adams, a New Englander who in the 1780s compiled a remarkable "dictionary" of the world's religions, boasted that Jews in America "have never been persecuted, but have been indulged in all the rights of citizens."[6] And Robert Baird, an American Presbyterian leader who in the 1840s surveyed his country's religious ways and sought to explain them to Europeans, depicted the blessings of freedom and respect as being showered upon virtually all opinions, including non-Christian and antireligious ones:

> The Christian—be he Protestant or Catholic—the infidel, the Mohammedan, the Jew, the Deist, has not only all his rights as a citizen, but may have his own form of worship, without the possibility of any interference from any policeman or magistrate, provided he do not interrupt, in so doing, the peace and tranquility of the surrounding neighbourhood.[7]

A few enthusiasts seemed to go even farther—for example, by implying a prevailing acceptance of the Indians and their various cultures. Among many artistic expressions of the myth of pluralist success, the best known and loved was Edward Hicks's depiction of what he saw as the world's first great embodiment of the Peaceable Kingdom foretold in Old Testament prophecy. In that painting, which Hicks reproduced in some one hundred versions, Indians as well as lions, lambs, and white settlers are seen to be dwelling together in harmony.

Edward Hicks, *Peaceable Kingdom*. A version done sometime between 1840 and 1845. Courtesy Brooklyn Museum, Dick S. Ramsey Fund (40.340).

This painting, with its references to William Penn and late-seventeenth-century history, might seem also to be suggesting that pluralist triumphs were achieved immediately in the New World environment; but Hicks was a Quaker who knew enough of his sect's history to recognize that things had not been that easy. Most of those who promulgated the myth of pluralist success not only recognized early difficulties; they emphasized them. Theirs was a story not so much of instant successes as of steady progress.

Baird, accordingly, acknowledged that intolerance and persecution in the earliest years had affected many besides "the descendants of Abraham." After chastising the founders of New England and Virginia, who had been "unwilling to accord to others [the religious freedom] they so highly prized for themselves," he recounted a slow, painful, progress that had occurred at different rates in different places. Only with great difficulty had the colonists been freed from the necessity of attending an established church, and then from having to pay taxes to support it. Dissenters had been obliged to battle for the right to hold public meetings.[8]

By the time when Baird wrote, however, the states had, one after another, followed the example of the federal Constitution and ended governmental support of religious establishments; and all but two of them (Baird mistakenly cited only one exception) had discontinued what he called the "barbarism" of imposing a religious test for office-holding. Given that impressive, or perhaps astounding, half-century of growth in legal toleration, it is no surprise to find that Baird was genuinely optimistic; and in this he spoke for most of his contemporaries. "In no part of the world," he wrote, "can we find any progress . . . which can be compared with what has taken place in the United States."[9]

Not only are we likely to read this kind of effusion as unduly optimistic; as in the case of Crèvecoeur we may want to ask how people of Baird's generation could have missed what now seems like abundant evidence that legal toleration was incomplete, and in any case had not produced social tolerance. Although legal disabilities affecting inhabitants of European origin were nearly gone, those imposed upon native and African populations obviously were not. As for non-European religions, the very idea that blacks or Indians *had* religions of their own seemed absurd to most members of the dominant culture. Baird cited, as one of the unfortunate obstacles to progress and fair treatment for the Indians, the fact that "not a single noble aspiration seems ever to enter their souls."[10]

Within the European population, anti-Catholic and antiforeign "nativism" had been virulent in the 1830s, and was gaining political strength during the years when Baird was writing his book. In 1844, at about the time when his first American edition appeared, the founder of Mormonism was murdered in the jail at Carthage, Illinois. In July of that year, Philadelphia was convulsed with anti-Catholic rioting that, as one historian has put it, "turned the City of Brotherly Love into a chaos of hatred and persecution." Two churches were burned to the ground, and twelve people were killed.[11] In the calmer city of Baltimore, John Quincy Adams, the congressman and former president, took charge of a National Lord's Day convention whose purpose was to promote observance of a Sabbath that was not the Sabbath of the Jews or of the Seventh Day Baptists.[12]

The failure of people like Baird to discern that toleration had not

Robert Baird. Engraving by J. C. Buttre. Courtesy Fine Arts Library, Harvard University.

stamped out intolerance, and that persecutions would continue, should not be attributed solely to wishful thinking or American boosterism. As I have suggested, the reality of rapidly achieved toleration in the young country, and its novelty in the Western world, could easily convince Americans and their overseas admirers that a peaceable kingdom had indeed been established—or was just over the horizon. What they could not grasp, with anything like the clarity available to privileged hindsight, were the effects of another kind of reality. This was the reality of a sudden, rapid diversification—ethnic, cultural, religious—that was at least as unusual in its time as were the new nation's constitutional and other commitments to religious freedom.

It was ironic, almost suspicious: during the very years in which constitutional and legal toleration was advancing—step by step and state by state—bigotry and social intolerance plainly were spreading as well, or at least were becoming increasingly visible. One can perhaps see this situation as an indirect effect of the very toleration that beckoned so many "strangers" to the young country. Alexis de Tocqueville, the most astute of the nineteenth-century European observers, speculated that the fluidity built into their institutional and social structures was making Americans nervous, disoriented, and inclined to seek supposed alternative ways of restoring social cohesion.[13] That argument is relevant here. An equally plausible explanation, however, is that a pluralist reputation achieved in one kind of world was being asked to maintain itself within a world that was changing rapidly and in fundamental ways. Advances achieved within the earlier mostly Protestant culture were not readily transferable, intact, into the new demographic situation.

CHANGING WHAT IT MEANT TO BE AN AMERICAN: THE GREAT DIVERSIFICATION

Traditionally, historians have flagged a somewhat later period—that of the "new immigration" from southern, central, and eastern Europe—as the time of greatest and most disruptive social change in American history. Or, in recent years, we have supposed that our own era can claim that distinction as a result of an influx of new Americans, from all parts of the world, that has owed a great deal to the Immigration and Nationality Act of 1965—a piece of legislation that ended most of the immigration restrictions imposed forty years earlier.

In many respects, however, the early nineteenth century was a time of more radical upheaval than one can find in any other period in American history; and the upheaval was especially evident, hence especially traumatic, in relation to religion. More specifically, one result of the unprecedented amount and rapidity of demographic change that marked this era was a severe reduction in Protestant Christianity's numerical dominance in the American population. The phrase "decline of Protestantism" was first used in a prominent way not, as most people would suppose, in the last decades of the twentieth century but in the middle of the nineteenth.[14]

What made the religious changes of the era so traumatic, and subjected ideals of tolerance to so much stress, was not simply the presence in the American population of people who were markedly different; it was the contrast with what had been the case in the colonial period. Colonials had thought of their society and culture as diverse, but in fundamental ways it had been broadly homogeneous for more than two centuries.

The types of diversity that existed in British-colonial America are certainly not to be slighted. The historian Mark Noll has pointed correctly to a "mosaic of Christian faiths" and "a terrific jumble of religious practices." As he remarks, even within the dominant Calvinist tradition, regional and other differences contributed to the jumble: "John Adams of Massachusetts could barely understand John Witherspoon of New Jersey when the former heard the latter preach," and "both were very different from anything on the ground in the southern colonies." [15] With equal cogency, our history books have traditionally placed a great deal of emphasis on the strivings—sometimes successful, sometimes not—of radical dissenters toward recognition and the right to practice their faith. We have looked back in amazement and often amusement at battles over belief or practice that, although they may now seem trivial, clearly aroused passions in public life, and frequently in private lives as well. Was all of this not religious diversity?

It was. Most historians today, amused or not, continue to think that the sectarian battles of the colonial era, and especially the trials and triumphs of an Anne Hutchinson or a Roger Williams, deserve a good deal of attention. In some ways, in fact, we now go beyond our predecessors by stressing types of demographic and religious diversity that they slighted; indigenous peoples, African slaves, and free blacks are now all seen as genuine players in the drama of American colonial development.

Within the colonial Euro-American population, however, dissent and difference had found expression within a framework of broad but powerful commonality. In the words of Horace Kallen, the twentieth-century philosopher who coined the term *cultural pluralism*, white Americans at the time of the Revolution "were prevailingly like-minded. They were possessed of ethnic and cultural unity; they were homogeneous with respect to ancestry and ideals." [16]

With respect to religious origins—for the moment we are not talking about church membership or attendance—the European component in colonial society had been well over 95 percent Protestant. At least 90 percent of the colonists, moreover, had come out of the Calvinist rather than the Lutheran side of the Protestant Reformation; and this made for profound similitudes—not just in doctrine, but in much broader ways of thinking, and in religious and cultural practice. When the historian Winthrop Hudson wrote several decades ago that American society had been imprinted, early on, with "the stamp of Geneva," he was not referring merely to such Calvinist theological emphases as predestination and total depravity. He had in mind deeper propensities toward (for example) legalism, moralism, biblical literalism, and religious activism that had become embedded in the assumptions and folkways of the dominant European population.[17]

If we then recognize that the colonists had been at least 85 percent *English-speaking* Calvinist Protestants, and that this quite homogeneous population had spent two centuries constructing a culture to their own specifications, we can begin to understand nativist and other negative responses to post-1820 diversification, however much we may be prone to deplore those responses.

But what about the aforementioned instances of colonial-era dissent and disagreement? And what about all those groups we might now call "countercultural"—from Jews and "seekers" (those who acknowledged no "true Church") in the first decades to Shakers and other radical sects in the revolutionary era? The answer is that, however colorful, however significant in principle and example, they had been minuscule in numbers.

Some historians have made a case for an increased religious diversity in the eighteenth century.[18] But that point, if sustained, makes the persisting cultural similarities even more striking. To be sure, the colonies by the revolutionary era were awash with Baptists; but more than 95 percent of the Baptists were English, and those who had not been Calvinist from the beginning had become so by the late eighteenth century. The Baptists' 460 congregations, moreover, made them the only "dissenters" whose numbers were comparable with those of the dominant colonial bodies (the Congregationalists, Presbyterians, and Episcopalians). The figures for other sectarian and outsider groups were considerably more modest.

Out of the 3,200 religious congregations in the colonies in 1780, some 600, including 240 Lutheran churches, either were or had been non-English-speaking. Three hundred were Quaker meetings that might still, on some criteria, be considered nonmainstream. But beyond that the numbers plummet: Catholic congregations numbered 56 in 1780, and the Methodists (who a century later could boast that they were "building two [churches] a day") stood at 65. The historically significant pietistic sect called Moravians had only 31 churches in 1780, the Mennonites a very localized 16. Although radical sects like the Dunkers and the followers of the Scottish reformer Robert Sandeman are sometimes placed in the same listing as Baptists and Quakers as examples of eighteenth-century diversity, the Dunkers had a mere 24 churches, the Sandemanians 6. There were only 5 Jewish congregations at the time of the Revolution, and no rabbis at all. Shaker communities by the 1790s, after a great spurt of organizing, numbered 12.[19]

As for diversification in language: Although it is clearly in order to stress the arrival of non-English-speaking settlers over the course of the eighteenth century, we must also take note of the rate at which non-Anglophone congregations and communities adopted the English language. In this era as in later centuries, this seems to have occurred at least as regularly as boatloads of immigrants arrived from various European countries. Around the middle of the eighteenth century, a visitor to the New York colony reported that "most of the young people now speak English and would even take it amiss if they were called Dutchmen and not Englishmen." A Swedish minister told his parents in 1743 that "most of our people [along the Delaware River] are ashamed of the Swedish language and despise it"; and a church elder in Germantown, Pennsylvania, wrote that "the Swedish language is disappearing entirely in Pennsylvania," and that "exactly the same thing is going to happen to our German language." Henry Melchior Muhlenberg, the prominent Lutheran leader, confirmed that insight when he observed, in the 1770s, that younger citizens of Philadelphia wavered between German and English "until the old people are out of the way." There were many exceptions, especially in isolated settlements; and congregational leaders often fought fiercely to maintain the old language in the church as it faded away in the surrounding community. But Tower of Babel metaphors probably suit the late eighteenth century even less well than they work for preceding eras in colonial history.[20]

So all in all, when we celebrate the religious and cultural diversities of the colonial era, we should be careful not to buy into illusions that

First prayer in the Continental Congress. Engraving by H. S. Sadd, 1848, after T. H. Matteson. Photograph courtesy Peabody Essex Museum (neg. #17122).

any part of the country—even, say, eastern Pennsylvania—swarmed with religious or cultural outsiders. Hicks's *Peaceable Kingdom* had depicted brilliantly the pluralist ideal, but another mid-nineteenth-century artwork, T. H. Matteson's depiction of *The First Prayer in Congress* (meaning the First Continental Congress, 1774) does a better job of conveying the reality.

Matteson, a nineteenth-century Norman Rockwell, painted numerous patriotic scenes that, like this one and his wildly popular *Spirit of '76*, were distributed widely as lithographs. In his *First Prayer* portrayal (which once adorned Christ Church, Episcopal, in Philadelphia as a stained glass window), we find a diversity consisting almost entirely of Episcopalians, Presbyterians, and Congregationalists. Catholics? Jews? Baptists or other radical dissenters? Not in this picture and not, of course, in the gathering it depicts. The most eccentric—identifiable because the artist portrays him with his hat on—is Stephen Hopkins of Rhode Island, the one member of the First Continental Congress who at least *had* been a Quaker. (Hopkins had been "disowned," a year before the Continental Congress, for refusing to free a slave.)[21]

CATHOLICS AND OTHER OUTSIDERS

White, Christian, and mainline Protestant dominance (also, of course, male dominance) were still very much in evidence when artists fashioned group portraits of influential Americans fifty or seventy years later. But by that time such portrayals were less true to demographic and religious realities. By the 1850s any "true record" of the society's development would have reflected an astonishing degree of diversification.

In the nineteenth-century story, as in the colonial one, raw numbers are interesting and important even though they provide only a beginning. Old-stock Americans, like old-stock elements in almost any society, were prone to react one way to a few newcomers, quite another way to a flood of newcomers; while the former had often been seen as quaint and picturesque, the latter seemed menacing. And the population of the new country grew, between 1790 and 1860, by a factor of eight, which translates to an increase of more than 35 percent in every decade. The three million immigrants who arrived in just one ten-year period (mid-1840s to mid-1850s), and who added themselves to a population of only twenty million, represented by far the largest proportional increase experienced in any period of American history.[22] Because this kind of growth, in any society, has usually produced wrenching social change, we can suppose that the explosion in numbers would have brought fear and social disruption even if most of the immigrants had been British Protestants.

But of course most of the in-flooding immigrants were not British Protestants. These were not simply new people; to an unprecedented degree they were "different" people.[23] To be sure, Englishmen and Scotsmen and the so-called Scotch-Irish (Scots who had lived for two generations in Ulster) continued to immigrate in large numbers. A huge portion of the immigrants, however, together with most of those added by territorial expansion, were people who struck old-stock European Americans as not just different, but exotic—about as exotic as Russian Jews would later seem to the established Americans of the 1890s, or as Muslims and Buddhists would seem a century after that.

Nor was this rapid diversification limited to the European component of American society. Although the count of Indians and Africans decreased in this era—the first numerically, the second in proportion to total population—its final decades brought the first substantial immigration from East Asia. Some fifty thousand Chinese arrived in the late 1840s and the 1850s.

Few of these Asian immigrants were "coolies"—if that term is used to denote a kind of indentured servitude. Low-paid manual laborers they were, and many came heavily indebted to those who had paid their way. By and large, however, exactly like European immigrants of the time, the Chinese came for a better life, and came on their own volition; the first of them, in fact, came to dig for gold. Nor did all settle in one place, or a few places. Although nearly 80 percent settled in Pacific Coastal areas, the Chinese also spread out. By 1870 they constituted nearly 30 percent of Idaho's (admittedly small) population, and about 10 percent of Montana's. Some Chinese immigrants found employment in the eastern and southern states.[24]

In this period, however, it was not the relatively few Chinese laborers, mostly off in California, whom old-stock Americans had in mind when they worried about rapid diversification. Nor were most people conscious of the rise in Roman Catholic population that came with territorial acquisitions in the West and Southwest. Those distant challenges to Anglo-Saxon Protestant hegemony did attract the worried attention of establishment figures like the Hartford theologian Horace Bushnell, who discussed them in an ominously titled treatise of 1847, *Barbarism the First Danger*.[25] But the forms of population increase that produced the most widespread and malevolent responses were of course those that were visible "in the neighborhood."

Here we are talking especially about the rapidly growing numbers of Germans and Irish in the American population. In 1790 fewer than 9 percent of white Americans were of German ancestry, and the percentage of Irish, especially of Catholic Irish, was well below that. Sixty years later, both percentages had risen significantly. Whereas British and Canadian immigration had continued, through that period, at something like the old rates, that of the Germans and the Irish had risen phenomenally. By 1850 these two ethnic groups accounted for nearly 70 percent of a foreign-born cohort that, in proportion to total population, was possibly the largest in American history.[26]

Because more than half of the German newcomers were Lutheran (as were nearly all Scandinavian immigrants), even the Protestant elements in the new population growth deserve some notice. Along with a small but significant effect on linguistic balances (as in earlier times, a short-term effect), the arrival of the Germans contributed in rather visible ways to a chipping away at the Calvinist hegemony within American Protestantism. In a rapidly expanding society like that of the early United States, the growth in the number of Lutheran congregations (from eight hundred in 1820 to more than two thousand by 1860) was not surprising in itself; Lutherans were just keeping pace. Somewhat more noteworthy, however, is the fact that this also involved the founding of something like one thousand non-English-speaking churches and communities, and that the numbers of Lutheran colleges and theological seminaries increased from none at all in 1790 to a dozen in 1860.[27]

Still, with respect to religious change the most important and portentous statistics, by far, were those that reflected the growth of Roman Catholicism from the status of tiny minority to that of very substantial minority. About one-third of the German immigrants and nearly all of the Irish were Catholic. Their advent, even if we ignore other increases occasioned by the acquisition of territories in the West and Southwest, meant that within seven decades the almost unanimously Protestant population of 1790 had been reduced to roughly 75 percent. And most of this change had occurred in one intense forty-year period, from the 1820s to the early 1860s.

The decline in Protestant numerical dominance is even steeper if we do figure in the territorial acquisitions of the mid-nineteenth century. Although the number of Catholic settlers and converts in California or the Southwest is difficult to gauge, this factor should not be ignored completely, as it usually has been, in relation to the shifting Protestant-Catholic balance.

One other index to this change is at least worth noting. Calculations proceeding from actual church membership, as opposed to those based on ethnicity or religious origins, yield a Protestant figure of only about 60 percent. Or even less: Baird, in the 1856 edition of his *Religion in America*, reported that Protestants accounted for only 57 percent of the membership of Christian churches.[28] To be sure, the Catholics defined membership differently, but that offered little comfort to Protestants already apprehensive about their loss of cultural power. The fact that church members and churchgoers were now about 60 percent Protestant instead of nearly all Protestant was, to them, highly and frighteningly relevant.

In our own day, a number of world societies have experienced grave apprehensions and some degree of violence in response to immigration rates well below that of early-nineteenth-century America. In Germany at the end of the twentieth century, Turkish immigrants amounted to 2 percent of the population, and the total for all foreigners came to 9 percent. In Great Britain, "non-white ethnic minorities," taken together, accounted for a mere 6.4 percent of the population.[29] So whichever way one does the math, changing proportions in the early national period can justly be seen as *the* great diversification in American history, certainly with respect to religion.

COMMUNITARIANS AND OTHER INNOVATORS

Religious diversification in the first half of the nineteenth century took other, less dramatic, forms that nonetheless tested Americans' much-touted commitment to pluralist principles. The form that attracted most notice at the time, and that has held the attention of historians ever since, was the proliferation of radical, communitarian, reformist, or simply unorthodox religious groups. Like the diversities introduced through immigration, those represented in religious and quasi-religious experimentation were not qualitatively new. What was new was the number and variety of such projects, and perhaps the enthusiasm of their founders and participants. Ralph Waldo Emerson told his Scottish friend Thomas Carlyle in 1840 that "we are all a little wild here. . . . Not a reading man but has a draft of a new community in his waistcoat pocket." Something of an exaggeration, to be sure, but the actual numbers would have sounded almost equally remarkable. Some 120 experimental communities were founded during the first half of the nineteenth century, and as Sydney Ahlstrom reports, as many as several dozen "became celebrated through transient successes." At least one, that of the Mormons, "became a major American cultural force."[30]

Supplementing these communitarian efforts to reform society were those of the numerous voluntary associations that formed around such objectives as prison reform or peace activism or antislavery advocacy. Together, the utopian ventures and the reform organizations presented an enormous range of deviations and heresies. Although we could catalogue them, it may be better to turn again to Emerson, who approached the phenomenon with his usual wit and acumen. He began a lecture of 1844 by asserting that religious impulses formerly confined within churches were now finding expression "in temperance and non-resistance societies, in movements of abolitionists and of socialists, and in very significant assemblies . . . composed of ultraists, of seekers, of all the soul of the soldiery of dissent."[31]

On the fringes of these movements Emerson found not just diversity but contradiction. "They defied each other, like a congress of kings, each of whom had a realm to rule, and a way of his own that made concert unprofitable." Sounding, to modern ears, like some sardonic observer of the reformist scene in the 1960s, Emerson exclaimed about the "fertility of projects for the salvation of the world!"

> One apostle thought all men should go to farming; and another, that no man should buy or sell . . . another, that the mischief was in our diet, that we eat and drink damnation. . . . Others attacked the system of agriculture, the use of animal manures in farming. . . . Even the insect world was to be defended, —that had too long been neglected, and a society for the protection of ground-worms, slugs, and mosquitoes was to be incorporated without delay.

Still others, as he said, "attacked the institution of marriage, as the fountain of social evils." Veering back toward more mainstream reforms, Emerson drew attention to those who "assailed particular vocations, as that of the lawyer, that of the merchant, of the manufacturer, of the clergyman, [and] of the scholar."[32]

The historian Leo Ribuffo has remarked that by the middle of the nineteenth century the influx of immigrants, and especially of Roman Catholic immigrants, "was changing what it meant to be an American."[33] We could add that communitarians, reformers, and nontraditional sectarians were helping to change what it meant to be religious. The question, in both cases, was the extent to which older-stock Americans, bearers of a tradition that included the celebration of diversity, were prepared to acknowledge these changes. How did the society respond to dissenters and outsiders who were often forced to ask, in effect, "What must I do to be tolerated?"

2 Just Behave Yourself:
Pluralism as Selective Tolerance

How did mainline Americans, those we would not call either outsiders or dissenters, respond to this extensive diversification in the first half of the nineteenth century? I think it is already evident that my initial, perhaps too flippant, answer would be: "Not very well." But we need to probe further. Why was this so, considering the society's multiple and world-famous commitments to religious and other freedoms?

G. M. Young, the mid-twentieth-century historian of Victorian British culture, offered a simple-sounding explanation of his own approach to complexities in the writing of social history. The rule he always tried to observe, he wrote, was to "go on reading until you can hear people talking."[1] If we utilize a similar method in scanning the literature and subliterature relating to immigration in this period, what we "hear" is a kind of double-mindedness or ambivalence. It is the ambivalence of old-stock inhabitants who, although they reveled in what seemed a remarkable onward march of religious freedom, were also genuinely worried about social stability and the moral health of the young nation.

The result was not simply a confusion of mind. It was also a curious mix of practical responses. Some radical dissenters—whether sectarian, communitarian, or individual— were tolerated and even celebrated, while others were denounced, or beaten down, or driven out.

What can explain these discrepancies? Class difference? Degrees of foreignness? Doctrinal divergences that in some cases, but not others, appeared noxious and dangerous? I think it was all of the above—or better, in given cases could be any of them. Out of the welter of reasons, however, a fairly clear pattern emerges, one that rests on the distinction between radical religious beliefs on the one hand and radical or allegedly radical behavior—religious and/or social—on the other. Behavior, it seems, was much more of a problem than beliefs.[2]

Robert Baird alluded to this distinction in an almost offhand way, yet quite explicitly: Everyone, he wrote, including the "infidel," could count on toleration and the rights of citizenship as long as he or she did not "interrupt . . . the peace and tranquility of the surrounding neighborhood." As Brigham Young and his followers moved west in the late 1840s under the close scrutiny of the federal government's Office of Indian Affairs, the head of that agency assured one of his field officers in Iowa that as long as the Mormons "conduct[ed] themselves with propriety" he would not want to "embarrass their movements." And a few years later, Philip Schaff, probably with the Mormons at the front of his mind, was explaining candidly to Europeans that in the United States religious liberty was allowed to those "who do not outrage . . . the public morality."[3]

Objections to unusual behavior cannot always be disentangled from disapproval of unorthodox views; yet in most cases the distinction seems quite clear. On the turbulent religious scene of the early republic there were numerous indications that cultural insiders could hold really extreme beliefs—reaching even, on occasion, to atheism—as long as they behaved themselves. Nineteenth-century Quakers and Unitarians, the latter especially, held doctrinal views seriously at variance with the dominant forms of Protestant orthodoxy; but this neither diminished their high social standing in their respective strongholds (eastern Pennsylvania and eastern Massachusetts) nor subjected them to disabilities elsewhere.

More unorthodox dissenters and sectarians, such as the Transcendentalists in New England and radical millenarians or utopians in the Middle States and the West, might be treated with condescension or amusement and be denounced in press and pulpit. And some of these doctrinal radicals complained about persecution as well. The Transcendentalist Theodore Parker fell back on such terminology when ministerial colleagues in the Boston area refused to engage with him in the customary pulpit exchanges. So did Abner Kneeland, a former Universalist minister who by the 1830s had become a publicist for skepticism and, at some points, for atheism.

In both instances, however, and in most others like them, those who administered the penalty (collegial shunning for Parker, a stint in the Suffolk County jail for Kneeland) were plainly objecting to manner at least as much as to matter. Parker's theology, as he never tired of pointing out, was no more extreme than those of several other Transcendentalists; but his language was far less polite than, say, Emerson's. He had what would now be called an attitude. His behavior was not up to the standard set by other radical Boston ministers. As for Kneeland, his radicalism got him arraigned under an old Massachusetts law that prohibited blasphemous religious views but seemed even more concerned about "cursing" and other public expressions of such views. Certainly Kneeland himself thought that he had been prosecuted less because of his views (which he denied were atheistic) than because of what one of his biographers calls the "smug good manners" of the Bostonians.[4]

In other words, a dissenter could hold wildly heretical opinions and yet be tolerated so long as he or she was "our sort of person." Crèvecoeur's observation about the homeowners on that polyglot country road—they were good sturdy farmers and family men, so who cared what they believed?—seemed to be validated, fifty and sixty years later, on the larger stage of the early American republic.

DREADFUL INFIDEL/GLORIOUS PATRIOT

A limited but striking example of this pattern is the thin red line of military and political heroes who were also detractors of the faith and practice held dear by the vast majority of their countrymen. To be sure, religious radicals such as Jefferson, Paine, and Ethan Allen were denounced and caricatured. Little children were warned against the anti-Christian wickedness that allegedly had destroyed "Mad Tom" Paine and others of his ilk. Yet they were exposed, in books and on schoolhouse walls, to the elegant Romney portrait of the "other" Paine, the one who had championed the American Revolution and thus had helped found their country. Their schoolbooks featured an intrepid Allen, the hero of Ticonderoga, and glowing patriotic treatments of Jefferson, despite the fact that both were reviled as dangerous deists. (Two decades after Jefferson's death, Baird was still calling him "the arch infidel.")[5]

Again we are dealing with a kind of double-mindedness (not to say double-talk). A few biographers, such as Gilbert Vale in his *Life of Thomas Paine* (1841), were single-minded enough to identify their subjects "with the glories of our Revolution" and also to lavish praise upon their religious radicalism. Vale thought that Paine's deism "breathes as pure a spirit of morality and philosophy, as anything that was ever written on the subject, in either ancient or modern times." More commonly, however, writers tolerated the heretic for the sake of his heroics. Jared Sparks, a prominent historian and Unitarian minister, called Allen's *Reason the Only Oracle of Man* "a crude and worthless performance," but then excused Allen's religious errors as the result of scanty education and went on to make him sound almost saintly: "Few have suffered more in the cause of freedom, few have borne their sufferings with a firmer constancy or a loftier spirit. . . . He was eccentric and ambitious, but these weaknesses, if such they were, never betrayed him into acts unworthy, dishonorable, or selfish."[6]

Somewhat earlier, Ezra Stiles, Yale's president and a pillar of the Congregational "standing order," had managed the same easy dichotomy in remarks following the death of Stephen Hopkins, the renegade Quaker who appears in the Matteson painting of *The First Prayer in Congress*. Hopkins, Stiles wrote, had been "rather a Quaker" (making him suspect) and at heart a deist (worse). He had been an infidel to whom Jesus, at the Last Day, "[would] say . . . *I know you not.*" Yet he had also been "a Man of a Noble fortitude & Resolution . . . a glorious Patriot."[7]

As that example suggests, the mental gymnastics required for this brand of toleration were not undertaken merely by fellow deists or by Unitarian liberals. Nearly everyone, including people more conservative than Stiles, made allowances for dangerous radicals who were also national heroes, particularly if, like Allen at Ticonderoga, they had had the decency to challenge enemies "in the name of God and the Continental Congress" or if, like Paine and Jefferson, they professed to be saving true religion rather than destroying it. Martin Marty is surely correct that preachers and writers like Sparks and Stiles expressed ways of thinking—and of tolerating—that were standard "in much of evangelical Protestantism."[8]

Le Fameux Empyrique. Thomas Paine as medicine man. Courtesy American Philosophical Society.

Thomas Paine. Engraving by William Sharp, 1794, from the Romney portrait. In Thomas Clio Rickman, *The Life of Thomas Paine*, 1819.

THE TEASING OF THE HERETICS

But what about others among the "radical but respectable"—that large majority among religious mavericks who, like some of today's politicians, had lacked the foresight to enlist and become heroes? In general, they were spared persecution nonetheless. The most common and widespread response, even to very radical opinions, seems to have been an amused (or bemused) tolerance.

In 1831 William Miller, a Baptist lay preacher and former deist, began preaching about Christ's Second Coming. After a dozen years of laborious biblical study he had come to believe, as he told his rapt hearers, that this would occur in March 1843. The response was extraordinary, surprising even Miller and extending far beyond his base in upstate New York. Before the appointed time, many thousands had heard the message, or

Ethan Allen as revolutionary hero. Courtesy Vermont Historical Society.

had read it. (Miller gave hundreds of lectures each year, and in addition had the help of a remarkable publicist named Joshua Himes.) When the event did not occur, the Millerite leadership revised their calculations and announced a second date, and then a third. When that date, in October 1844, had passed, the movement declined. Although it had tapped a rich vein—the idea or feeling that all must prepare for Christ's return—and although later premillennial bodies owed a great deal to Miller and the Great Disappointment, Millerism itself became permanently installed as the leading example of an American religious movement treated with amused tolerance.

Or, of course, mistreated. One newspaperman thought that the preacher often called "crazy Miller" had been "the object of more abuse, ridicule, and blackguardism than any other man living."[9] His followers fared little better. Some of them, their numbers probably augmented by village pranksters anxious to discredit all the faithful, had donned white robes and climbed hills or steeples to await the end; but these and other supposed happenings were exaggerated mercilessly at the time, and continued long after to be taken as hilarious hallmarks of the movement.*

Some of the stories were well attested; for example, it seems to have been true that certain "highly-bred ladies" of what is now called the Philadelphia Main Line refused to gather in a downtown building lest they be taken up to heaven "with the common crowd." Other less credible stories, to the shame of some leading American literary figures, were committed to print on the basis of prejudice and hearsay; Cooper, Longfellow, and Holmes all, on such grounds, derided Millerism as evidence of the rising mob mentality and mass lunacy that they thought was about to devastate American society. But true or false, fair or unfair, the point for us would be the same: this was a movement—one among dozens or perhaps hun-

---

*Not surprisingly, many of those who considered Miller crazy were equally convinced that his followers must be mad. Recent work has shown that most Millerites were more "mainstream" than we had thought—quite like other revivalistic Christians in their denominational affiliation, their social standing, and even their ideas concerning Christ's return. Just as striking, however, is the persistence with which opponents insisted on a linkage between Millerism and insanity. The Millerites themselves, of course, were likely to see this sort of "ridicule" as crossing the line into persecution. Doan, *Miller Heresy*; Numbers and Butler, *The Disappointed.*

Kidding the Millerites. (The Devil prevents the ascension of Miller's publicist: "Joshua V., you must stay with me.") Courtesy American Antiquarian Society.

dreds—that was tolerated and allowed to run its course, that was "persecuted" only through ridicule, and that achieved this degree of toleration because, whatever the heated imaginings of a Fenimore Cooper, the Millerites on the whole behaved themselves.[10]

Among major dissenting groups, the other lucky winners of the Amused Tolerance award were the transcendentalists of New England (and, later, of selected spots in the Midwest). These Boston-area intellectuals, most of whom either were or had been Unitarian ministers, began in the mid-1830s to promote interpretations of Christian doctrine that most Unitarians, to say nothing of other Christian believers, found utterly foreign. ("Foreign" in both senses; the philosophies and theologies they most relied upon were German in origin, and to a large extent had been brought to their attention by British and French think-

A MILLERITE PREPARING FOR THE 23ᵈ OF APRIL.
"Now let it come! I'm ready!"

"Now let it come! I'm ready." By permission of the
Houghton Library, Harvard University.

ers.) Adherents favored theories of knowledge that placed a great deal
of trust in "transcendent" human capacities for discerning religious and
other truths. They were therefore doubtful about human reason, as most
people defined that quality, and were much inclined to reject miracles, or
at least to question their importance, as validations for Christian truth.
Reducing the status of Christ more than did the Unitarian movement out
of which they came, most of them revered Jesus as little more than an
outstanding or perhaps a uniquely inspired exemplar of the divinity common to humankind. For much of Christian doctrine they substituted what
seemed to most other Christians a high-flown romantic individualism.

In the popular mind the term *transcendentalism* stood for "any view that
is enthusiastic, mystical, extravagant, impractical, ethereal, supernatu-
ral, vague, abstruse, [or] lacking in common sense." It stood for many of
the same things in the minds of theological and philosophical critics, so
much so that transcendentalism's most famous or infamous critic, Professor Andrews Norton of the Harvard Divinity School, at first disdained
even to refute its arguments. In a scathing response in 1839 to Ralph
Waldo Emerson's "Divinity School Address" of a year earlier, Norton asserted that "it is not necessary to remark particularly on this composition.

It will be sufficient to state that the author professes to reject all belief in Christianity as a revelation." In the title of his discourse he called the new views, quite simply, *The Latest Form of Infidelity*.[11]

Norton, obviously, was not amused. But most other critics were. The usually somber theologians at the Presbyterians' college and seminary in Princeton offered detailed scholarly refutations, along with a heavy dose of what Germans would call *Schadenfreude* (in effect: "Ha! We told you this would happen among those wild-eyed New England liberals"). But even the sober Princetonians managed some lighter notes. Professor A. B. Dod prefaced denunciation of the movement with a tongue-in-cheek admission, on his own behalf and that of his Princeton colleagues, that he did not know what the transcendentalists were talking about (and wondered whether they did either):

> What is this vaunted German philosophy, of which our young men have learned the jargon? We shall endeavor to give an intelligible answer to so reasonable an inquiry . . . [but] it is far from our purpose to profess to be adepts. We have seen a little, heard a little, read a little . . . and understood perhaps as much as some who have become masters; yet we disclaim a full comprehension. . . . We have tried the experiment, and proved ourselves unable to see in a fog. Our night glasses do not reach the transcendental.[12]

In less formal contexts, including a great many parodies of the writings of Emerson and others (especially Bronson Alcott, Henry David Thoreau, and Margaret Fuller), transcendentalism was accorded the full treatment of light-hearted derision unalloyed with serious argument. In 1842 the New York magazine *Brother Jonathan* published the imagined response of a transcendentalist called Moonshine Milkywater to a simple dinner invitation. Among its many pretentious passages was the following: "A dinner is, and it is not. Savory, committee-gentlemen, is the order of the fried smelts, pork-fat in potatoism pan-borne, harmoniously liquidating. But wherefor fried? Are not gridirons extant in perennial parallelism? Is there lack of culinary capacity in copper stew-pans? . . . Gentlemen, I incline not dinner-wise."[13]

Emerson, who as lecturer, essayist, and poet was by far the most famous transcendentalist of his time, was the one most extensively teased. In his poem "Brahma," the best known lines are

If the red slayer thinks he slays,
   Or if the slain thinks he is slain,
They know well the subtle ways
   I keep and pass and turn again.

And, toward the end,

I am the doubter and the doubt,
   And I the hymn the Brahmin sings.[14]

Lines like these proved irresistible to several generations of parodists who composed such gems as "If the grey tom cat think he sing" and "If the fat butcher think he slays," and quite a few others. One cricket-inspired takeoff, by the Scottish poet and historian Andrew Lang, opened with:

If the wild bowler thinks he bowls,
   Or if the batsman thinks he's bowled,

and concluded with the lines:

I am the batsman and the bat,
   I am the bowler and the ball,
The umpire, the pavilion cat,
The roller, pitch, and stumps, and all.[15]

Other overseas notables piled on. Thomas Carlyle, in the closing pages of his *Past and Present* (1843), expressed both appreciation and amusement about the doings of the young Americans whom he had helped inspire. He was plainly most ambivalent about those among them who had established Brook Farm, the famous back-to-nature communal experiment south of Boston: "My Transcendental friends announce there, in a distinct, though in a somewhat lankhaired, ungainly manner, that the Demiurgus Dollar is dethroned. . . . Socinian [extreme Unitarian] Preachers quit their pulpits in Yankeeland, saying, 'Friends, this is all gone to coloured cobweb, we regret to say!'—and retire into the fields to cultivate onion-beds, and live frugally on vegetables. It is very notable." [16] By the 1880s, when Gilbert and Sullivan made a "transcendentalist" the chief character in their comic opera *Patience*, lankhaired effeteness, augmented with elements from several British models, was a bit more prominent, but the emphasis was still on verbal obscurity and general pretentiousness. According to the foppish Bunthorne,

> If you're anxious for to shine in the high aesthetic line, as a man of culture rare,
> You must get up all the germs of the transcendental terms, and plant them ev'rywhere.
> You must lie among the daisies and discourse in novel phrases of your complicated state of mind.
> The meaning doesn't matter if it's only idle chatter of a transcendental kind.
> And ev'ryone will say,
> As you walk your mystic way:
> "If this young man expresses himself in terms too deep for me,
> Why, what a very singularly deep young man this deep young man must be."

Such constant raillery, directed against colorful religious radicals who conceivably wished to be taken seriously, might have counted as a mild form of persecution had the transcendentalists themselves not joined in the merriment. But they did. They were secure enough as a group that they felt free to both criticize and tease each other.

James Freeman Clarke, although he had been a founding member of the Transcendental Club, remembered later that the group had called itself "the club of the like-minded; I suppose because no two of us thought alike." And Emerson, functioning as the teaser as well as the teased, delighted in anecdotes about the more mystical of his colleagues, and about the kind of language they used. Elizabeth Peabody, he claimed, had walked straight into a tree and, when asked why she had not seen the tree, responded loftily that "I saw it but I didn't *realize* it." A bit more seriously, in a Boston lecture of 1842 on "the Transcendentalist," Emerson tried to distance himself somewhat from his longtime associates by acknowledging "a great deal of well-founded objection to be spoken or felt against the sayings and doings of this class." They had, he said, "[laid] themselves open to criticism and to lampoons," and some could be indicted for "cant and pretension . . . subtilty and moonshine." [17]

He added, seemingly in agreement with Carlyle, that some transcendentalists "betake themselves to a certain solitary and critical way of living, from which no solid fruit has yet appeared to justify their separation." Philanthropists, he remarked, "inquire whether Transcendentalism does not mean sloth; they had as lief hear that their friend is dead, as that he is a Transcendentalist; for then he is paralyzed, and can never do anything for humanity."[18]

Other transcendentalists, in their turn, indulged in mild criticisms of Emerson. Christopher Pearse Cranch, a younger member of the group, used the medium of cartooning to make sport of Emersonian metaphors that he, like some of the parodists I have cited, considered especially rare-fied. Emerson in his most famous prose piece, "Nature," had averred that "standing on the bare ground . . . and uplifted into infinite space,—all mean egotism vanishes. I become a transparent eyeball." Later in the same essay he reported, "I expand and live in the warm day, like corn and melons." Cranch produced a set of drawings that pretended to take such metaphors literally (see pp. 44–45).[19]

For Emerson, Cranch, and other transcendentalists who indulged in self-criticism and self-mockery, final judgments on the movement were, of course, highly affirmative. Emerson implored his listeners to "tolerate one or two solitary voices . . . speaking for thoughts and principles not marketable or perishable," and assured them that the transcendentalists' strange-seeming impulses would "abide in beauty and strength."[20] But the ready acknowledgment of weaknesses indicates how secure—how un-beleaguered—radical dissenters could feel in the atmosphere of the new republic.

It is worth noting, too, that Emerson, principal spokesperson for the transcendentalist "infidels," spent most of his later years on the lecture circuit, and was accepted and applauded all over the country—in cities, towns, and hamlets that were a great deal more conservative than Uni-tarian Boston and the Harvard Divinity School.

REVIVAL BEHAVIOR

A handful of other religious radicals and "infidels"—for example, the Englishwoman Frances Wright and the Scotsman Robert Dale Owen—barnstormed the country in these years. Not all were so enthusiastically received in the hinterlands as Emerson was, or as "Colonel Bob" Ingersoll would be somewhat later. But they were treated at least as tolerantly as another class of religionists whose theologies were far closer to the main-

"Standing on the bare ground, — my head bathed by the blithe air, & uplifted into infinite space, — all mean egotism vanishes. I become a transparent Eyeball." *Nature*. h. 13

Emerson as a transparent eyeball. Cartoon by Christopher Cranch. By permission of the Houghton Library, Harvard University.

I expand and live in the warm days,
like corn & melons.

Nature. p. 73.

Emerson expanded. Cartoon by Christopher Cranch. By permission of the Houghton Library, Harvard University.

stream. Evangelical revivalists, though almost never "persecuted," had to endure a great deal of the kind of invective and abuse that foreign observers like Mrs. Trollope lavished upon them. And their alleged offenses were nearly all behavioral rather than theological in nature.

The "new revivalism" in frontier areas (and after 1830 in eastern cities as well) was doctrinally innovative mostly on points related to free will. Even on those points it was less extreme than much of the rapidly liberalizing Congregationalism of New England, to say nothing of Unitarianism. But revivalism underwent intense and vitriolic attacks from virtually all "orthodox" quarters, and from these liberals as well; and the problem was largely, though not entirely, a matter of religious practice. A whole litany of complaints arose about such revivalistic techniques as the provision of an "anxious bench," where nearly persuaded sinners parked and wept as they awaited the moment of conversion. The revivalists were castigated, as their eighteenth-century predecessors had been, for promoting overly emotional reactions and, supposedly, sanctioning licentious behavior that masqueraded as religious ecstasy.

The best known among American critics of the new revivalism was the liberal Congregational leader Horace Bushnell, whose *Christian Nurture* (1847) inveighed in a relatively polite way against practices that he thought placed too much emphasis on a supposed moment of conversion. Others, such as the theologians at Princeton and in the German Reformed Seminary at Mercersburg, Pennsylvania, were inclined to use stronger language that came close to what one could find in the secular press. John Williamson Nevin, Philip Schaff's Mercersburg colleague, argued that the seemingly simple anxious bench procedure actually led to "the very worst excesses." It was, he charged, a high-pressure system that dragged people "theatrically into public view," made the pulpit itself into a stage, encouraged preachers to be full of themselves rather than filled with the Holy Spirit, and in general promoted "vulgarism of feeling." The preaching that accompanied such goings-on was at best rude, coarse, and vapid. Little wonder, he concluded, "that the religion which is commenced and carried on under such auspices, should show itself to be characteristically coarse and gross. Wanting true reverence for God, it will be without true charity also towards men. It is likely to be narrow, intolerant, sinister, and rabidly sectarian. All that is high will become low, and all that is beautiful be turned into vulgarity, in its hands."[21]

This, whether or not we consider it fair, was one of the more eloquent statements of objection to revivalistic behavior. Nevin footnoted it with an equally poignant complaint that he attributed to Professor Archibald Alexander of Princeton. In a letter to a friend, Alexander had written that "fanaticism often blazes with a glaring flame, and agitates assemblies as with a hurricane or earthquake; but God is not in the fire, or the wind, or the earthquake. His presence is more commonly with the still small voice.

There is no sounder characteristic of genuine devotion, than reverence."[22] Both of these assaults on revivalistic religion testified to a religious and cultural divide that showed itself repeatedly, in one form or another, long before the term *culture wars* was invented in the late twentieth century. More to the point here, however, is the fact that revivalism, whether in eastern cities or on the frontiers, tended to be treated less politely than liberal or even radical expressions; and that the objections related more to religious behavior than to religious belief.

Somewhat surprisingly, a particularly nasty version of antirevivalism arose among people whom the historian James Bratt refers to as "regionally dispersed populists." In their eyes national evangelical figures like Charles Grandison Finney were part of "a monstrous combination" that concentrated power in the hands of a few individuals and thereby posed a threat to "the liberties, both civil and religious, of our country." In 1827, Primitive Baptists in Virginia denounced the "pharasiacal, money-loving, money-hunting, money-begging, mesmerizing, passion-exciting . . . Baptists of the present day" who promoted revivals out of self-interest. And a Lutheran pastor felt forced to inform the folks back home in Germany about the "wild worship, manipulative preachers, excessive and unstable emotionalism, sectarian divisiveness, [and] sheep-stealing" that he was encountering on the Michigan frontier.[23]

None of this is to say that objections to revivalism were not also doctrinal in nature, in the South or West as well as in Horace Bushnell's Connecticut. Behavioral issues were prominent, however, both at home and on the various mission fields abroad.[24] Where they arose, they seem to have been argued with more vehemence than was usually expressed in doctrinal disputes.

CULTURAL FEAR AND FULL-SCALE INTOLERANCE

If Americans in the early years of their republic could manage casual attitudes toward religious radicals, and even toward the antireligious, why did so many withhold the same easy tolerance (or, often, any tolerance at all) from Roman Catholics, Mormons, and others? Why is it that more than half of the experimental communities founded during this time experienced persecution in the form of violence or economic discrimination?[25] The quick but also accurate answer is that, like T. S. Eliot's J. Alfred Prufrock, they were plagued by feelings only partly explicable in any rational terms. They were, "in short . . . afraid."

Again Robert Baird is a barometer, at least for those old-stock Americans who were worried but who also deplored violence and nativism. Baird took care to acknowledge that some Irish immigrants, and quite a number of Germans, were respectable folks; and he thought these and some others could be made into true-blue Americans. (Those who were not Protestant would become so.) But clearly he was more than mildly worried. He feared that the new hordes of immigrants were not, on the whole, coming to America because of religious persecution or high idealism. Even the best of them, he thought, were merely seeking economic advantage—to make a better life for themselves and their children—while the worst were people who had left their countries "for their countries' good." (Much of the crime committed in America, he pointed out, "is the work of foreigners.") And between the best and the worst stood the largest number, people who, discouragingly, were "not only very poor, but ignorant, also, and depraved"—people plainly "ill qualified to succeed in a new country." Baird, who clung to a long-range optimism, called on the churches to provide the immigrants with "the means of grace" that would promote their assimilation and ensure that their children would "grow up Americans in their feelings and habits."[26]

In these hopes regarding assimilation and also in his belief that intolerance was ending, Baird almost certainly spoke for a majority in the old-stock population. But a vigorous and noisy minority, those usually called nativists, proved him wrong on the second point, the supposed ending of intolerance. Nativists not only were less confident than Baird was about assimilation; they also brought forward concerns that he had barely acknowledged—concerns about Rome's supposed ability to dictate to the American church and thereby to control Catholic voters. The nativist political parties of the 1840s and 1850s sought such things as literacy tests for prospective voters, a tighter rein on states and territories that were allowing noncitizens to vote, and a radical lengthening of the naturalization process (from five to twenty-one years). "*Americans must rule America*," the 1856 platform of the American Party insisted. Nativists trumpeting such objectives achieved control, very briefly, of several state legislatures

"A Nun at Confession." In Samuel B. Smith, *The Escape of Sainte Francis Patrick,
Another Nun from the Hôtel Dieu Nunnery of Montreal* (1836).

in the mid-fifties, and the American Party won 21 percent of the popular
vote in the presidential election of 1856.[27]

In the vast anti-Catholic literature that was spewed out on the fringes of
the nativist movement, the specter of Roman encroachment in American
affairs was prominent; and we may well see that as more a political issue
than either a religious or a directly behavioral one. But behavior was immensely and directly prominent in other anti-Catholic arguments. Catholics were stereotyped as drunkards (or at least as unfriendly to temperance crusades) and as Sabbath breakers. More strikingly, one finds in the
popular literature of nativism an obsession with Catholic "immorality,"
sexual immorality in particular, that was at least equal to the preoccupation with Popish plots. Ray Allen Billington, whose meticulous work on
antebellum nativism involved laboring through virtually all the sources,
went so far as to say that the immense volume of writings about Rome's
alleged grasp for temporal power was "dwarfed by the still larger volume
of books and pamphlets attacking the immorality of the papal system"
and "the degrading effects of Popery."[28] Allegations concerning Catho-

"The Priests in Pursuit of the Nun." In Samuel B.
Smith, *The Escape of Sainte Francis Patrick, Another Nun
from the Hôtel Dieu Nunnery of Montreal* (1836).

lic clergy and the members of Catholic orders were severe, sinister, and
minimally grounded in any sort of evidence. The spurious *Awful Disclosures
of Maria Monk* (1836), supposedly penned by an escapee from a Montreal
nunnery, was merely the most notorious example of hundreds of publications that described and pictured priests, nuns, and monks in general
debauch and very specific sexual transgressions.

The American Party was already confused and divided before it
launched into the 1856 elections. There were numerous reasons for that
party's decline, and for the short and unhappy careers of most nativist
legislators in the states. A surprisingly typical incident—one that also
bears striking resemblance to a Keystone Kops scenario—points to several of these reasons.

Nativists in Massachusetts, having won complete control of the state
government, and caught up in the crusade to stamp out Catholic im-

morality, established a Nunnery Committee to investigate the goings-on in convents. When some legislators advised their excited colleagues that there were no convents in Massachusetts, the mandate was broadened so that committee members could roam the state, frightening Catholic schoolchildren and, on at least one occasion, dining and drinking at state expense and consorting with ladies of easy virtue. The Know-Nothing majority, by replacing nearly all of its 1854 candidates, managed to win again in 1855; but the less-eventful record of the new body was also devoid of accomplishment. The end of the Know-Nothing phenomenon—though not, of course, the end of anti-Catholicism—was in sight.[29]

MORMONISM AND THE FREEDOM
TO GO ELSEWHERE

In a lecture of 1852, John Hughes, the puckishly astute Archbishop of New York, criticized mainstream America's pretensions as originators and protectors of religious pluralism. He chided not only the oft-chided Puritans of Massachusetts Bay but also the usually spared Pilgrims of Plymouth: "They had no objection that others should enjoy liberty of conscience; but it was not to be in their colony. They judged that those others, if they wished liberty of conscience, might imitate their example and find themselves a Plymouth Rock in some other bay."[30]

Hughes's witticism contained some sober truth. Religious freedom for "others" had frequently consisted in freedom to go elsewhere. The banishment of Roger Williams and Anne Hutchinson, and the execution of Mary Dyer and other Quakers who refused to be banished, had been early and particularly egregious instances; but the pattern had remained an important one. In Hughes's time, the Mormons, driven by persecution as well as economics from place to place across the country, and the Oneida Community, originally sited uncomfortably in Vermont but forced to migrate to upper New York State, were clear-cut examples of what he was talking about. (This is not to say that Hughes had positive feelings about either of these; he excoriated the Mormons, seizing the occasion to blame them on Protestantism.)[31] And some, including Mormons and Oneidans, continued to be persecuted or harassed after they had exercised this limited kind of freedom.

In the case of anti-Mormonism, religious and social behavior stands out with special clarity as the source of difficulty. It was, on the whole, permissible for Mormons to believe that an angel had led their founder, Joseph Smith, to mysterious golden plates on the Hill Cumorah, and that Mormons on their journey westward had been fed miraculously by tame quail on the Mississippi shore. Such beliefs were tolerated even if thought wrong and peculiar.

The point at which critics and public drew the line was the one defined by the Mormon leadership's championing of "plural marriage" (the Mormon term for polygamy) and, still more, what was thought to be its extensive or universal practice. (Although only 10–15 percent of the Mormons actually acted on this particular belief, the public perception was that most Mormons did so.)[32] Citizens in New York, Ohio, Missouri, and elsewhere along the path of the Mormons' westward flight also resented the Saints' economic success, and mainline spokespersons like Baird considered them fraudulent and dangerous. "The annals of modern times," Baird wrote, "furnish few more remarkable examples of cunning in the leaders, and delusion in their dupes."[33] But it was the practice of plural marriage, together with Mormon pretensions to "kingdom" status, that marked the movement off from most other new religions and that, more than anything else, accounts for the level and intensity of the opposition.

To be sure, the Mormons were subjected to teasing just as the transcendentalists and Millerites were. A typical lampoon, published after the death of Brigham Young, Smith's successor as principal leader, shows an enormous bed with an open space in the middle. The great man's boots stand forlornly at the foot, and twelve widows in nightcaps weep into very large handkerchiefs. The caption quotes Sir Walter Scott's *Lochinvar*: "The place which knew him once shall know him no more."

For Mormons, however, as for Catholics and some others, the experiences of intolerance and belittlement went well beyond either humor or mere theological disagreement. In Salt Lake City one can view a panorama, painted between 1869 and 1890 by a Danish immigrant named Carl C. A. Christensen, that depicts major episodes in Mormon history. Christensen emphasized miraculous events (Smith discovering the golden plates, the Mormons fed by tame quail) and heroic struggles (immigrants struggling across the plains with handcarts containing their worldly

Young's wives in mourning. Cartoon by J. Keppler in *Puck*, September 5, 1877.

goods), but also showed some of the better-known moments in a long history of rejection and persecution: the destruction of one Mormon settlement in Missouri; the Hauns Mill massacre in October 1838, in which seventeen Mormons were killed; the murder of Joseph Smith in 1844; the torching in 1846 of their temple in Nauvoo, Illinois.

This is sacred history. In keeping with usual practices in that genre, these paintings tell only one side of a more complicated story. Violence engaged in by Mormons, whether or not provoked by their enemies,[34] is not depicted. But Christensen's overall message is well supported by the historical evidence. The artist could have shown two dozen dramatic, disheartening scenes of riots, of Mormon leaders being tarred and feathered, of much more extensive conflagrations, and of Mormons being forced from their settlements.[35]

In relation to the subject of religious and cultural pluralism, an important reason for recounting the Mormon story is that it offers such a clear example of the way behavior operated to provoke intolerance or induce tolerance. "What goes around comes around." The earliest Mormons were denied acceptance because their religious practices threatened the communities in which they tried to settle. They fared better once they

C. C. A. Christensen, *Burning of the [Nauvoo] Temple.* Courtesy Brigham Young University Museum of Art. All rights reserved.

could pursue these practices in their own back yard (Utah) instead of someone else's. Within a few short decades after that, an official renunciation of the chief offending practice—polygamy—ended most of the hostilities, and a great deal of the ill feeling, between Mormons and the rest of American society.

Mormon folk songs composed barely a decade after the settlement at Salt Lake offer evidence—circumstantial, but rather surprising and of great interest—that Mormons already, by that time, were feeling more secure, though not necessarily more "tolerated." These songs alluded to the sect's history of persecution; but they seemed just as ready to acknowledge its idiosyncrasies—usually in a rather humorous way. "Tittery-Irie-Aye," a song of the 1850s, stressed the intolerance of earlier decades— "the way they have been treated, I think it is a sin"—but also referred to Mormons as a "strange people" and offered a bit of ammunition to detractors (in case they should need any):

> There is another item, to mention it I must,
> Concerning spiritual women that make a hell of a fuss.

C. C. A. Christensen, *The Handcart Company.* © Intellectual Reserve, Inc. Courtesy Museum of Church History and Art, Church of Jesus Christ of Latter-day Saints.

Some men have got a dozen wives, and others have a score,
And the man that's got but one wife's a-looking out for more.
Sing tittery-irie-aye, sing tittery-irie-o.[36]

Mormon songs of the 1860s pursued the same themes but also offered evidence of a rapid adjustment that was in large part behavioral. What they showed, in particular, was a reversal of attitude concerning Mormon relations to the "gentile" world. In the late 1850s, immigrants from Europe and the East reached Salt Lake City by hiking across the plains, pushing or pulling handcarts that Brigham Young had designed. Although the rationale for Mormon insistence on that mode of migration was in part economic, the words of "The Handcart Song" expressed distinct pride in the physical isolation that the farmers' carts symbolized:

Ye saints who dwell on Europe's shore, prepare yourself for many more
To leave behind your native land, for sure God's judgments are at hand;
For you must cross the raging main, before the promised land you gain,
And with the faithful make a start to cross the plains with your handcart.

. . . .

For some must push and some must pull, as we go marching up the hill.
So merrily on our way we go, until we reach the valley-o.

All did not go merrily. Some immigrants died on the plain, and Young had to send rescue parties in aid of others. What is striking, however, is how rapidly Mormons began to shed their sense of being despised, isolated, separated radically from the gentile world of Europe and the East. Those traditions did not disappear; yet in scarcely more than a decade Mormon songsters were celebrating the railroad that by then connected the Saints with the gentile world. Gradually Mormons had become less inclined to make a virtue of the trials an immigrant must undergo in order to leave the world behind and join them. By 1868, they were reporting that

The great locomotive next season will come
To gather the saints from their far distant homes,
And bring them to Utah in peace here to stay
While the judgments of God sweep the wicked away.

The refrain tried to make it clear that the Mormons' leader no longer felt quite the same about handcarts: "Hurray! Hurrah! The railroad's begun! Three cheers fr'our contractor; his name's Brigham Young." And another song of the same year, "The Utah Iron Horse," showed complete self-consciousness—spiked with self-deprecating humor and taken-for-granted racism—about the larger change this signified. The song exulted that "the iron horse is coming, with a train in his wake," and continued:

We have isolated been, but soon we shall be seen;
Through this wide mountain region, folks can learn of our religion;
. . .
"Civilized" we shall be, many folks we shall see,
Lords and nobles, quacks and beggars, anyhow we'll see the niggers;
Saints will come, sinners too, we'll have all that we can do,
For this great Union railroad it will fetch the Devil through.

During the next few decades, the Mormons' physical and intellectual isolation—and, even more, their sense of isolation—was diminished further. I would not suggest that this was merely a matter of changed behavior, or even of changed attitudes. The Mormons' theology, for example, and their ideas about the Hebrew and Christian scriptures, by the end of the century had shifted visibly toward the mainstream, and particularly in the direction of Protestant evangelicalism.[37] But behavior continued to be the sticking point. In the midst of repeated rejections of statehood for Utah, both the Congress and the Supreme Court of the United States acted to outlaw polygamy; and statehood was not approved until 1896, when the Mormons themselves renounced plural marriage.

As one historian of Mormonism puts it, a long-standing political ambition had thus been achieved "amid the defeat of the peculiar Mormon dream of their own Zion in the mountains." Mormons, having agreed to behave themselves, had sealed their entitlement not merely to toleration but also to an ampler, less patronizing form of acceptance: inclusion. Before long they would be widely regarded as satellites of the cultural and religious mainstream—indeed, by some measures, as mainstays of that mainstream.[38]

At the end of the next century, the denomination's president confirmed in an interview that Mormons thought of themselves that way, but he was quick to add that "we haven't lost our distinctiveness. We have not set aside the uniqueness of our doctrine, our organization, or our practices."[39] That statement was too casual (or amnesiac) with respect to the doctrine and practice of plural marriage, which—"unique" practice or not—had been rather forcefully set aside, but otherwise it was in accord with the facts as most non-Mormons saw them.

What can we conclude about responses to the new diversities of the early nineteenth century?

From later vantage points, but also in the eyes of many at the time, it was clear that the American reputation for religious freedom and social liberality had been compromised, though not destroyed. In the midst of largely unanticipated social upheaval, Americans had managed to apply their pluralist ideals in very visible ways, and usually in perfectly genuine, committed ways. Just as visibly, however, they had applied limits. They had said, "Thus far, and no farther." I have argued that, time and again, they drew the line at what they perceived as socially threatening behavior.

In practical terms, this meant that if you were a cultural insider, you could be about as different as you wished in actual religious views. And it meant that if you were an outsider, acceptance depended to a large extent upon your willingness to adjust, to become assimilated, especially in matters of religious and general behavior. Those outcomes, together with the fact that improved acceptance would often be related to changed material or political conditions — for example, an "outsider" group's advance in numbers, economic status, and voting power — could lead us to conclude that in the early nineteenth century the pluralist ideal, as an ideal, was almost without effect.

My own view is closer to the one the historian David Potter held with respect to the place of values in social development. Potter's *People of Plenty* (1954) was a study of the part played by economic abundance in shaping the American character. Yet Potter, despite that emphasis, refused to discount the power of the society's formal commitments to individualism, equality, and other leading values. According to his formula, which is the one I would apply to the case before us, favorable material conditions enabled Americans in some measure to "pay democracy's promissory notes."[40]

Double-minded responses to diversity were, of course, to continue. But so were the echoes, ringing down the years since the Declaration of Independence, the Virginia Statute of Religious Freedom, and the Federal Bill of Rights, of some less ambiguous expressions of respect for religious difference. These and other promissory notes of religious pluralism, only partly made good in the years of the early republic, would remain on the books as commitments that could never entirely be ignored.

3

Marching to Zion: The Protestant
Establishment as a Unifying Force

A funny thing happened on the way to the twentieth century: the Americans, who were noted for overthrowing religious establishments, and were delighted with themselves for having done so, developed a very effective religious establishment of their own. This extraconstitutional arrangement constituted a brake upon pluralism even while at some points nurturing and promoting it. As a brake it bore a cousinlike resemblance to such strident and often violent movements as nativism; but the Protestant establishment was larger, more powerful, and significantly more benign.

European observers recognized that the Americans had not disestablished religion after all. Alexis de Tocqueville's analysis of American society, *Democracy in America* (1834–40), confirmed that impression. Tocqueville reported that "there is no country in the world where the Christian religion retains greater influence over the souls of men than in America. . . . In the United States, Christian sects are infinitely diversified and perpetually modified; but Christianity itself is an established and irresistible fact."[1]

Many admirers thought that the Americans had been very clever and were having it both ways. A delegation of British Congregationalists, at about the time of Tocqueville's visit, remarked that although the United States had "no law for the regulation or observance of the Sabbath . . . public sentiment secures its sanctification better with them than with us." Others were not so complimentary. John Henry Newman (the Anglican cleric and future Roman Catholic cardinal) acknowledged the reality of the American nonestablished establishment, but found it hypocritical as well as anomalous. Newman snorted that despite the Americans' boast "that their Church is not, like ours, enslaved to the civil power," it was thoroughly enslaved to the laity. "And in a democracy what is that but the civil power in another shape?"[2]

Americans generally denied the entire allegation, even when it was kindly and admiringly meant. But surely the foreign observers were right. As Tocqueville explained, life was unsettled and unsettling on the frontiers and in American society generally. He wrote that "when there is no longer any principle of authority in religion any more than in politics, men are speedily frightened at the aspect of this unbounded independence. The constant agitation of all surrounding things alarms and exhausts them."[3] American aspirations toward unity, which were enshrined in such formal principles as *e pluribus unum*, were grounded more fundamentally in the people's yearnings for order, coherence, and certitude. A religious establishment, even if its legal sanctions were scattered and miscellaneous, as in the American instance, could serve as a vehicle of social as well as religious coherence.

America's informal arrangement also, in the manner of hegemonic structures generally, served to draw "others" toward—or even into—the ambit of the dominant culture.[4] To the dismay of the most independent spirits among them, Catholics and Jews, for example, acquiesced in the Protestant hegemony, at times buying into it in quite concrete ways. As the historian Catherine Albanese puts it, Protestant dominance

> was related to the continuance of a certain community, the early settlers and their offspring, who were of Anglo-Saxon and North European stock. But it was also related to the widespread adoption by others of the creed, code, and cultus that the original community handed on. Although many times they were unaware of it, [others] could and did share in public Protestantism.[5]

STRUCTURES OF PROTESTANT INFLUENCE

The idea of an "informal establishment" sounds elusive, but the American arrangement was not very different in that respect from the constitutional establishments of Europe. For one thing, in the nineteenth century the latter were becoming more difficult to define in any but the most superficial terms. Gradually, but steadily, nearly all of Europe's church-state alliances were going the way of the Cheshire cat—becoming mere faces with less and less of a substantial body of powers and perquisites behind them.[6] For another, the American arrangement turns out, on inspection, to have been definable in fairly concrete institutional terms.

The institutions were of several kinds. The religious establishment involved, first and most obviously, the more powerful Protestant denominations, especially those of the Baptists, Congregationalists, Episcopalians, Methodists, and Presbyterians. Second, it included the multitude of voluntary associations, both interdenominational and nondenominational, that promoted missions, peace, temperance, and numerous other kinds of moral and social reform. Third, it derived authority from a large and dominating world of English-language cultural, literary, educational, and journalistic entities that were Protestant in personnel and outlook. Finally, the establishment must be understood as a personal network of Protestant leadership that extended across the churches, controlled most of the nation's political life, and managed virtually all of the major secular institutions and entities in American society.

We may want to think of this personal network as an institution only in the sense in which we identify the family as an institution. But that analogy would be apt, as is the further observation that the personal network was also built upon institutions—families, colleges, churches, and such great amorphous entities as business and government.

Another figurative term for what I have called the structures of Protestant dominance would be *fabric*, because what we have here is something like the weaver's warp and woof. One can picture, using that image, vertical threads that represent such things as churches, governments, economic institutions, and social elites; and, running across these horizontally, the more personal relationships of family, intermarriage, collegiality, and friendship—indeed personal relationships of all kinds.

A PROTESTANT ETHOS

Institutional structures, however, important as they were, make up only part of the picture. The continuing dominance of Protestantism amid the new diversities of the American nineteenth century depended upon the existence and compelling force of a national ethos whose religious elements were heavily Protestant. (Also Calvinist, even though the tougher Calvinist theological points had been widely modified by the middle of the century.) This ethos, although it affected different groups of Americans in different ways and intensities, nonetheless gave powerful support to the various structures of mainline Protestant dominance. It was, at the same time, nurtured and perpetuated by those structures. They were mutually supportive.

Here again, as in the case of other volatile terms like pluralism, it is helpful to start with a dictionary definition: An ethos is not just a vague atmosphere; the term refers to the "attitudes, habits, [and] beliefs" that are dominant in a given culture, and that exercise some degree of power or influence in diverse communities within it. Albanese, making this kind of generic definition specific to the nineteenth-century American situation, and catching the interaction between ethos and structures, writes that "public Protestantism" as a dominant tradition embodied "acknowledged ways of thinking and acting supported by most institutions in the society."[7]

What, exactly, were these common traits that allegedly stood out, and performed a unifying function, in the midst of great and growing diversity? Philip Schaff, the Swiss historian and adoptive American, can be particularly helpful at this point. Schaff, who penned his observations two decades after Tocqueville published his, described the distinctive elements in American religion more astutely, perhaps, than any other European observer before or since.

Schaff emphasized diversity as itself a distinguishing feature of American life and institutions; but he also identified commonalities in thought and action—not all of which he found praiseworthy—that he attributed in large part to the abiding influence of Calvinism. There were only two countries, he wrote, Scotland and the United States, where one could "obtain a clear view of the enormous influence which Calvin's personality, moral earnestness, and legislative genius have exerted on history." In America, this influence, which "modifies . . . even the Lutheran Church," had produced a religious life that Schaff characterized as "uncommonly practical, energetic, and enterprising . . . entering into the relations of the world, organizing itself in every variety of form; aggressive and missionary." America's Calvin-infused culture, he added, "places the Bible above everything else, and would have its church life ever a fresh, immediate emanation from this, without troubling itself much about tradition and intermediate history."[8]

Schaff expressed astonishment at the concrete results of this enterprising spirit. "It is amazing, what a mass of churches, seminaries, benevolent institutions, religious unions and societies, are there founded and supported by mere voluntary contributions." In Europe, by contrast, church building and "general religious progress" had fallen far behind population growth, especially in cities; and Schaff thought his fellow Europeans "could learn very much from America." He also thought, however, that people on both sides of the water should simply recognize that the American style was different. American religion, Schaff said, is more in the mold of the activist St. Peter than of the mystic St. John,

> more like busy Martha than like the pensive Mary, sitting at the feet of Jesus. It expands more in breadth than in depth. It is often carried on like a secular business, and in a mechanical or utilitarian spirit. It lacks the beautiful enamel of deep fervor and heartiness, the true mysticism, an appreciation of history and the church; it wants the substratum of a profound and spiritual theology. This is especially evident in [a deficient] doctrine of the church and of the Sacraments, and in the meagreness of the worship.[9]

In a similarly detached but more negative tone, the Swiss-born churchman described the "restless reachings into the future" that suffused the general consciousness and the religious thinking of the average American. The dream of a vast, ever growing, benevolent empire, Schaff remarked, "flatters his vanity, it stirs his ambition, it rouses his energy, it constantly excites and strengthens in him the impression that his nation is one day to be the greatest of the earth, to attain the perfection of church as well as state, and then to react with regenerating power on Europe, and from California to convert China and Japan."[10]

RELIANCE ON BIBLICAL AUTHORITY

From such observations—and we could find quite a number that resembled Schaff's—one can distill a consensus list of the most prominent elements in the Protestant ethos of nineteenth-century America. The five elements that observers emphasized at the time, and that stand out in retrospect, are biblicism, individualism, moralism, activism, and millennial optimism.

What I am calling biblicism took varying forms, the most common of which was the moderate stance Schaff described—simply a greater reliance on Scripture than on other sources of authority. It also, however, assumed other, more extreme shapes as the century wore on and defenders of biblical authority reacted to scientific and other challenges.

Many people today, even if they have some knowledge of America's religious past, assume that the Puritans of the seventeenth century must have been much like modern fundamentalists in their attitudes toward the Bible; but Puritan divines would have blushed and fumed if told about the lengths to which some successors had carried their reliance on scriptural authority. Leading Puritans had expressed confidence that "the Lord hath more truth yet to break out of his Holy Word."[11] But Charles Hodge, the leading theologian of nineteenth-century Presbyterianism, expressed the growing hostility among conservatives of his own era to any ideas of "human" interpretation or a continuing revelation. Hodge insisted in 1857 that "everything which the Bible affirms to be true is true. . . . Its declarations . . . as to facts and principles, are the declarations of God."[12]

Several decades later, Hodge's son and other Princeton theologians had moved farther in the direction of a strict "verbal inerrancy." So had popular revivalists. The leading evangelist of the late nineteenth century, Dwight L. Moody, put in simpler language virtually the same ideas; and such academic and pastoral utterances, as the historian George Marsden has written, thrust the doctrine of scriptural inerrancy into "a more prominent role in modern America than it has had at almost any other time or place in church history."[13]

But relatively moderate claims about scriptural authority (ideas that, in their seeming concessions to modernity, helped in turn to provoke the more rigid formulations of biblicism) were at least equally common. Henry Boynton Smith, a Presbyterian theologian who differed from the Princetonians on this and many other matters, gave a much wider berth to biblical interpretation. The object of inspiration, he wrote, "is the communication of truth in an infallible manner, so that, when rightly interpreted, no error is conveyed."[14] And among the growing number, both within and outside of Presbyterianism, who were more liberal than Smith, words like *infallible* were disappearing from the lexicon.

Taken together, these differing forms and intensities of biblicism, especially if we include allusions to Scripture in political speeches and other forms of public discourse, fully confirmed Schaff's perceptions about the American deference to biblical authority. This deference was as striking on the American scene, and as much a contrast with European patterns, as was the relative weakness of concern about creeds, liturgies, institutional structures, or, in Schaff's words, "a profound and spiritual theology."

INDIVIDUALISM

In religious terms, *individualism* was focused on each person's responsibility to work out his or her own salvation. This was expressed in almost countless forms of sermonic, artistic, musical, and literary discourse. But popular art may be the place to start; nothing else made the point so forcefully and at the same time, perhaps, naively. (That is, one feels that individual striving simply *was* the formula for the conduct of life.)

In hundreds of depictions like the two reproduced below, the idea, as in the revival sermon, was that humans, born as sinners and surrounded by inducements to remain in that condition, must somehow find the road — or ladder — to virtuous lives. And the assumption was that the desired result, even though the grace of God is fundamentally involved in bringing it about, cannot happen without a decision on the part of the individual.

The *Ladder of Fortune*, a Currier and Ives lithograph printed in 1875, is quite typical in presenting the moral life as a matter of clear choices between good and evil, God and Satan. The young man poised to climb the ladder (the principal figures were invariably male when the immediate subject was "getting ahead") not only will set his feet on rungs like *integrity* and *prudence*; in doing so he will reject wicked alternatives. It is a zero-sum game.

The *Ladder of Fortune* artist obviously, when he thinks about wickedness, is preoccupied mainly with pursuits like gambling and labor agitation. The other artist, whose depiction of *The Way of Good and Evil* appeared in 1862, presents an entire menu of evil choices and practices, beginning

"The Ladder of Fortune." Currier and Ives print, 1875. Prints and Photographs Division, Library of Congress (LC-USZ62-36515).

"The Way of Good and Evil." Drawing by John Hailer, 1862. Prints and Photographs Division, Library of Congress (LC-USZ62-49490).

with the foundational sin of "disobedience to parents and teachers" and culminating in felonies that lead to the gallows and eternal damnation.

The same rhetoric of choice recurred constantly in the hymns sung in churches and camp meetings. A prominent example is James Russell Lowell's majestic "Once to Every Man and Nation," which he composed in 1845 and set to an equally majestic Welsh melody:

Once to every man and nation comes the moment to decide,
In the strife of truth with falsehood, for the good or evil side;
Some great cause, God's new Messiah, offering each the bloom or blight,
And the choice goes on forever 'twixt that darkness and the light.

Some of the most striking, unqualified expressions of the same zero-sum religious individualism occurred in the preaching of Charles Grandison Finney, the leading evangelist of the mid-nineteenth century. As a theologian, a former lawyer, and in his later career a prominent educator, Finney clearly represented the establishment elite; but as a preacher he ran close to the ground of popular consciousness. As one historian of revivalism has put it, Finney "did not study the popular mind; he had it." [15] This was nowhere more evident than in those early sermons and theological writings in which he pressed the point that sinners were "bound to change their own hearts."

That kind of demand for individual choice would be unlikely to surprise anyone a few decades later—not, at least, when it was posed in a revivalist context. But that was because of the influence of Finney's generation of neo-Calvinist leaders, and the enormous popular resonance of Finney himself. Back in 1831, however, when the young evangelist mounted the pulpit at Boston's Park Street Church to urge that sinners change their own hearts, this was a startling and dangerous admonition. Most evangelists retained at least some of the outlook of their great predecessor, Jonathan Edwards, who had made it fearsomely clear that sinners are "in the hands of an angry God"—in other words, that their salvation is entirely dependent upon God's grace.

To be sure, Finney conveyed his own brand of fearsomeness. Tall, rangy, personally magnetic and compelling, he portrayed the sinner's situation in terms almost as grim as those Edwards had insisted upon, and with far more compelling body language. During the Park Street performances, and in others throughout his evangelistic career, people on the speaker's platform ducked as Finney, with his long arms flailing and his intense gaze sweeping the hall, dramatized the Creation by flinging the Earth and other planets into space. It was reported that those in the back seats rose involuntarily to follow his finger as it described the path of the sinner down to Hell.[16]

But when it came to the question of what it was that sinners (by which he meant virtually everyone) could and must do to achieve salvation, Finney's answer was milder, or at least more reassuring, than that of Edwards. Sinners, Finney insisted, are not helpless in the face of God's anger. For the landmark sermon of 1831 he drew his text from the book

Charles Finney in 1850. Courtesy Oberlin College Archives, Oberlin, Ohio.

of Ezekiel: "Make you a new heart and a new spirit, for why will ye die?" And he really did mean, "*You* must do it!" He warned his hearers not "to be passive, to wait for some mysterious influence, like an electric shock, to change [your] hearts." They could wait until the day of judgment; God would not do their duty for them. "The fact is, sinners, that God requires you to turn, and what he requires of you, he cannot do for you. It must be your own voluntary act. . . . Do not wait then for him to do your duty, but do it immediately yourself, on pain of eternal death." [17]

Finney's exhortations—this one included—also had their calmer moments. Indeed, some of those back-row sinners at Park Street may have risked eternal damnation and gone out for a smoke as the ex-lawyer offered sixteen lengthy, carefully numbered reasons why individuals must *act* before God could or would save them.

But act in what way, exactly? Point seventeen, which was Finney's peroration, rose to an especially high pitch:

Throw down your rebellious weapons—give up your refuges of lies—fix your mind steadfastly upon the world of considerations that should instantly decide you to close in with the offer of reconciliation while it now lies before you. Another moment's delay, and it may be too late forever. . . . Hear then, O sinner, I beseech you, and obey the word of the Lord—"Make you a new heart and a new spirit, for why will ye die?" [18]

MORALISM

The characteristic usually called moralism was connected closely to religious individualism, because it related to one of the many other duties that fell to aspiring Christians once they had chosen between God and Satan. This, simply put, was the regenerated individual's imperative responsibility to save others. A gospel song written toward the end of the century, "Throw Out the Lifeline," stated this obligation in especially graphic terms:

> Throw out the lifeline across the dark wave;
> There is a brother whom someone should save;
> Somebody's brother! Oh, who then will dare
> To throw out the lifeline his peril to share?
>> Throw out the lifeline! Throw out the lifeline!
>> Someone is drifting away;
>> Throw out the lifeline! Throw out the lifeline!
>> Someone is sinking today.

This suggests another point at which individualism and moralism were deeply interconnected. In theory at least, the responsibility to save others involved persuasion, not some kind of coercion. If the saved individual was to save or help others, he or she was obligated first of all to recognize those others as individuals, as people capable of making free choices. The responsibility was to help them work out their salvation.

Broadened out into concerns about a Christian or Christianizing society, however, this sometimes did become coercive. A redemptive social order helps people to do the things that make for their own salvation and the advancement of God's kingdom. But at some points it may have to force them to do these things.

Timothy Shay Arthur's "Ten Nights in a Barroom" was an extended temperance tract widely read in the 1850s and more widely viewed, in the form of lantern slides, later in the century. In this famous story, a town's more sober citizens spend ten years trying, and in general failing, to reform the worst of its drunkards. But in the end, the very worst, one Joe Morgan, has seen the light; and the town, under his leadership, opts for prohibition—in other words chooses to enforce morality by means of a clearly coercive kind of legislation.[19]

The tenth night: the reformed drunkard exhorts the townspeople. From lantern slides of "Ten Nights in a Barroom," reproduced in *American Heritage*, June 1964.

RELIGIOUS ACTIVISM

Together, individualism and moralism added up to the kind of religious activism that Schaff considered central to the American style and that Finney harangued his hearers about. The American was *expected*, it seemed, to be "more like busy Martha than like the pensive Mary." In theory, Christians could be individualistic, or moralistic, or both, and yet just sit there, waiting piously for God "to do their duty for them." Clearly that was not the way of Finney revivalism. It came to be seen as not the American way.

The term *activist*, especially as employed in European critiques of the American style (in Germany, *Aktivismus* and *Amerikanismus* became synonyms), referred to a deep-seated reliance on what theologians called human agency. To most foreign observers, and some domestic ones, this human self-confidence seemed almost as evident in American revivalistic religion as it was in an emerging American liberalism that was usually at odds with revivalism. By midcentury, many revivalists besides Finney were insisting that sinners must take action on behalf of their own salvation. In the same era, religious liberals (and this was true even before the emergence of a "social gospel" toward the end of the century) were more and more open to strategies that seemed to bypass or postpone individual salvation in favor of social salvation. But in both contexts, human beings were relied upon to take action toward the advancement of God's kingdom on earth.

This unusual degree of trust in human agency, although it always encountered dissent, was strikingly common at the level of theology and intellectual discourse. In more popular forms—for example, in the constant jesting and complaints about American braggadocio—it was legendary. In one story that made the rounds of regions (and accents), but that was most often told about a Vermont "fahmer," the parson compliments a parishioner on "the verdant farmland that you and the Lord have made out of this rocky hillside." "You can put it that way, preacher," the farmer answers, "but you should have seen it when the Lord was tryin' to fahm it by himself."

One of the best expressions of the activist spirit was the camp meeting hymn "You Must Be a Lover of the Lord," which was written in 1866.[20] In this hymn, a rollicking American version of a much staider piece by the eighteenth-century hymnist Isaac Watts (who might not have acknowledged paternity), most of the verses express a scornful attitude toward all passive forms of Christianity:

> Am I a soldier of the cross?
> A follower of the Lamb?
> And shall I fear to own His cause,
> Or blush to speak His name?
>   Oh, you must be a lover of the Lord,
>   You must be a lover of the Lord,
>   Oh, you must be a lover of the Lord,
>   Or you can't go to heaven when you die.
> Must I be carried to the skies
> On flow'ry beds of ease?

While others fought to win the prize,
And sailed through bloody seas?
  Oh, you must be a lover of the Lord . . .
Are there no foes for me to face?
Must I not stem the flood?
Is this vile world a friend to grace,
To help me on to God?
  Oh, you must be a lover of the Lord . . .
Since I must fight if I would reign,
Increase my courage, Lord;
I'll bear the toil, endure the pain,
Supported by Thy word.
  Oh, you must be a lover of the Lord . . .

MILLENNIAL OPTIMISM

A final, highly important, element in the Protestant ethos was the one Schaff identified as "restless reachings into the future." Among the several forms of future-mindedness that Schaff's phrase referred to, none was more potent, or more a subject of criticism from abroad, than the millennial optimism that featured Americans as a chosen people—in fact, as the chosen people of the modern age.[21] One finds, underlying and invigorating the ever-present themes of individual and collective striving, an overwhelming sense that God's kingdom is advancing, and that the American nation and society are the special instruments of this advance.

In more technical theological terms this was postmillennialism, the idea that Christ will not return until after the sanctifying of human society. But those called premillennialists, who were a growing minority by the end of the century, and who in theory foresaw little or no earthly improvement before Christ's return, managed to use much of the same language. According to either version triumph was inevitable; the thousand-year reign of Christ is coming, whether before or after his physical return.

The process, however fraught with troubles and obstacles, is inexorable; and we are part of it insofar as we are really Christians. Those of us who are saved and, collectively, the chosen society we represent and lead, are "marching upward to Zion." That phrase dominated the chorus in another hymn of the 1860s that Americanized poor Isaac Watts. The great Englishman's prayerful "Come We That Love the Lord," which had been composed in 4/4 time, with no chorus, became a surging and—dare we say it?—swinging burst of enthusiasm in 6/8 time.[22]

> Come, we that love the Lord
> And let our joys be known,
> Join in a song with sweet accord, [sung twice]
> And thus surround the throne. [×2]
>> We're marching to Zion,
>> Beautiful, beautiful Zion;
>> We're marching upward to Zion,
>> The beautiful city of God.
> Let those refuse to sing
> Who never knew our God;
> But children of the heav'nly King, [×2]
> May speak their joys abroad. [×2]
>> We're marching to Zion . . .
> Then let our songs abound,
> And ev'ry tear be dry
> We're marching thro' Immanuel's ground [×2]
> To fairer worlds on high [×2]
>> We're marching to Zion . . .

This millennial optimism, with its seemingly inevitable accompaniment of confidence about a secular national mission, has provoked more comment and historical analysis than any other feature of the nineteenth-century Protestant ethos. Its expressions ranged from echoings of Jonathan Edwards's cautious (and soon revoked) speculation that the hoped-for redemption of the world "will begin in America" to the chauvinism of the Reverend Josiah Strong at the end of the nineteenth century. In 1885 Strong's best-selling *Our Country* announced that the "Anglo-Saxon race," led by the Americans, was about to conquer the world for Christ:

> Is there room for reasonable doubt that this race, unless devitalized by alcohol and tobacco, is destined to dispossess many weaker races, assimilate others, and mold the remainder, until, in a very true and important sense, it has Anglo-Saxonized mankind? . . . I believe it is fully in the hands of the people of the United States, during the next ten or fifteen years, to hasten or retard the coming of Christ's kingdom in the world by hundreds, and perhaps thousands, of years. We of this generation and nation occupy the Gibraltar of the ages which commands the world's future.[23]

Strong, who later drew back both from the hyperoptimism of such out-bursts and from the biological racism they implied, had spent much of his earlier career as an active promoter of the mission enterprise on the American continent. The story of the "home missions" he pursued and supervised would provide a telling case study of the workings of millennial optimism in religious outreach.[24] The overseas missions of the time, however, provide a still better crucible, for here it is more obvious that the aspiration is to aid and convert the entire world.

Once again, popular hymnology tells us a good deal about the assumptions implanted in the thinking and actions of ordinary people. Late in the century, with the foreign mission movement booming, versifiers used Strong-like language about the "nations crowding to be born" ("Fling Out the Banner," 1894) and about heathens "bound in the darksome prison-house of sin" ("O Zion, Haste, Thy Mission High Fulfilling," 1894). But a similar confidence had appeared in the hymnology of the early nineteenth century, when the foreign mission movement had been young, small, and ill-supported. Various lyrics set to music, in the 1820s and after, by the New England composer Lowell Mason expressed acute anguish about the little-known "lands that in darkness have lain" ("Hail to the Brightness of Zion's Glad Morning," 1832). And Mason's setting, dating from 1832, of Bishop Heber's "From Greenland's Icy Mountains" rang the changes on the idea, later made notorious by Rudyard Kipling, of a "white man's burden." These far-off peoples are pleading for help:

> From many an ancient river, from many a palmy plain,
> They call us to deliver their land from error's chain.

Efforts to heed their call will prove burdensome. They will not show gratitude, and many will persist in their wickedness:

> In vain, with lavish kindness, the gifts of God are strown;
> The heathen in his blindness, bows down to wood and stone.

Yet we, the chosen and favored ones, must persist:

> Shall we, whose souls are lighted by wisdom from on high—
> Shall we to man benighted the lamp of life deny?
> Salvation! oh, salvation! The joyful sound proclaim
> Till earth's remotest nation has learnt Messiah's name.

The notion that the heathen are pleading with us, urgently, "to deliver their land" was an especially important part of the rationale for foreign missions. It helped, somewhat at least, to deflect charges of what would now be decried as religious and cultural imperialism.

Like most elements in the argument for foreign missions, this one had roots in a much earlier period. The supposed summons, "Come over and help us" had been imprinted, along with an image of the American aborigine, on an official seal of the Massachusetts Bay colony. And, like the Heber-Mason "missionary hymn" itself, it was an assertion that persisted into the twentieth century.*

This imperative was pressed also in relation to allegedly civilized peoples. They too, it was argued, want us to reform their rotten civilizations. When those "marching to Zion" were enjoined to "speak their joys abroad," this meant, for some, not only carrying the Word to a highly civilized Japan but also preaching Protestantism in Roman Catholic areas of Europe and Latin America. Echoing the old refrain, the mission executive Robert E. Speer quoted a Brazilian's plea: "I beg you to arouse your country to come to our help." [25]

All of these themes and elements of the Protestant ethos were contested within American society—especially in nonmainstream ethnic, racial, and religious contexts. [26] We might suspect that most "outsiders" lacked any awareness of the Protestant establishment and its values; and that might be true, just as it would be true that most Protestants were unaware of a dominance they simply took for granted. Aware or not, however, the people in nonmainstream communities could scarcely avoid being affected by the continuing white Protestant domination of the newspapers, the educational system, and most city governments. Nor could Catholics, Lutherans, and others remain indifferent to such neo-Calvinist moral pre-

---

*A very similar rhetoric, in fact, turned up in attempts to justify American activities abroad at the opening of the twenty-first century. In April 2002, a writer for the conservative *Weekly Standard* declared that "troubled lands cry out for enlightened foreign administration." In response to this, William Pfaff, the syndicated foreign affairs columnist, remarked that "to some in Washington, empire seems a career opportunity." He added, however, that "to the ordinary American, I suspect, it simply looks like trouble." Boston *Globe* (April 8, 2002), A13.

"Come and help us." Left, a 1630 seal of the Massachusetts Bay Colony, from Nehemiah Adams, *The Life of John Eliot* (1847). Right, a May 1920 cover illustration for *Missionary Review of the World*, Courtesy Publications Office, World Council of Churches.

occupations as temperance or sabbatarianism, given the fact that these and other elements in the dominant culture provoked turmoil and dissension within their own communities.[27] So mainstream influences and encroachments were widely perceived. Often they were welcomed, or at least absorbed without complaint. But nearly as often they were resisted, and such resistance is an important element in the overall story.

None of the "Protestant" characteristics, moreover, should be seen as exclusively or even singularly American; often they grew out of European experience as well as contrasting with it. Max Lerner, the journalist and historian who in the 1950s attempted to define *America as a Civilization*, took the position that many apparently distinctive American traits have been such not because they have run contrary to European patterns but because they have exhibited those same patterns in bold relief. "The American is . . . the concentrated embodiment of Western man, more sharply delineated, developed under more urgent conditions, but with most of the essential traits present."[28]

Lerner's formula is helpful in any attempt to sort through the more universal and the more parochial elements in the Protestant ethos. American biblicism presented impulses of the Protestant Reformation in sharpened form, while American millennial optimism extended, and on the whole outdid, a spirit of euphoric expansionism in nineteenth-century Europe. The individualism, moralism, and activism that stood out as traits in American religion all carried forward and exaggerated identifiable European impulses—especially those of Protestant Europe and, most of all, those of British civilization.

RUNNING WITH IT: THE DRIVE FOR A
CHRISTIAN AMENDMENT

The institutional structure of the Protestant establishment, together with the skein of essentially Protestant moral and religious ideas that pervaded so much of the society, helped maintain a high degree of unity in a diverse and diversifying culture. Protestant unifying elements were not capable of penetrating every ethnic subculture, and not nearly enough to dissolve sectional and other rivalries, even within the churches.[29] Yet they did unquestionably exert a powerful hegemonic force.

They represented, in any case, about as much of a religious establishment as most Americans wanted or would tolerate. (The Confederate Constitution, unlike its federal predecessor, did give passing recognition to a deity. Its preamble invoked "the favor and guidance of Almighty God.") One of the symptomatic developments of the late nineteenth century, nonetheless, was the aggressive attempt by a well-organized minority to seize upon the existing Protestant hegemony and run with it— more specifically, to formalize the informal establishment.

In 1863, during the darkest days of the Civil War, an organization was formed that bore the broad and liberal-sounding name of National Reform Association. The purpose of this organization, however, was one that most contemporaries did not consider liberal. The purpose was to write the Christian religion into the United States Constitution.

What the reformers had in mind was not an end to church-state separation. They went to some lengths to reaffirm that arrangement; and they insisted that they intended no restrictions at all on religious liberty. In a statement set before the president of the United States in the hope of gaining his support, the association assured Mr. Lincoln that "we ask for no union of Church and State — that is a thing which we utterly repudiate; we ask for nothing inconsistent with the largest liberty, or the rights of conscience in any man."[30]

All they wanted — but they wanted this very badly indeed — was a constitutional amendment affirming that the United States is a Christian nation. The petition to Congress that they showed Lincoln included a new wording for the preamble to that Constitution. (I have italicized the proposed additions.)

> We the people of the United States, *humbly acknowledging Almighty God as the source of all authority and power in civil government, the Lord Jesus Christ as the Ruler among the nations, and His revealed will as the supreme law of the land, in order to constitute a Christian government and,* in order to form a more perfect union, establish justice, insure domestic tranquility, provide for the common defense, promote the general welfare, and secure *the inalienable rights and* the blessings of liberty, *and the pursuit of happiness* to ourselves, our posterity, *and all the people,* do ordain and establish this Constitution for the United States of America.[31]

This proposed preamble not only incorporates language about Jesus and Almighty God but also lifts phrases from the Declaration of Independence that might not seem essential to a confirmation of Christian nationhood. For that there appear to have been two reasons: because the Constitution makes no mention of God, the petitioners wanted to give special recognition to a document that does so. Secondly, they wished, in the wake of Lincoln's Emancipation Proclamation, to emphasize in the revised Constitution the "inalienable rights [of] all the people."

If Lincoln, himself a consummate stylist, objected to the resulting 109-word sentence, no complaint of that sort is recorded. The presidential response we do have bespeaks, instead, Lincoln the practiced politician:

> Gentlemen: The general aspect of your movement, I cordially approve. In regard to particulars, I must ask time to deliberate, as the work of amending the Constitution should not be done hastily. I will carefully examine your paper, in order more fully to comprehend its contents than is possible from merely hearing it read, and will take such action upon it as my responsibility to our Maker and our country demands.[32]

The association asked for such other changes in the main body of the Constitution "as may be necessary to give effect to these amendments in the Preamble." And over the next ten years, as they struggled to get their proposals before Congress, the reformers came up with a number of other ways to make explicit the nation's commitment to Christianity. They lobbied for strengthening the Christian Sabbath. They demanded presidential proclamations and oaths of office that would recognize Jesus Christ as well as God the Father. And some went so far as to demand that the federal government institute, for what would have been the first time, the restrictions on office-holding that had once existed in a number of states. But the idea of amending the Constitution, and in particular its preamble, remained central.

Resolutions passed at the 1873 convention of the Reform Association made it clear that, despite their constant assurances concerning rights of conscience, these citizens were driven more by a unitive instinct than by any sort of pluralist ideal. "A nation and an administration of government," they asserted, "can no more exist without moral character . . . than without a [common] language. . . . Any attempt to do so is not only absurd but dangerous." The results of trying to get along without a legally sanctioned common faith were, they thought, already starkly evident: "The signs of the times, the rapid deterioration of public morals, and the bold demands of organized public infidelity, show conclusively and impressively, that the alternative now presented to the American people is Atheism or Christianity."[33] Failure to adopt the proposed amendment therefore "involve[d] ultimately general immorality and anarchy." There could be no social or national health without moral consensus; and such consensus would be impossible without a fully recognized special position for Christianity.

That this also meant a special position for Protestantism seems clear. The word *Protestant* did not appear in the association's literature or proposals, and one reason for that may well have been that leaders of the movement hoped for Roman Catholic support. If so, however, they were disappointed, because the response from that quarter was an eerie silence. Catholics thought they knew what a "Christian" establishment would be like.

The Congress, and probably a comfortable majority of those who elected congressmen, found the amendment idea unworkable; some found it downright abhorrent. In 1874, when Christian Amendment legis-

Thomas Nast weighs in against governmental support for "any religious creed or doctrine." From *Harper's Weekly*, February 25, 1871. Prints and Photographs Division, Library of Congress (LC-USZ62-127553).

lation reached the Judiciary Committee of the House of Representatives, that body answered with a powerful reaffirmation of what legislators believed had been the Founders' intentions. The Constitutional Convention, the committee advised, had decided "after grave deliberation" that because this country "was to be the home of the oppressed of all nations of the earth, whether Christian or pagan," it would be inexpedient "to put anything into the Constitution or frame of government which might be construed to be a reference to any religious creed or doctrine." They went on to point out that, over the long history of the amending process, no amendment "has ever been proposed to the States by which this wise determination has been attempted to be changed." The Judiciary Committee recommended that further discussion or action was not called for, and asked "that this report, together with the petition, be laid upon the table."[34]

Tabled they were. This did not necessarily mean that either the Congress or most Americans tabled the unitive principle, or that everyone renounced the idea and rhetoric of a Christian America. Proposals for writing God and Jesus Christ into the Constitution kept surfacing well into the twentieth century, and these initiatives always won some support from prominent public figures. Anson Phelps Stokes, who in 1950 produced a massive history of American church-state relations, was probably right that "millions of thoughtful Americans" were sympathetic with the movement's broader objective, which was, as he explained, "to retain the Christian basis of our national life."[35]

Stokes, an Episcopal priest, made it clear that he was one of those millions; and his reasons for nonetheless disapproving of the amendment idea are therefore of special interest. He not only thought a reversal of the Founders' intentions would be unwarranted and unwise; Stokes held that, "from the standpoint of emphasizing the Christian ideal of our government," it would be "unnecessary."[36]

In the midst of booming diversification during the years of the early republic, the pluralist principle had run into two powerful competitors. One of these was the impulse toward societal unity that had been around, and had been notably visible and active, since the beginning of the revolutionary period. The other was a formerly sleeping giant that was promptly recognized as an informal establishment of the Protestant religion.

Explanations of this unusual occurrence—the emergence of a non-established establishment—have always been numerous and varied. The evangelist Lyman Beecher was one among many Protestant leaders who thought the formal ending of church-state alliances had revitalized the Protestant churches, and that this accounted for their enormous and growing power in American society. Beecher eventually, in fact, celebrated legal disestablishment (which had occurred in his own state in 1818) as "the best thing that ever happened in the State of Connecticut."[37] Others, however, especially historians writing several generations later, attributed the continuing dominance of Protestantism, throughout the nineteenth century, to the power hunger and machinations of people like Beecher himself—that is, to Protestant leaders, in both religious and secular pursuits, who feared the loss of personal and class privilege, and who would have pursued these unseemly goals whether the churches were formally established or not.[38]

People like Lyman Beecher and Robert Baird seem to have assumed,

however naively, that they and their kind would remain in charge whatever might happen. No midnight machinations on their part would be
necessary. So the most sinister explanations of the solidifying of an establishment are less plausible than others we have noticed—less persuasive,
for example, than analyses of the rootlessness people experience in an
unstructured society, or of popular convictions that a common religion is
essential to nation building.

A revised, less cynical version of the "loss of status" explanation can
also, however, remain in the mix: The self-conscious process of perpetuating the Protestant establishment was indeed partly defensive. It was a
circling of the wagons.

That having been acknowledged, however, the motivations for this defense—the extent of Beecher's concern for Connecticut and the common
good, the extent of his concern about Beecher—are much more difficult
to discern. At best, I think, we gain reliable insight into these motivations
case by case.

What we can say, in sum, is that Protestant dominance continued not
just in spite of diversification but also because of it. The arrival in the
society of more or less unexpected groups was a burr under the saddle
of a dominant Protestantism that previously had taken its dominance for
granted. A burr can immobilize the horse or make her gallop. The new diversities caused this animal, if not to gallop, at least to proceed at a stately
canter.

4 "Repentance for Our Social Sins": Adjustments Within the Establishment

The post–Civil War era in the United States deserves its reputation as a time of unusually rapid social change. Immigration proceeded at a lesser rate than before, relative to total population; but new forms and degrees of diversity were introduced as people swarmed in from southern, central, and eastern areas of Europe. And in other elements of national development, industrialization and urbanization in particular, rates of growth showed marked increases over those of the early part of the century. Taken together, the three phenomena of industrial, urban, and demographic change, playing upon and stimulating one another, produced serious challenges for religious bodies of all kinds. The challenges were especially acute and complex, however, for Protestant churches—white and, beginning in about 1910, black as well—that had been accustomed to serving the spiritual and other needs of rural populations.

One question for this chapter is how these churches and their people responded. A second question, following upon that, is how their varied responses affected the development of pluralism within and beyond the dominant Protestant establishment. Historical accounts have often made it sound as though everyone reacted either as a ruthless conservative Darwinian—"If the poor and others are crushed by these new social forces, that's too bad"—or as a valiant social gospeler who championed fundamental changes in the system. But there were of course numerous positions between those poles. In addition, many churches and people in a still-rural America took no notice at all, or did so only in a detached way.

Given that variety of responses and blank stares, it is safe to estimate that the system changers were a minority, even after a new "social gospel" in the Protestant churches had begun to attract wide notice around the turn of the century. The reformist minority, however, had a disproportionate effect in altering the official stance on social issues of nearly all the mainline Protestant churches. We may be a bit skeptical about "official stances," but such public commitments made a difference. Among other important things, they opened the way for pluralist gains, or even produced such gains in a visible way.

That an establishment venture might actually give aid and comfort to pluralism may, at first blush, seem surprising. The fundamental reason for its doing so in this case is that the social gospel, even in its more moderate or individualistic forms, placed a heavy emphasis on ethics. It advocated a Christianity that would be a matter of living and doing, not just a matter of believing and confessing, or of close adherence to creeds and the Bible. Wherever this shift in theological emphasis prevailed, or made gains, it helped in a major way to open American Protestantism to collaboration with Catholics and Jews (in both cases, old hands in the business of adjusting to urban settings), and with secular reformers. These forms of collaboration, in turn, stimulated greater appreciation in Protestant sectors for alternative faiths and ideologies.

The social gospelers also, in the course of their work, forged specific links to black or ethnic ministers and leaders, and to ordinary people in virtually all outsider groups. To be sure, the mostly white Protestant reformers, despite appreciable outreach in black communities of the South and North, were usually not very aggressive about racial questions—certainly not by modern standards. Too often they were not thinking about those matters at all, and when they were they could be just as paternalistic as conservatives might be. But such leaders of the social movement as Washington Gladden and (surprise) Josiah Strong were more active, and more advanced, in matters of race than historians once assumed.[1] At the very least, social gospel activity meant exposure to minorities and their problems. Quite often, it involved exposure to their religious forms and religious experience.

In spite of these pluralistic adjustments within the Protestant establishment—but also, in part, because of them—the more liberal responses to the new urban-industrial order helped to maintain the preeminence and cultural authority of the Protestant churches. Certainly the social gospel leaders took that to be the case. Walter Rauschenbusch, the most celebrated and influential of these leaders, disliked "ecclesiasticism" too much to say, or even think, that a social gospel should be pursued because this would help perpetuate a religious establishment. What he and others did say repeatedly, however, was that the Christian churches must respond to "the call of a great historical situation"; and that if they failed to do so the churches would be ignored, increasingly and deservedly.[2] In that sense, he and others clearly did think that Protestant authority and prestige were at stake. And as the movement advanced, it seemed evident that Protestant leaders were in fact gaining new visibility and respect—not least because of their close association with a largely successful political progressivism.

Opponents of course disagreed, principally about the propriety and theological soundness of the new social reform emphasis, but also about any idea that such an emphasis was bolstering the Protestant Christian presence (as opposed to that of a debilitated pseudo-Christianity) in American society. Most conservatives thought that social problems and all other problems—certainly including those of the survival of Protestantism and of religion—could best be solved if the churches stuck to their true business, that of saving souls.

CONSERVATIVE REMEDIES

Those who defended the status quo, like those who wanted to change it, relied for a good many of their arguments on nonreligious sources—even though some of them deplored such reliance and tried to avoid it. This seemed especially evident in the 1870s and after, an era in which Charles Darwin's theory of evolution had become thoroughly embedded in American public consciousness and public discourse, and when both liberals and conservatives sought the support of evolutionary ideas for their social theories. (Darwin's lieutenant, Thomas Huxley, complained about that in a famous lecture of the 1890s that chided all of them for trying to apply purely biological findings to their own social-theory agendas.)[3] What conservatives, in and beyond the churches, were most inclined to appropriate—or, if one agreed with Huxley, misappropriate—from Darwinian science was its apparent confirmation of older forms of determinism.

In theory, at least, these earlier determinisms, notably the one embodied in Calvinism, had limited individual autonomy and looked askance at all schemes for humanly engineered social change. But conservatives in this later era seemed even more anxious than Calvinist thinkers and preachers had been to have it both ways: They did think that the inevitability of cosmic processes like "survival of the fittest" made pleas for social restructuring dangerous or futile; yet they also believed passionately that the individual, like the young man in that *Ladder of Fortune* poster, could and must strive toward virtue and material success. Although the resulting formulas could (and did) seem oxymoronic to many critical minds, they could be made to work given a certain will to believe, plus a goodly amount of rhetorical and logical fiddling.

William Graham Sumner, a political economist at Yale University, was the principal fiddler. He was a highly persuasive one, especially for the many who either had achieved secure status in the new industrial elites or felt some confidence that they could do so. In an essay of 1884 that is still a standard item on conservative bookshelves, Sumner explained *What Social Classes Owe to Each Other*. His answer was, in effect: not very much. People of different class standings and differing degrees of wealth, he thought, owe each other nothing more than "good-will, mutual respect, and mutual guarantees of liberty and security." In a later treatise with a notably in-your-face title, "The Absurd Attempt to Make the World Over" (1895), he inveighed against all proposals involving governmental intervention in those natural processes that, as he readily acknowledged, make some rich and others poor.

> It is repeated until it has become a commonplace which people are afraid to question, that there is some social danger in the possession of large amounts of wealth by individuals. I ask, Why? . . . Everyone of us is a child of his age and cannot get out of it. . . . The tide will not be changed by us. It will swallow up both us and our experiments. . . . That is why it is the greatest folly of which a man can be capable, to sit down with a slate and pencil to plan out a new social world.[4]

When legislative bodies are the ones wielding slate and pencil, that is far worse. For Sumner, quite unlike Franklin D. Roosevelt several decades later, the "forgotten man" was not a poor or unemployed worker, or an impoverished farmer. He thought these allegedly downtrodden people were not forgotten at all. Quite the contrary: foolish legislators remembered them constantly and tiresomely, thus squandering time and effort that should go into the undoing of preceding bad legislation. The truly forgotten man, according to Sumner, was the hardworking person of great or adequate means who is commanded by do-gooders and legislators to hand over his earnings to people who should be making it on their own.

The former Episcopal priest acknowledged that some among the poor or the marginalized could not make it on their own, however hard they might work or try to get work. The answer, however, was neither "social planning" nor the wicked legislation that grows from it; the answer was a carefully meted-out private philanthropy.[5]

The industrialist Andrew Carnegie agreed, but voiced the philanthropic part of Sumner's solution with greater thoroughness and far greater enthusiasm. Starting with an assertion that "the man who dies rich dies disgraced," the millionaire Scottish immigrant fashioned a "gospel of wealth" to soften the hard effects of a process that he, like Sumner, believed could not be changed. In hundreds of lectures on this theme, Carnegie insisted that the successful entrepreneur is "but a trustee for the poor; entrusted for a season with a great part of the increased wealth of the community, but administering it for the community far better than it would or could have done for itself."[6] In his own financing of hundreds of libraries and other institutions devoted to human betterment, he adhered to this highly paternalistic plan of action.

Both Sumner and Carnegie—especially the latter, the rags-to-riches Scottish farm boy—were card-carrying individualists. Yet both were rather somber about it. In their mental world, one darkened by cosmic determinism, the individual's best hope lay in grim determination. But that was much less the case with other conservative spokesmen; and, understandably, those who did manage to convey a more cheerful message about human possibilities were the ones most widely read and heard. Sumner attracted some popular following, and Carnegie attracted considerably more, but the clear winners with the public were those who managed to mute or transform the emphasis on what Lord Tennyson had referred to as "nature red in tooth and claw."

How could people of any sort—social theorists, popular publicists, or

Andrew Carnegie spreading his gospel.
Drawing by Bernard Partridge in *Punch*,
May 29, 1901. Courtesy Punch Ltd.

just ordinary folks deciding whether or not to get up in the morning—
find a place for individualism or human striving in a universe reputed to
be a matter of inexorable processes? To some extent the answer to that
puzzling question was the well-known "bumblebee" explanation: In aero-
dynamic terms, this creature is unable to fly; but the bumblebee simply
ignores this inconvenience and flies anyway.

Social theorists, or even popular writers and lecturers, could not be
quite that cavalier about the plight of the individual in a harsh Darwinian
environment. But if they could not ignore Darwinian determinism, they
could try some logical stretching and bending; they could reinterpret determinism to suit their needs. And they did. Most commonly, they held
that the predetermined order of things, although it brings hardship and
death, also presents opportunities that the individual can grasp or fail to
grasp. Even Sumner allowed for what he called "chances"; and there were
dozens of popular writers, plus thousands of preachers of all faiths, who

Cover drawing for Horatio Alger's Luck and Pluck series, 1869.

stressed this part of the formula more than Sumner did. One leading example was the fabulously successful adviser to upwardly mobile American
boys, Horatio Alger, Jr.

Alger's term for the opportunities that come unbidden—that one cannot create—was, quite simply, *luck*. The counterpart term, for Alger, was
pluck (which of course made for good titles). The individual must rely on
the fates to supply him (it was almost always "him") with luck; but he
also needs character, and the individual enjoys enough autonomy to work
at shaping his own character. In the Luck and Pluck series of books, and
in most of the rest of Alger's 120 volumes, the hero rises in the world because of unexpected opportunities that fate places in his path, but also
because he is a boy of character who is therefore prepared to seize these
opportunities.

Alger, born in 1834, had graduated from Harvard College in 1852 and from the Harvard Divinity School—where he was known as Holy Horatio—eight years later. After a short and unhappy Unitarian pastorate in Brewster, Massachusetts, he moved to New York City, where he wrote his stories, and labored with street urchins, until his death in 1899.

In the typical, not to say predictable, Alger story, the plucky, observant lad not only will glimpse the diamond necklace that a wealthy widow has chanced to throw out with the garbage; he will demonstrate character by returning the necklace. Provided that he does that, he will be rewarded (with a job; that was always important), and presently will become chief clerk of the company and then vice president.

In *Ragged Dick; or Street Life in New York*, the young protagonist "chanced" to go for a boat ride with his friend Henry Fosdick, and was lucky enough to pull from the swirling waters not Fosdick, and not even a middle-class drowning boy, but a rich boy whose father could not swim. "'My child!' [the father] exclaimed in anguish—'who will save my child? A thousand—ten thousand dollars to any one who will save him!'" The series of fate-ordained events then continues:

> There chanced to be but few passengers on board at the time, and nearly all these were . . . standing forward. Among the few who saw the child fall was our hero. . . . Little Johnny had risen once, and gone under for the second time, when our hero plunged in. . . . He reached him none too soon. Just as he was sinking for the third and last time, he caught him by the jacket.[7]

Even so, they nearly drown, and would have drowned "had not a row boat been fortunately near." When the boys have been hauled on board, a boatman says, "You've had a pretty narrow escape, young chap. It was a pretty tough job you undertook." "Yes," Dick responds, "that's what I thought when I was in the water."

Alger explains carefully that Dick had not heard the offer of ten thousand dollars, and that if he had it would not have caused him to act any faster. In any case, Mr. Rockwell—for that was his name—says nothing more about the money. With emotion, probably laced with gratitude that Dick had not heard him, he simply exclaims, "My brave boy, I owe you a debt that I can never repay." Dick answers modestly that "it wasn't any trouble. I can swim like a top."[8]

Why this breach-of-contract by Rockwell/Alger? The explanation is

"He caught him by the jacket." Illustration for *Ragged Dick*, 1868.

probably not, despite my slighting remark, stinginess or meanness on their part. The point is that it would not be *good* for Dick to have ten thousand dollars. Instead, Mr. Rockwell offers Dick a comfortable bed, a new suit of clothes, and a writing test; and, after all that, he offers him the ultimate reward: "How would you like to enter my counting-room as clerk, Richard?"

As Dick leaves Mr. Rockwell's office, "hardly knowing whether he stood on his head or his heels," his first thought is not about a coming life of comfort, or even about further successes. His first thought is about others: "I wish Fosdick was as well off as I am."[9]

That was *character*, and it was also "in character." Dick had habitually made the right life choices. He had been ready for the breaks. He had learned to write, and to swim. He had been industrious. Alger had introduced this last point earlier, in a conversation between Dick and a fellow bootblack, Johnny Nolan, whom Dick had chanced to meet in front of the post office. Johnny asks what in the world Dick is doing there. "Mailin' a letter," Dick answers. "Who writ the letter?" "I wrote it myself." "I didn't know you could write. I can't." "Then you ought to learn." "I went to school once, but it was too hard work, so I give it up." "You're lazy, Johnny—that's what's the matter." "I can't learn." "You can," Dick assures him, "if you want to."[10]

Alger's commentary on this incident manages to touch all the bases in a succinct description of the individual's confrontation with a world he cannot fundamentally change. Johnny Nolan, he writes, "was a good-natured boy . . . nothing particularly bad about him, but utterly lacking in that energy, ambition, and natural sharpness, for which Dick was distinguished. He was not adapted to succeed in the life which circumstances had forced upon him. . . . It was easy to see that Johnny, unless very much favored by circumstances, would never rise much above his present level. For Dick, we cannot help hoping much better things."[11]

Indeed. It will take more than a drowning millionaire to get Johnny Nolan on the path to a vice presidency. Johnny isn't ready for the breaks—probably hasn't even learned to swim like a top.

BRIGHTEN YOUR CORNER: DR. CONWELL'S
SOCIAL PRESCRIPTION

From these mostly secular formulations as presented by two former ministers, Sumner and Alger, and by the agnostic Carnegie, it is not a huge step to religious statements of the same themes. Here the leading example is a public lecture, "Acres of Diamonds," that the Baptist minister and educator Russell Conwell gave six thousand times between the mid-1880s and his death in 1925. Conwell's version of individualism perhaps placed more emphasis on virtue than Alger's did; but his language is not noticeably more pious, nor do Christian doctrines or scriptural allusions show themselves any more frequently. And Conwell's own social activism resembled Alger's; the Baptist leader devoted much of his effort to workers' education—a brand of social amelioration that, like Alger's work with urban youth, was consistent with a highly individualistic pro-capitalist stance.

As a student at Yale, Conwell had been an atheist, but he had experienced a conversion during army service in the Civil War. After engaging in the law and in business, he became a pastor first in Lexington, Massachusetts, and then at Grace Baptist Church in Philadelphia, which was popularly known as Baptist Temple. During the 1880s one of his educational projects—another was the theological seminary that was eventually named for him—evolved from night school classes in the church basement. This became Temple University, which he headed until his death.

But Conwell was most widely known for "Acres of Diamonds." Here we find all the conservative themes, including, quite prominently, that of the inexorable nature of cosmic forces. But in Conwell's vocabulary, as in Alger's, determinism appears in one of its kinder, gentler forms. The terrible, crushing force of cosmic inevitability can be trumped by virtuous behavior. And at this point in the argument Conwell offers a neat, indeed nifty, explanation that we particularly need to notice, because it expresses, almost offhandedly, how the assumptions underlying a fundamentally optimistic social outlook can solve the old determinist/individualist conundrum: "The very laws of nature," he insists, are on the side of the virtuous individual.

Conwell, despite the arthritis that troubled him during most of his lecturing career, was a handsome, mustachioed fellow who cut a dashing figure at the lectern. Perhaps more important was a booming voice that was nonetheless well modulated, and a skilled extemporaneous delivery. Teddy Roosevelt, who was less favored in these departments, remarked that "I'd give ten thousand dollars to have a voice like that."[12] Quite wisely, given the obvious dangers in repeating the same speech thousands of times, Conwell constantly varied the stories and rhetorical strategies in the body of his lecture. But his audiences might have turned nasty had he altered the opening tale that gave "Acres of Diamonds" its title.

This was a cautionary tale, featuring a protagonist named Ali Hafed who resembles Johnny Nolan more than Ragged Dick; that is, he is too limpid in character to seize opportunities that fate places before him. An ancient Persian described as "wealthy because he was contented, and contented because he was wealthy," Ali submits to materialistic advice from a Buddhist priest. This nefarious character tells him that "many mines of diamonds are yet undiscovered. All you have to do is to start out and go somewhere—away, away." (A Buddhist holy man counseling acquisitiveness and restless discontent? Well, meet the Westerner's "knowledge" of non-Western cultures.) Avarice awakened, Ali has become poor; for, as Conwell remarks, "poverty is only discontent." The formerly prosperous and contented Ali does roam the world; but of course he never finds the treasure he seeks, and he dies in his self-induced poverty. In the meantime, the diamond mines of Golconda have been discovered back in his old neighborhood. "Had Ali Hafed remained at home," Conwell pointed out, "had he dug in his own garden . . . instead of poverty, starvation, death in a strange land, he would have had acres of diamonds."[13]

In each rendition of the speech Conwell followed this tale with as many as twenty-five other anecdotes or testimonies. Most of these came from letters or reports penned by grateful auditors and readers. A typical testimony averred that "it was the lecture of Dr. Conwell on 'Acres of Diamonds,' delivered fifteen years ago in Reynoldsville [Pennsylvania] that . . . ultimately resulted in the founding of the Reynoldsville Brick and Tile Company." Another told of a young Connecticut farm lad who was given up by his teachers as too weak-minded to learn. "Today," Conwell exulted, "he is a respected professor of zoölogy in an Ohio college." The speaker also liked to tell about the unlettered slave who, inspired by "Acres of Diamonds," had become "the highest Negro official in South Africa." In all these instances, the central message was very much like Alger's: whether you are poor or wealthy, do not fret about your lot in life; be of good cheer and good character, and take advantage of the opportunities fate places before you. Then wealth, or greater wealth, may well come to you. If you ask, "Where can I get rich?" the answer is "Right where you are. At home. Not somewhere else. Not a man has secured great wealth by going away who might not have secured it as much by other means if he had stayed at home."[14]

At that point, Conwell always worked himself up to a peroration in defense of honest acquisitiveness and the status quo. This final segment of "Acres" is perhaps the best popular or idiomatic summary we have of late-nineteenth-century moral and social conservatism in its response to the realities of the new industrial era. He began it as follows: "To secure wealth is an honorable ambition, and is one great test of a person's usefulness to others. Money is power. Every good man and woman ought to strive for power, and to do good with it when obtained."

Conwell then offered his own version of the linkage between chance and choice. Opportunity, he insisted, is out there for anyone who can see and use it. Blind fate has *placed* it out there. Yet lazy and characterless people, he complained, quite unfairly berate the rich for seizing these opportunities. Such whiners contend that it's all a matter of luck; but it is not, because those successful people—most of them—are virtuous.

> Tens of thousands of men and women get rich honestly. But they are often accused by an envious, lazy crowd of unsuccessful persons of being dishonest and oppressive. I say, Get rich! get rich! But get money honestly, or it will be a withering curse. Money being power, it ought to be entirely in the hands of good men and women. It is *now*, more largely than many are willing to admit.[15]

Conwell, although his name lives on today in a major evangelical seminary (Gordon-Conwell, in Massachusetts), "was not known for evangelistic fervor."[16] Many evangelical revivalists of his day, however, along with some theological liberals, concurred in his message and put their own spin on it. Homer Rodeheaver, who was the songmaster for Dwight Moody's ebullient successor Billy Sunday, popularized a gospel hymn that located spiritual riches where Conwell located material ones—that is, "where you are." Don't go searching (in the words of a James Russell Lowell hymn) for "some great cause, God's new Messiah"; just look to your everyday evangelistic duties. Be ready to throw lifelines to perishing sinners. If you save even one of them, that will be your reward:

> Do not wait until some deed of greatness you may do,
> Do not wait to shed your light afar.
> To the many duties ever near you now be true,
> Brighten the corner where you are.
> > Brighten the corner where you are!
> > Brighten the corner where you are!
> > Someone far from harbor you may guide across the bar,
> > Brighten the corner where you are.
> Just above are clouded skies that you may help to clear,
> Let not narrow self your way debar,
> Tho' into one heart alone may fall your song of cheer.
> Brighten the corner where you are.
> > Brighten the corner . . .
> Here for all your talent you may surely find a need,
> Here reflect the bright and morning star,
> Even from your humble hand the bread of life may feed.
> Brighten the corner where you are.
> > Brighten the corner . . .[17]

AFFLICTING THE COMFORTABLE: TOWARD A
SOCIAL GOSPEL

Exhorters like Sunday and Conwell, and songsters like Rodeheaver, barnstormed the world telling people to stay home, and urging them to apply brighten-your-corner solutions to social problems. At the other extreme, "structural" reformers took dead aim against anyone who expected to save society via individual conversions; and it was these more thoroughgoing reformers who eventually monopolized the term *social gospel*. As I have suggested, however, there were important intermediate positions. More moderate reformers, while remaining nearly as individualistic as the evangelists and the self-help enthusiasts, were quite vigorous in calling upon the churches to turn some real attention to social problems — to wake up and smell the potent new coffee being brewed in post–Civil War America.

Some of the most articulate publicists in this middle category were novelists rather than theologians or social theorists. Whether or not these moderate advocates deserved inclusion in *the* social gospel — that point has often been disputed — certainly they could claim to be preaching a new (or renewed) social Christianity, and they fashioned a brand of religious fiction that has, in fact, usually been referred to as the social gospel novel.

The flourishing of this genre was not a minor phenomenon. A close student of the subject estimates that nearly one hundred social gospel novels appeared between 1886 and 1914. Cumulatively, moreover, they enjoyed about as large a readership as did the self-help literature I have been describing; and one social gospel novel, Charles Sheldon's *In His Steps* (1897), in some years was a best-seller that ranked second to the Christian Bible. (Because of many pirated editions in English and other languages, a total figure is hard to come by, but it seems clear that at least two million copies of *In His Steps* were sold in the United States before World War I, and some estimates have run much higher.) The novel, subtitled *"What Would Jesus Do?"* became a stage play and, as its popularity continued almost full force in the 1930s, was produced as a movie, albeit a distinctly third-rate one that embarrassed the book's author.[18]

Sheldon, raised in New York State, educated at Brown University and Andover (Massachusetts) Theological Seminary, had left a rural Vermont pastorate in 1889 and taken one in the more industrial and polyglot setting of Topeka, Kansas. There, as the founding minister of Central Congregational Church, and one who cared little for the formalities of conventional worship (for example, he eliminated recitation of the Apostles' Creed), Sheldon frequently substituted stories for sermons; and the stories for the most part grew out of his own experiences as what we would now call a participant observer in the slums and working-class areas abutting his very middle-class parish. At one point he enlisted 150 of the young people in his church for a project in the black ghetto; at another, he spent an entire week, dressed as a tramp, in an almost entirely futile search for work.[19]

The story Sheldon derived from these experiences is still widely known. (As I write, nineteen editions of his novel are in print, and a new What Would Jesus Do? movement is large and active.) It is also a story that is too simple to require much elaboration or explanation. During a Sunday morning service in Henry Maxwell's staid Protestant church, after a beautiful performance of "the best music money could buy," a stranger comes forward out of the shadows at the rear of the elegant sanctuary. Sheldon describes the visitor as consumptive, worn, unkempt, and unshaven (although, as you see, the illustrator got him cleaned up for the 1899 edition). On the whole, he looked much like the carpenter of Nazareth as commonly depicted. This stranger puts an unsettling question to the congregants—followed by a provocative observation. Having heard them sing, "All for Jesus, all for Jesus," he asks what this may mean. "It seems to me there's an awful lot of trouble in the world that somehow wouldn't exist if all the people who sing such songs went and lived them out."[20]

The vagrant dies, but his challenge lingers on and, under Maxwell's goading and guidance, a number of parishioners respond to it. An editor decides, at considerable sacrifice to his paper and his own prosperity, to exclude gossip and sensationalism, to refuse ads for liquor and tobacco, to cease reporting on prizefights and other gambling ventures, and to stop publishing a Sunday edition. An heiress decides that Jesus, had he come into great wealth, would have donated part of it to the newspaper and the rest to the building of a settlement house and the founding of a rescue mission. A singer named Rachel rejects a lucrative offer from the National

"What do Christians mean?" Y. W. Kennedy illustration for the 1899 edition of In His Steps.

Opera in order to perform at tent meetings in a tenement district called the Rectangle, and to teach music at the settlement house.

And so on. Sheldon was neither a great writer nor a deep and complex thinker. But he was also not a wild-eyed optimist, even though we may think his trust in human nature and in top-down social solutions makes him a candidate for that honor. His story, while it conveys an indubitable faith in the long-range workability of what he proposes, also recognizes the difficulties: Most of Maxwell's parishioners fear to take the pledge, and some who do take it fail to follow through. The heiress's ne'er-do-well brother concludes that Jesus would have kept his country club memberships in order to spread the "What would Jesus do?" message among other rich and shiftless people. At the other extreme, socialists and agnostics (who, Sheldon hints, tend to be the same people) deride the whole idea. At a mass meeting in the Settlement Hall, a "large, black-haired, heavily-bearded" socialist rises to insist that "we've got to have a new start in the way of government. The whole thing needs reconstructing." When another "big, brawny" metalworker follows with a plea for trade unionism, people applaud; but the moderator, horrified, silences this second dangerous speaker and calls upon Rachel for a calming anthem.[21] Jesus would not approve of social engineering—certainly not the kind championed by brawny black-haired agitators.

As you see, I do not think one must be dead serious when recounting Sheldon's story and his well-intended proposal for solving social problems. But neither should we dismiss the message and effect of this appeal, nor of the many similar ones we find in the new socially aware novels, preaching, and hymnody. (Washington Gladden's "O Master, Let Me Walk with Thee," in 1879, was one of the first of many hymns that summoned the Christian to "lowly paths of service.") The approach to social problems remained individualistic, indeed conversionist; each of Sheldon's heroes experiences a form of conversion, and each sets out to make converts of others. But it also demanded direct and serious attention to fundamental social issues. It declared and lamented the inadequacy of any gospel that encourages preoccupation with "me"—whether this means "my conversion" or "my virtuous pursuit of riches."

Especially the latter. Sheldon's message offered vigorous answers, indeed rebukes, to the various Sumner-Conwell rhetorical questions: Can there be any social danger in the accumulation of great wealth? (Indeed there can be, Sheldon answered.) Does one social class owe much to another? (Yes, a great deal.) But why? Aren't the very laws of nature on the side of the virtuous individual? (No. Virtuous, even Christlike, individuals fail, sicken, and die; and no law of nature serves to protect them.) But can we not, following Mr. Carnegie, give it all away, keeping only necessities like our castles in Scotland and on East 91st Street? (Nice try; but still not enough.) Perhaps, the Sheldonites proposed, we are obligated to follow Jesus along paths of genuine sacrifice.

Sheldon, in other words, along with most of the others who sought to awaken a comfortably dozing establishment, clung to traditional solutions, yet did build an important bridge. Within the history of Christian social reform he represents a transition—from a gospel that had seemed to work on the frontier and in rural settings, to one that might stand a chance of working in a newly urban and industrial America.

THE SOCIAL GOSPEL IN FULL

Sheldon's experience and his famous book are instructive in at least one other way. Even if we saw In His Steps as representing only a stopping place on the path toward the "real" social gospel, it would still signal something important about that fuller, more aggressive social awareness: that one of its major sources, perhaps the major source, lay in day-to-day experience.

The Protestant social gospel has always captured the imagination and usually gained the approval of historians. For a long time, in fact, secular analysts saw it as one of the few religious movements that seemed at all consequential or admirable. But these chroniclers, probably including the present writer, often left the impression that the idea of a new social Christianity sprang from the heads of a few American spokesmen and their European—especially their British—colleagues or predecessors.

Stories like In His Steps, if taken at all seriously, correct that impression. They imply—accurately, I believe—that the social gospel also arose out of adjustments forged on the ground by congregations and their pastors.[22] A good many of these pastors—Rauschenbusch is an excellent example—then became theorists and spokesmen for more radical models of social amelioration.

Jane Addams, the great leader of the settlement house movement, took this insight a step further. Addams testified in her memoirs to the importance of day-to-day experience in actually changing the attitudes with which she and her coworkers had entered upon their careers in social work. The assumptions about such things as race, poverty, immigrants, and "welfare" that they held when they went into the ghettoes were materially changed by life and work in the ghettoes.[23]

That insight may not seem startling. Yet it is a neglected one, even as applied to people like Addams herself (or, a more graphic example, Josiah Strong), whom we're likely to picture carelessly as having held the same ideas all their lives. But it may be even more useful as it applies to such collective bodies as churches and reform organizations. In many cases (to be sure, this did not seem to work in Henry Maxwell's congregation), they were led by their experience—often by trial and error—to move beyond the older individualistic kind of reform. They came to accept the necessity for reform legislation, for example, not so much because they were reading liberal social theory but simply because of a certain internal logic that pressed upon them as they sought to discern and carry out their obligations as Christians.

In a previous chapter I mentioned in passing that even Timothy Shay Arthur's "Ten Nights in a Barroom," a midcentury temperance tract that took for granted an emphasis on personal conversion, concluded with the principal convert demanding legislation. Two contrasting pieces of temperance literature, one from the 1860s and one from the 1890s, also serve to illustrate the workings of this internal logic. In a modern reconstruction of a nineteenth-century song, "Father's a Drunkard and Mother is Dead," a piping voice like that of Broadway's "Annie" records the plight of "poor little Bessie":

> Out in the gloomy night, sadly I roam,
> I have no Mother dear, no pleasant home;
> Nobody cares for me—no one would cry
> Even if poor little Bessie should die.
> Barefoot and tired, I've wandered all day
> Asking for work—but I'm too small they say;
> On the damp ground I must now lay my head—
> Father's a Drunkard, and Mother is dead!
>
> Mother, oh! why did you leave me alone,
> With no one to love me, no friends and no home?
> Dark is the night, and the storm rages wild,
> God pity Bessie, the Drunkard's lone child!

Bessie launches into two more verses that chronicle a descent into ruin even more pathetic than that of Arthur's crumbling community. "We were so happy till father drank rum. / Then all our sorrow and trouble begun." When Mother sickened and died, "baby and I were too hungry to play." Now "baby" has died, and Bessie is on the streets. Is there hope for her? Yes. It lies in private-sector charity:

> Oh! if the "Temp'rance men" only could find
> Poor wretched Father, and talk very kind—
> If they could stop him from drinking—why, then
> I should be so very happy again!
> Is it too late? "Men of Temp'rance," please try,
> Or poor little Bessie may soon starve and die.[24]

Although private-sector "temp'rance men" would still be featured in similar ditties thirty years later, a song written at that later time displays how one thing had led to another as thousands of Little Bessies and their would-be saviors roamed the slums of the burgeoning cities. From the words of "When the Girls Can Vote" we gather that, for many reformers, both temperance and temperance men have proved inadequate. Temperance *women*, at any rate, want "prohibition" — in other words, legislation. They also believe that prohibition will make it into the Constitution, and then into an act of Congress, only after the approval of still another massive piece of legislation, one mandating women's suffrage:

Young Fellow, don't you come too near,
With swearing, drinking, smoking;
For girls don't like the breath of beer
But long to do the voting.
  When girls can vote, hurrah, hurrah!
  Saloons will not be here; (hurrah!)
  There won't be one in all the land
  Old Rummy's heart to cheer.
So hasten on, ye blithesome day,
When we'll be grown to women;
We mean to vote ere very long,
And stop the boys from drinking.
  When girls can vote . . .[25]

GOING (PRACTICALLY) ALL THE WAY: THE "REAL" SOCIAL GOSPEL

Among the best known social gospelers, one man in particular illustrated in his own career how one thing could lead to another in the emergence of a Christian social program. This was Washington Gladden, a vigorous, brawny man of great energy who wrote forty books and innumerable articles and sermons, and who was still preaching at age eighty-two. Born in 1836, Gladden graduated from Williams College, then held ministerial and editorial positions in New York State and Massachusetts before settling in as pastor of the First Congregational Church in Columbus, Ohio.

Gladden's first proclamation of a social gospel, in *Working People and*

Their Employers (1876), was individualistic and moralistic; and his social solutions were roughly as conservative as those of Charles Sheldon would be two decades later. Like Sheldon, the young Gladden stood out as one who demanded that the churches confront social problems. In addition, unlike Sheldon, he voiced a number of objections to laissez-faire economics and offered support to labor unions. But this Gladden of the seventies was arguing in the main for the application of the Golden Rule on both sides of the labor-capitalist divide. He thought that employers, applying that standard, would cease their heartlessness and restrain their greedy impulses. Workers, for their part, would be good-hearted enough to take whatever work was offered, would wear simple clothes, would avoid frivolous entertainment, and would restrain their consumption of liquor and tobacco. "Of all the enemies of the workingmen," he thought at this time, the worst were not conservative economic doctrines or ruthless capitalists. "The worst is strong drink."[26]

The more Gladden experienced the turmoil of industrial life, however, first in the factory towns of Massachusetts and then in the mining regions of Ohio, the more he favored specific reforms that, by and large, resembled those being promoted by the populist and progressive movements that were gaining prominence and political success after 1890. Up to the mid-nineties, Gladden's social program featured various cooperative schemes, such as profit sharing, that relied upon mutual goodwill. After that, however, he turned his attention to wage and hour legislation and other measures that would force employers to provide the kind of justice that, as he now realized, they would not provide voluntarily.

By 1911, when Gladden published The Labor Question, he had turned at least 180 degrees. He had come to favor, and also to anticipate as the shape of the future, a mixture of social and and private ownership. If forced to choose, he then asserted, he would prefer even a thoroughgoing socialism to anything more individualistic—whether the individualism was that of the anarchist or that of conventional, unreformed capitalism.[27]

Others in the new social movement had, by that time, traveled by various routes to about the same point. This became evident in 1907, when Walter Rauschenbusch's manifesto, Christianity and the Social Crisis, was published to great and mostly unanticipated acclaim. In the earlier chapters of that book, we hear the voice of Rauschenbusch the biblical scholar and church historian. He burrows into the historical record to show that Jesus taught a social creed, and that Christianity had then fallen away, radically and grievously, from Christ's own prescriptions. But it is in the final chapter, a lengthy one called "What to Do," that the prophet speaks, setting forth the program that he believes is not only responsive to contemporary social needs but also in conformity with the mind and intentions of Christ.[28]

Being responsive meant, for Rauschenbusch, that the church must support and learn from the champions of "social redemption"—quite definitely including secular champions—wherever they might be found; when necessary, it should back their resort to legislative remedies. It must promote working-class solidarity, be sympathetic to some degree of common ownership of the means of production, and not back down when conservatives used scare words like communism to discredit such social remedies. Just what degree of common ownership was called for, "the common sense of the future will have to determine."[29] All such determinations were to be guided by tradition as well as by immediate situations; but Rauschenbusch wanted no one to forget that responsiveness to human need was itself an historically vital Christian tradition.

The other part of this double-barreled brief was an insistence that the church must retain its own voice. Thus, for example, the starting point must be personal regeneration, just as the evangelical tradition had contended, even though regeneration needed to be defined more broadly than it had been among evangelical revivalists. "In personal religion," Rauschenbusch wrote, "the first requirement is to repent and believe in the gospel. . . . Social religion, too, demands repentance and faith: repentance for our social sins; faith in the possibility of a new social order." Work was to be seen as invested with divine purpose; and everyone's work or profession, including those of professing Christians, was to be understood as coming under divine judgment.[30]

The social gospel preacher, therefore, although he would of course address issues of public morality, would also exercise enough Christian humility to avoid attacking individuals. Those whom Theodore Roosevelt, in a 1907 speech, had called "malefactors of great wealth" were not merely malefactors. Like the poor and everyone else, they were also the products of malign social forces. Those forces should be the objects of attack.

Along the same line, the preacher was to avoid becoming the "mega-phone" of a political party. Such restraint was called for if the church was to retain its independent prophetic voice, but also because neither a political party nor the church itself was likely to hold a monopoly on righteousness for any significant period of time.

Rauschenbusch thought that it was time for the church to reassert the true doctrine of stewardship. Those who manage the mining companies and the railroads, he wrote, may be "owners," as they insist, but they are also stewards for the community. "A mining company owns the holes in the ground, for it made the holes; it does not own the coal, for it did not make the coal."[31]

In a small book that he wrote several years after *Christianity and the Social Crisis*, the Rochester Seminary professor worked his dual emphases into a revised form of the thirteenth chapter of First Corinthians. Here are some of his verses:

> If I create wealth beyond the dream of past ages and increase not love, my heat is the flush of fever and my success will deal death. . . . Though I give of my profits to the poor and make princely endowments for those who toil for me, if I have no human fellowship of love with them my life is barren and doomed. . . . For now we see in the fog of selfishness, darkly, but then with social vision; now we see our fragmentary ends, but then we shall see the destinies of the race as God sees them. But now abideth honor, justice, and love, these three; and the greatest of these is love.[32]

INSTITUTIONALIZATION AND IMPACT

How could appeals like those of Gladden and Rauschenbusch, embodying ideas that at many points crossed the line into Christian socialism, achieve any resonance at all in a society that turned out large crowds for Carnegie and Conwell, and that kept Alger and Sheldon on the best-seller lists? Many social gospelers, despite their passionate hopes for a new order, had their own doubts about whether their message could gain support. Rauschenbusch reported that he had entered on the writing of his most celebrated book "with a lot of fear and trembling. I expected there would be a good deal of anger and resentment." After sending it to the publisher, he had left for a year in Europe. But he came back a hero, even a popular hero, "swamped with work and demands for lectures. . . . To my great astonishment, everybody was kind to [the book]. Only a few 'damned' it."[33]

Clearly the social gospel prophet had caught a moment. He had articulated — with special brilliance, to be sure — reform ideas that had achieved some currency in the churches and the political world. Within months of his book's publication, the Methodist General Conference confirmed this by voting in favor of a "social creed" that, going well beyond pious generalities, called for a living wage, the abolition of child labor and of sweatshops, arbitration in labor disputes, and a number of other specific reforms.[34]

This Methodist statement was then adopted, in expanded form, by the Federal Council of Churches during the first four years after its establishment in 1908. For the originators of this body, to which thirty-three Protestant denominations adhered, social action was not merely something that a new federation could facilitate; it was a principal reason for bringing such an organization into being. The tone of the FCC's founding statement was aggressive on the point: "Not for its own sake, but in the interest of the kingdom of God, the Church must . . . acquiesce in the movements outside of it which make for human welfare." More than that, the church must "demonstrate not by proclamation but by deeds its primacy among all the forces which seek to lift the plane and better the conditions of human life."[35]

Minority movement or not, the social gospel had achieved solid institutional embodiment. More than that, it had put a new face on long-standing Protestant claims to a special place of leadership in American society. The "progressive moment" that Rauschenbusch had captured, seemingly by accident, was one of those times in American history when a new religious movement has converged — not really by accident — with an equally new and dynamic political movement.

Up to that time, the most striking instance of such a convergence had been the one between Jacksonian democracy and Finneyite revivalism ("cast your vote for God or for Satan"). In this later case, as in the earlier one, the encounter was stimulating and beneficial not just to reformers in the churches but to those in the political world. Henry May, who wrote one of the classic histories of the social gospel, remarked that "the ability to justify social change in terms of Christian doctrine [gave] American progressivism authority, power and a link with tradition," and added that "these gifts were particularly valuable during the difficult first adjustment of the American liberal tradition to the age of giant industry."[36]

May's point is amply illustrated in the public careers of such leading social gospelers as Gladden, Rauschenbusch, Strong, Lyman Abbott (editor of *The Independent*), and the economist Richard Ely. Each of these key figures, along with many lesser ones, became a frequent consultant on public policy, and some were drawn into secular forms of public service.

Gladden's relationship with Theodore Roosevelt had begun in the 1890s when Roosevelt was New York's police commissioner. The ideas and rhetoric of the two reformers were so similar that it is not always easy to remember which one coined which Progressive slogan. ("Malefactors of great wealth" was Roosevelt's invention; "tainted money" was Gladden's.) Rauschenbusch, soon after his meteor-like appearance on the public scene in 1907, was consulted on social policy by President Roosevelt, by the British liberal statesman David Lloyd George, by Governor Woodrow Wilson of New Jersey, and by twenty other state governors.[37]

In one of the Rauschenbusch-Roosevelt conversations, according to Dores Sharpe,

> Rauschenbusch informed the President that it [was] apparent to many thoughtful minds that socialism was coming in the United States. . . . "Not so long as I am President [Roosevelt responded], for I will sail the ship of state alongside the ship of socialism and I will take over everything that is good in socialism and leave the bad. What will socialism do then?" Rauschenbusch replied, with a chuckle, "I suppose the ship of socialism will sink, but that is no matter, if you really save her valuable cargo. . . . Do you propose to write into the laws of the nation the social theories of socialism?" "Precisely that," replied the President, "at least in so far as those theories are wise and practicable for the nation's well being."[38]

Given the enormous popular following of the revivalists, plus that of the various spokesmen for social conservatism, one could argue that defenders of the status quo contributed at least as much as their rivals did to the perpetuation of a Protestant establishment in and beyond the new industrial era. But the social gospel, in its several forms, seems to have played a larger role in that process. It injected more into American reli-

Washington Gladden and Theodore Roosevelt, 1912. Myron T. Seifert photo. Courtesy Ohio Historical Society.

gious life that was new and, quite literally, rejuvenating. Perhaps more important, this newness was very much in tune with the exhilarating intellectual and reformist currents of the Progressive Era. The social activists were fond of quoting Wordsworth's reminiscence of his revolutionary past: "Bliss was't in that dawn to be alive; to be young was very heaven!" Many people in the churches, and far more people in the colleges and seminaries, responded to that kind of enthusiasm and shared it.

As for the impact of differing social attitudes on the development of religious and cultural pluralism, it seems to me that the gap between conservatives' contributions and those of the social liberals is a larger one. Although we can find some instances in which social-economic conservatives supported the more "pluralistic" side of an argument—for example, in Sumner's opposition to imperialism and to restrictions on immigration—the contacts between pluralism and the social gospel are more direct and far more numerous. Social liberalism, almost as much as the theological brand that I shall discuss in the next chapter, was linked strongly to internal changes, and changes in public image, that helped keep the Protestant establishment in place well into the twentieth century. But the changes the social gospelers championed did far more—usually indirectly, but often quite directly—to provide openings into twentieth-century religious and cultural pluralism.

5 In (Partway) from the Margins: Pluralism as Inclusion

For seventeen days in September 1893 a pathbreaking World's Parliament of Religions was held in Chicago as part of a great world's fair, the Columbian Exposition. During one of the sessions of this extraordinary interfaith gathering, the poet and reformer Julia Ward Howe reacted testily to the views of the preceding speaker, one Professor Wilkinson. Wilkinson, a Baptist minister who taught at the new University of Chicago, had denied the possibility of even partial truths in non-Christian religions, and Howe asserted that she could "never agree with any person, no matter who, who enunciates such principles." Christ's sacrifice, she asserted, was an act "not . . . of exclusion but of an infinite and endless and joyous inclusion."[1]

The next day, a writer for the Chicago Herald reported that the response from an audience of some four thousand had been overwhelmingly in Howe's favor. "Seldom, if ever," he wrote, "have the huge rafters and girders of Columbus Hall creaked under the pressure of such a storm of applause." As the meeting broke up, "someone, it is not known who, touched the keys of the great organ" and played the notes and chords of Howe's famous hymn, "Mine eyes have seen the glory of the coming of the Lord."[2]

One must be careful not to read too much into this little drama. The self-selected audiences at the World's Parliament were clearly more open to pluralist ideas—of whatever kind—than were most American Christians. Many of the latter, probably a solid majority, would have found Wilkinson's ideas more congenial than Howe's.

What the encounter did reflect accurately, however, was the way in which public discourse about religious diversity and religious pluralism was changing. Within American society, although the struggle against intolerance was far from over, many Catholics, Jews, nonmainstream sectarians, and religious radicals no longer considered toleration a sufficient remedy; and the same can be said about a great many of the enthusiasts for pluralism in the majority culture itself. With respect to American attitudes toward Asian and other world religions, the very convening of a meeting like that of 1893 signified a readiness to recognize and "include" these religions (though not necessarily to offer anything beyond that).

The Parliament, in some ways a rather modest venture, achieved epochal status because it was almost completely unprecedented. Intellectual and other leaders of the various non-Western religions had never before been invited to such a gathering. Not only that; American Protestants had never included Jews and Catholics in a conference on religion, and almost never in meetings concerning other subjects of supposedly common concern. A mere seventy or eighty years earlier the idea that Hindus or Muslims might have intellectuals to send, or even that these religions might be real ones with something to offer, would have been considered laughable.

This is not to say that "inclusion," as a goal for outsiders seeking fair treatment, or of others favoring positive responses to diversity, was a concept that appeared suddenly at the end of the century. But the term (or terms with similar meaning) had most often been used in relation to groups marginalized for other than religious reasons. Women whose religious views were perfectly in accord with those of their churches or sects had usually been prevented from preaching, and in nearly all cases had been denied ordination and excluded from other positions of authority. For them, the issue had always been inclusion, and "a voice," not mere toleration. The same is true of black Christians, who much more often than not had been either excluded from the white churches or provoked to withdraw from them. Both women and blacks had been rebuffed regularly by institutions for ministerial and professional education.

By the middle of the nineteenth century, some women, some blacks, and a scattering of white male supporters were applying the concept of inclusion in campaigns for recognition that made important incremental

Anna Howard Shaw, c. 1915. Photo by Ellis. Courtesy Schlesinger Library, Radcliffe Institute, Harvard University (A-68-369-9).

gains over the next half-century. Among women, one of many personal exemplars of the process was Anna Howard Shaw, who fought her way into the ministerial and medical professions and who then, as a powerful leader and lecturer in the suffrage movement, helped lead women into the political mainstream. Among blacks, a leading example was Alexander Crummell, a prominent Episcopal priest and Cambridge-trained scholar who had had to battle exclusionary practices at every stage of his education and ministry.[3]

Among those marginalized on religious grounds (at least ostensibly so) rather than on the basis of race or gender, some had also employed inclusionary arguments from an early date. But Jews, Catholics, and other religious outsiders increased their use of the vocabulary of inclusion—as did liberal Protestants—in the late nineteenth and early twentieth centuries, the age of "melting pot" enthusiasm.

NEW AND NEWLY VISIBLE DIVERSITIES

Not by accident, this era in which Americans embraced the melting pot as their brave new metaphor for inclusiveness was another era of dramatic diversification. Along with the industrial and urban growth that provoked innovations in the churches' programs of social outreach, post–Civil War generations experienced both a new spurt in immigration rates and a new round of ethnic shifts within the immigrant population. In directly religious terms, it was a time in which new, sharply divergent movements sprang up at least as regularly as they had earlier in the century and, more often than their predecessors, attracted large followings and became fixtures on the religious landscape.

After 1850, but especially during the period of "new immigration" that began about 1880, Catholic and Jewish participation in American life increased in highly visible and much publicized ways. Between 1850 and 1920, the Roman Catholic population expanded at nearly three times the rate of overall population growth, while the number of Jews rose spectacularly—from fifty thousand to more than three million. The immigrants who accounted for most of this expansion, moreover, differed from those who had preceded them in European background and in a number of other ways. The new Jewish immigration was far more working class, eastern European, and Orthodox than the American Jewish community already in place; and Catholic immigrants were much more likely than their predecessors to have come from southern or central Europe. So "diversification" on this front involved much more than increased numbers, however impressive those numbers.

The principal new currents of piety in the era—adventism, intensified forms of premillennialism, the "holiness" movement, pentecostalism, and what is usually called mind cure—affected thought and life within existing churches, but they also contributed new organizations to the already rich mix of American denominations. The Seventh-Day Adventist Church, the Church of the Nazarene (holiness), the Church of Christ, Scientist, Jehovah's Witnesses (radical adventist), the Assemblies of God (pentecostal), and the Church of God in Christ (black pentecostal) all were organized between the 1860s and 1915.

In much of this chapter, I shall explore the meaning of inclusion as that goal was articulated by Jewish and Catholic leaders. But both the development of this ideology and its partial realization in practice were matters of, at the least, three-way collaboration; and Protestant liberals, given their numbers and cultural authority, necessarily led the way in developing what became a new common language for religious pluralism.

PLURALIST LEANINGS IN PROTESTANT LIBERALISM

Like its companion movement, the social gospel, the liberal theological surge of the late nineteenth century served both to shore up the Protestant establishment and to advance a religious pluralism that in the longer run would do much to undermine it.

Although evangelical revivalism, especially as led and personified by the great evangelist Dwight L. Moody, undeniably played a large part in keeping the United States a "Protestant country," the liberal movement may well have kept just as many people in the churches. Almost certainly, liberalism did more than evangelicalism could do to maintain the establishment's authority within the formal culture. As a movement that was both famous and notorious for trying to place religion in conversation with the world outside the churches, liberal Protestantism shared ideas and language with many of the most powerful institutions and personages in that wider world—most obviously with the new universities, but also with large segments of government, the press, the professions, and business.

Religious liberalism played another role that may have been even more important to the continuing viability of a Protestant establishment: it enabled great numbers of people, especially younger ones, to maintain a relationship with Christianity and the churches. Harry Emerson Fosdick, who between the world wars ranked as the best-known and most revered representative of popular liberalism, made this point when he recalled the process of vocational choice that he and others had undergone just before the turn of the century. As he said, opponents had been perfectly sure that the liberal movement would weaken, if not destroy totally, American

Protestantism and its influence in society. What they had failed to grasp, Fosdick thought, was liberalism's "absolute necessity to multitudes of us who would not have been Christians at all unless we could have escaped the bonds of the then reigning orthodoxy."[4]

Conservatives, of course, were ready with a rebuttal: "You folks would leave the churches if liberalism were prohibited? So leave. Good riddance." In the 1920s that was just what they did say to Fosdick and his liberal friends. What conservatives saw as the evisceration of Protestantism, and of religion itself, was too high a price to pay for the pleasure of such company.

But liberals themselves believed, just as firmly, that they were preserving and strengthening the essence of the faith—not destroying it, and not just making it easier for young Fosdicks to adhere to it. More than that, they were sure that their efforts to revise and restate particular doctrines were clarifying the true meanings and motivations behind those doctrines. Most located themselves within the category of "evangelicals"; and they were confident they were perpetuating, not discarding, the beliefs and symbols that made up the evangelicalism of their time.

Nearly all of the liberals' more distinctive emphases had a direct bearing upon the pluralist ideal. Their generally positive assessment of human nature, for example, involved appreciation of what Quakers had always called "that of God in everyone"; and this in turn implied strongly that non-Christian religions contain valuable truths. (*How much* valuable truth was another question; even liberals differed among themselves about that.) Their lack of enthusiasm for creeds and other formal structures, together with their rejection of biblical literalism, made the boundaries between Christianity and other faiths far less rigid than they were in any form of orthodoxy. And their emphasis on ethical behavior, which tended to supplant the orthodox insistence on creedal adherence, provided a bridge across the boundary lines that remained.

At the very end of the century, some liberals and most of their opponents began to use the term *modernist* for this cluster of ideas. What that term signified was an overall liberal commitment to religion's "cultural adaptation." So far as the opponents were concerned, this could just as aptly be called "capitulation to the secular"; but the liberals, of course, did not see it that way. Because they were also committed to the idea of a God who is "in everyone"—a God who is immanent in human nature and human cultures—they in fact refused to draw lines of that sort between the sacred and the secular. To do so, as the New Haven pastor Theodore Munger put it in the 1880s, is actually heretical! Tossing a well known bit of Scripture into the faces of the conservatives, Munger charged them with ignoring "the very process by which the kingdoms of this world are becoming the kingdom of the Lord Jesus Christ."[5] Whether or not one accepted that biblical rationale for what the liberals were up to, it is clear that the idea of religion's necessary cultural adaptation was an especially important element in the expansion of pluralism. As an idea, but even more as a matter of everyday practice, it meant that religious faiths in the process of adapting to the same culture—for example, Protestants, Catholics, and Jews in the United States—would gain more and more respect for each other, and would become increasingly aware of the extent to which they shared common ground; adaptation to the general culture would also be adaptation to each other. Thus the whole notion could, and did, help change the definition of pluralism from one that called for mere toleration to one that called for genuine inclusion.

THE LIBERAL METHOD

All of the distinguishing liberal positions, but most of all the rationale for religion's adaptation to culture, relied upon a theoretical distinction between form and substance: according to this understanding, creedal and other forms are temporary and changeable, while the substance of any faith is permanent and immutable. This distinction, like the various liberal doctrines, had been developing for a long time, especially during Western Christianity's encounters with the Enlightenment of the eighteenth century and then with romanticism in the nineteenth.

Characteristically, liberals revised or rejected particular forms—creeds, doctrines, rituals—that they thought had served as idioms for spiritual realities in earlier times but had become inappropriate or meaningless in the culture of their own day. During the many centuries when people had easily believed in miracles, miracles had been important as ways of authenticating the truth of an underlying belief—such as the power or goodness of God; but the liberal went on to insist (to use an idiom of our day) that "that was then, but this is now." We may still believe in miracles, they acknowledged, or adhere to some ancient creed; but if we do we should realize that the miracle or the creed is a matter of form, not of substance. It is legitimate, therefore, if not obligatory, for us now to express the power of God in "thought forms" that are natural and mean-ingful in our own day. Evolution, according to the popular philosopher John Fiske, is "God's way of doing things," and for most liberals the evo-lutionary hypothesis served as a leading example of the kind of modern thought form they were talking about.[6]

During the opening decades of the nineteenth century this "liberal method," like the various tenets I listed earlier, had been articulated and defended most noticeably within the Unitarian movement. The most fa-mous and controversial sermon of the Unitarian radical Theodore Parker had been constructed around the distinction between form and sub-stance. Parker's "The Transient and Permanent in Christianity," delivered in Boston in 1841, had proclaimed this distinction with utmost clarity.

If we take him at his word, Parker never intended, in that or his other pronouncements, to question the truth of Christianity. Quite the oppo-site: his avowed purpose was to underscore, vindicate, and promote that which is true and unchangeable in Christianity. In order to do that, how-ever, he had to be explicit about which elements of the traditional faith he thought were outdated and therefore eligible for the discard pile.

He was not loath to do so. To be sure, Parker gave most of his preach-ing time, in this sermon and elsewhere, to the permanent elements in Christianity, which he believed were centered in "love to God and love to man." But he also went on at great length and colorful detail about "transient" forms that other people—deluded ones, in Parker's view—took to be sacred and permanent. In the 1841 sermon we find him alleg-ing that Christian doctrines in general owe more to heathenism, Juda-ism, and "the caprice of philosophers" than to the teachings of Jesus. Becoming more graphic (and, seemingly, more angry), he insisted that many Christian doctrines are "the refuse of idol temples . . . wood, hay, and stubble, wherewith men have built on the cornerstone Christ laid." The pure stream of Christ's message had been "polluted by man with mire and dirt." Generations of mere human beings, Parker charged, had "piled their own rubbish against the temple of Truth."[7]

What did he have in mind, exactly? Which doctrines did Parker regard as mere heathenish rubbish? In a later sermon he listed them:

> Of course I do not believe in a devil, eternal torment, nor in a particle of absolute evil in God's world or in God. I do not believe there ever was a miracle. . . . I do not believe in the miraculous inspiration of the Old Testament or the New Testament. . . . I do not believe in the miraculous origin of the Hebrew Church, or the Buddhist Church, or the Christian Church; nor the miraculous character of Jesus. I take not the Bible for my master, nor yet the Church; nor even Jesus of Nazareth. . . . I try all things by the human faculties. . . . Has God given us anything better than our nature?[8]

Very few of Parker's fellow Unitarians, in his time or later, used this sort of dismissive language, or even agreed with him about what needed to be dismissed. Nearly all of them, however, concurred heartily in his distinction between form and substance (which they, like Parker himself, had derived in large part from German philosophies). And some enlisted this distinction quite forcefully in the project of extending a welcoming hand to non-Christian religions. During the half-century after Parker's controversial sermon, his fellow transcendentalist James Freeman Clarke, along with Samuel Longfellow (brother of the poet) and other younger Unitarians, penned appreciative studies of "the great religions," and wrote extensively about "the harmony of religions."[9]

In these pioneering forays into comparative religion, the connections between an antiformalist stance and the newer inclusive pluralism were abundantly clear. Liberals freed from the obligation to venerate the detailed doctrines and practices of any religion, their own definitely included, were commensurately free to stress those "permanent" elements —such as the divine presence in humanity—that they thought most religions shared.

Looking beyond Unitarianism, it is fair to say that the "Transient and Permanent" sermon ranked as a kind of keynote address for the much broader (and usually less strident) liberal movement that carried Parker's kind of antiformalism well beyond his own denomination.

POSTWAR—AND POST-DARWINIAN—LIBERALISM

When liberals in the post–Civil War period sought to recast the "permanent" truths of Christianity in the idiom of their own day, the language they found most readily at hand was that of Darwinian science. In theology, however, as in social theory, Darwinism offered both good news and bad news for those pursuing a liberal and pluralistic agenda. The bad news was that Darwinian ideas like natural selection and the survival of the fittest could be used to rationalize racism and imperialism. *The Origin of Species*, after all, had been subtitled *The Preservation of Races in the Struggle for Life*. It was true, as the historian Richard Hofstadter cautioned much later, that "Darwin had been talking about pigeons"; but others, in these areas as in the sphere of economic and social relationships, felt free to call on the great naturalist for support. "The imperialists," as Hofstadter says, "saw no reason why [Darwin's] theories should not apply to men." Wearing their militarist hats, they could use "the harsh fact of the elimination of the unfit as an urgent reason for cultivating the martial virtues and keeping the national powder dry."[10] In these and a number of other ways Darwinism could be distinctly unfriendly to notions that "others" deserve genuine respect and that diversity is a good thing.

All of that may cause us to doubt whether Darwinism could have brought any good news for pluralist advances; but clearly it did. For one thing, as I have pointed out, not all social Darwinism was conservative; some influential thinkers, by arguing that the human mind is an active agent in the evolutionary process rather than completely controlled by it, managed to enlist evolutionary science in the cause of social reform. More than that, as the Columbia University philosopher John Dewey wrote in 1910, Darwin's theories about the naturalness and inevitability of change in the biological world had given an enormous boost to the acceptance of change in all departments of thought and human action. Dewey thought that Darwin's achievement, in broadest terms, was that he had "conquered the phenomena of life for the principle of transition."[11]

That particular achievement, spelled out in theological terms, gave new ammunition to religious liberals who were already more than prepared to question the formalisms of the past. Especially among a younger generation of religious thinkers, the insistence of Fiske, Lyman Abbott, and others that evolution is a divinely directed, God-infused process was immensely liberating. William Jewett Tucker, a prominent theologian who became president of Dartmouth College, remembered the promulgation of Darwinism as a watershed event—in fact, as an "explosion" on the intellectual and moral landscape. He and his contemporaries, Tucker wrote in his autobiography, had felt keenly the need to break with the past; and "by common consent, the break came with the publication of *The Origin of Species.*"[12]

It would seem, however, given Tucker's own depiction of a younger generation already champing at the bit, that Darwinism was the match rather than the explosion. Much broader changes were going on, or at least were ready to happen. In virtually all cultural arenas, one could easily detect reactions—at least among younger intellectuals, but often reaching beyond them—against whatever had come to be considered traditional in those arenas. In architecture, for example, the movement called functionalism was rejecting classical rules that allegedly had produced buildings inappropriate to the real life in and around them, while in the new science of psychology the same term, *functionalism*, stood for a refusal any longer to treat the mind as a static entity. In literature, so-called realists and naturalists were busily revising a number of formalisms—for example, the rule that literature must be morally uplifting. In philosophy, several types of "pragmatist" objected to philosophical systems that, they thought, erred by picturing the world as more neat and unified than it really is.

What such movements (there were quite a few more of them) shared was first of all a sense of exhilaration and common purpose. But beyond that were some concrete ideas: the rejection of fixity; the farewell, with regret but also a sense of adventure, to comfortable expectations about the attainment of certainty.[13] There was a rising disbelief in the kind of universe whose goals and meaning were preordained and unchanging, and a widespread rejection—especially but not only among intellectuals—of the deductive modes of thinking that seemed to go with the insistence that ultimate reality is fixed and unchanging.

With such ideas and enthusiasms in the air, what Tucker called "an intellectual detachment from the past" would have occurred even without Darwin's intervention. Evolutionary theory, however, provided new, scientifically *au courant* explanations of what Parker had called "the transient"—of that which is changeable over time and of that which differs from one culture to another. Darwin could be, and was, read as saying that Parker and the pioneer comparativists had been right—that religions differ, for the most part, in their more transient or changeable features. Darwinism thus offered a new language and a new set of scientific justifications to religious thinkers who for a generation had been moving toward an inclusionary response to religious diversities.

REFORM JUDAISM AND INCLUSIONARY PLURALISM

Protestant liberals, however, could not have gone far down the path of inclusionary pluralism without a good deal of cooperation from those they sought to include. Not all offered this cooperation. Most of the newer nonmainstream groups—for example the Christian Scientists—were preoccupied with the problem of establishing their own somewhat separate identity; and a few, such as the sect that came to be known as Jehovah's Witnesses, were too busy defying the mainstream culture to give much thought to accommodations with it. Among the rest, however—which really means the outsiders of longer standing—inclusion, by the late nineteenth century, had become a principal goal and expectation.

That pattern was clearest among Jews and Catholics. More specifically, the drive for inclusion, complete with an argument for inclusionary pluralism as the American way, was central to the liberal movements within each of these major non-Protestant faiths. Through most of the century, but especially after 1850, both Jewish and Catholic liberals warned their coreligionists around the Western world that those faiths, if they were to survive at all, must adapt to modern conditions, and must look to America as the advance guard of everything good in modernity.

At many points, of course, "liberalism" looked and sounded quite different in these very different settings; but the pleas of Jewish and Catholic adaptationists were also strikingly similar, both to each other and to the arguments of Protestant liberalism. Each of the three was saying, in effect: "The essential, timeless core of our faith must be preserved; but we must also discard inessential doctrines and practices that are mere artifacts of some past time." Each insisted, in the face of furious objections from conservatives, that the resulting adaptations—such as, for

Catholicism, the adjustment to church-state separation—were not abject capitulations. On the contrary, these adjustments would make the ancestral faith stronger at its core, and in that sense more worthy of an equal place in society as well as more likely to achieve that status.

Among American Jews, the closest thing to an opening declaration in favor of cultural adaptation is a famous sermon preached in 1855 by David Einhorn, rabbi of Congregation Har Sinai in Baltimore. Einhorn, a religious and political liberal who had just emigrated from his native Germany, quickly became the intellectual leader of American Reform Judaism, and he retained that standing throughout the third quarter of the nineteenth century. An intense and notably determined man, he had been too radical even for the Reform faction in Germany; and his antislavery activities got him into nearly as much trouble in his adopted land. In 1861 he had to "flee for his life" from Baltimore and resettle in Philadelphia. Einhorn's radical views about Jewish adaptation to modernity were similarly unpopular during the early years of his American career. By the end of the century, however, they had become standard in American Reform.[14]

In the inaugural sermon of 1855, Einhorn's warning to Jews everywhere, but especially to the still vastly outnumbered American Jewish community, was that failure to adapt to modernity would cause defections and ultimate collapse. "Judaism," he argued, "has arrived at the critical stage when it must part company with dead and obsolete ceremonies, if it means to keep the Jews within the fold or prevent their moral decay." To be sure, this must be done "without deviating from the fixed principles of the divinely revealed word." But that cannot mean preserving obsolete forms. "Experience has shown," he said, "that all persuasion and pleading in favor of tradition—to galvanize dead forms into life—is ineffective." And he put it more strongly, at some points sounding as iconoclastic as Theodore Parker: "The remedy must be thoroughgoing. The evil [a too-rigid traditionalism] which is gradually draining our strength and sapping our life must be plucked up by the roots." This could be accomplished only by recognizing "what is decayed and untenable . . . and then, in the name of our faith, solemnly freeing ourselves from its authority."[15]

Thirty years later, nineteen Reform leaders gathered just outside of Pittsburgh under the leadership of Einhorn's son-in-law, Kaufmann Kohler. The purpose of this 1885 meeting was to codify or at least clar-

David Einhorn, c. 1857. Portrait by Fabronius. From *David Einhorn Memorial Volume*, 1911.

ify the points of agreement among these Jewish liberals and thereby to increase their movement's effectiveness.

The resulting "Pittsburgh Platform," which helped to define Reform Judaism for the next half-century, offered specifics about the practices and attitudes that most of these liberals wanted to discard (or had already discarded).[16] About some of these specifics there was already enough agreement that neither debate nor extensive definition seemed to be needed. In his opening remarks at the meeting, Kohler asserted that those who had ceased to insist upon circumcision and other "reminiscences of the remote past" were not merely a small dissenting faction within Reform Judaism. Far from it; "the overwhelming majority of Jews within the domain of modern culture disregard altogether the Mosaic-Rabbinical laws concerning diet or dress, concerning work or the kindling of lights on Sabbath, or any other ancient rite." The platform itself, in the fourth of its eight articles, repeated the same list, and added that these allegedly obsolete practices "fail to impress the modern Jew with a priestly holiness; their observance in our day is apt rather to obstruct than to further modern spiritual elevation."[17]

At least two topics, however, did arouse disagreement, and both bore directly on the issue of Jewish inclusion in American society. One of these had to do with the Sabbath, the other with Jewish attitudes toward Christians and other non-Jews.

The Reform leaders differed about the degree to which Judaism should alter traditional Sabbath practices—some holding that Sunday services should displace those traditionally held on Friday night and Saturday, others that services must be provided at all of these times. But no one doubted that something needed to be done. Adolph Moses, a radical Louisville rabbi who had, nonetheless, resisted a shift to Sunday services, said that he now thought things had "come to such a pass that, unless we boldly advocate and strenuously strive to introduce Sunday service, the future of Judaism in this country looks gloomy in the extreme." On Friday nights, Moses said, "most of us preach to about the sixth part of our congregation, at times outnumbered by the Gentiles present." On Saturdays, he added, we usually preach twice, but "to women, children, and a few old men." Meanwhile, the great mass of those who belong to a given congregation go "from year's beginning to year's end without religious and moral instruction." He and others thought that, although no congregation should be required to hold Sunday services, all should be permitted and encouraged to do so wherever conditions called for it.[18] A thoroughly pragmatic adaptationism could scarcely have gone farther.

As for relations with other religions, the words of the platform said it best: although "we hold that Judaism presents the highest conception of the God-idea," all religions are infused with divinity:

> We recognize in every religion an attempt to grasp the Infinite One, and in every mode, source, or book of revelation [we discern a] consciousness of the indwelling of God in man. . . . The spirit of broad humanity of our age is our ally in the fulfillment of our mission, and therefore we extend the hand of fellowship to all who co-operate with us in the establishment of the reign of truth and righteousness among men.[19]

The Jewish sense of belonging, of being included, gained its most emotional expressions whenever immigrant Jews portrayed America as the promised land of biblical prophecy. This theme had emerged as early as 1841, in an address by the spiritual leader of the congregation in Charleston, Gustav Poznanski. (There were some fifty synagogues in the United States by that time, but only one ordained rabbi, who had arrived a year earlier and was serving in Baltimore.) Later, anti-Zionists in the Reform wing of Judaism portrayed Poznanski as having rejected all ideas of a return to Palestine. That was not necessarily the case, but he had clearly elevated America's status as a Promised Land. He had assured the people of Beth Elohim that "this synagogue is our *temple*, this city our *Jerusalem*, this happy land our *Palestine*, and as our fathers defended with their lives *that* temple and *that* city and *that* land, so will their sons defend *this* temple, *this* city, and *this* land."[20]

As this idea was elaborated throughout the rest of the century, it acquired more specific meanings. In 1897 the Central Conference of American Rabbis reminded everyone that Jews considered themselves not merely as full participants in American life but also as having been players in the drama of the nation's origins: "We are unalterably opposed to political Zionism. The Jews are not a nation, but a religious community. . . . America is our Zion. Here, in the home of religious liberty we have aided in founding this new Zion."[21]

American Jewish spokesmen, like those representing many other immigrant religious groups, frequently urged the European cousins to change their ways and adopt "American" practices and characteristics. We find a striking illustration of this within the Jewish community of Great Britain, where a radical but highly respected rabbi named Israel Mattuck trumpeted this admonition for more than forty years after his arrival from the States in 1911. Like most other Reform spokesmen, Mattuck sought to do away with traditional practices that modern Jews could not accept. But he went farther along this line than any of his Reform colleagues in Great Britain or Germany—altering liturgies, abandoning the traditional sequence of prayers, opening his pulpit to women, and preaching the equal chosenness of all peoples. Such innovations were quickly and persistently objected to as "American."

Mattuck and his supporters not only accepted that designation; they assured everyone that in America these supposedly radical practices were standard ones—no longer considered radical, if they ever had been. Mattuck in his British setting frequently referred to himself as a missionary for the only kind of Judaism that would persuade Jews not to defect to Christianity or secularism. As he told a writer for the London *Jewish Chronicle*, in 1912, "the experience in America" had been that such innovations had kept Jews in the fold, "and I do not see that it will not apply here." [22]

The editors of the *Chronicle* had tried to remain neutral and to maintain an open forum, but this sort of claim—that American Judaism held the key to the survival of the faith—was simply too much. American and American-trained leaders like Mattuck, they conceded, had displayed Reform "as conceived in the United States, at its highest and best." What that highest and best amounted to, however, was "our great faith drained of its very life-blood."

The "one ideal" of Mattuck's kind of Reform, according to the *Chronicle*, was "assimilation to Americanism and conformity with American aspirations." Everything truly sacred to the Jew must give way to "the exigencies of American civilization and the demands of American 'hustle.'" It is far better, the editors wrote, to endure the terrible difficulties involved in maintaining Jewish language and practices in an alien environment than to "adopt the *manqué* Judaism—the neurotic, decadent, degenerate Judaism—presented by so-called American Reform." Jews need not flounder hither and thither "in what must at most be a doubtfully successful quest for—Americanization." [23]

LIBERAL CATHOLICS AND THE QUEST FOR INCLUSION

Roman Catholics also made their case—usually in an implicit way, but often in very direct fashion—for the sort of acceptance that would go beyond mere toleration. Most of this kind of advocacy came at the end of the century, when nativist intolerance seemed to have abated somewhat and when such Catholic clerics as Cardinal Gibbons had gained widespread recognition and respect. Like Jewish leaders, however, Catholics in the colonial and early national periods had occasionally entered public pleas for their own recognition as proven and trustworthy players in American public life.

The most famous public statement about Catholics' loyalty to the United States—or at least one that would have been famous had non-Catholics chosen to pay it much attention—had been a speech that John

England, the Roman Catholic Bishop of Charleston, delivered in the United States Congress in 1826. In this pronouncement, England had offered the sort of assurance about Catholic adherence to the American political system that most people imagine was first voiced by Al Smith or John Kennedy in the twentieth century. England confronted directly the assumption that Catholics should be treated as outsiders because they allegedly rejected the idea of church-state separation. He explained that "we have brethren of our church in every part of the globe, under every form of government," and that the Catholic Church had never asserted a right to dictate the details of government in those places. There was, he said, "no tribunal in our church which can interfere in our proceedings as citizens."

Coming even more directly to the point, England acknowledged that Americans had "wisely kept [church and state] distinct and separate," and that it would be "wisdom, and prudence, and safety to continue the separation." He had a short, sharp answer for those who kept insisting that American Catholics would have to heed Rome if the latter ordered them to overthrow or alter their government:

> Our answer to this is extremely simple and very plain; it is that we would not be bound to obey it, that we recognize no such authority. I would not allow to the Pope, or to any bishop of our church, outside this Union, the smallest interference with the humblest vote at our most insignificant ballot box.[24]

England was more strident in these matters than most of his fellow prelates, who in fact were critical of him for speaking out so boldly. But his fundamental assertion of Catholic compatibility with American principles, along with its implicit plea for full recognition and inclusion for Catholics, was reiterated throughout the nineteenth century and well into the twentieth.

By the 1880s, moreover, the so-called Americanists among the bishops and parish priests had expanded the rhetoric into enthusiastic claims, very similar to those of Reform Jews, that the American style was the wave of the future and must be so recognized in Europe. Like the arguments of their Jewish counterparts, theirs went well beyond a mere plea that "we must do these things to survive in America." The Catholic liberals got in serious trouble with the Roman authorities, and one reason for that was

John Lancaster Spalding. Courtesy University of Illinois Library.

their insistence that American experience and principles were superior to those of poor old Europe.

One of the more outspoken Americanists in this later period was John Lancaster Spalding, bishop of Peoria. Spalding—scholarly, rather severe, unfailingly direct in manner and argument—had worked strenuously for Catholic educational ventures and had been instrumental in the founding of the Catholic University in Washington, D.C. In 1888 he gave the principal address at the laying of the cornerstone for the university building.

After a long section, nearly half of the speech, praising almost every element of "modern progress"—scientific, social, spiritual—Spalding assessed the consequences of this progress for various traditions and habitual practices of his own church. Like Theodore Parker and most other religious liberals, Spalding clearly intended to stress the permanent elements of the faith more than those that deserved eradication. "Truth is unchangeable," he said repeatedly. "Many things, in this age of transition, are passing away; but true thoughts and pure love are immortal." Such assurances, however, attracted less attention than his colorful and largely disparaging references to nearly everything premodern—whether within the church or outside of it. (Aristotle took his licks along with Aquinas.) Compared with modern life, he asserted, "the life of Greece and Rome . . . was narrow and superficial"; and the labored doctrinal disputes occupying so much of the church's history were little better: "It is not to be imagined . . . that men should again become passionately interested in the questions which in the fourth and fifth centuries filled the world with the noise of theological disputation. [And] it were mere waste of time to beat now the waste fields of the Protestant controversy."[25]

None of that, however, seemed so sacrilegious, so direct an attack on traditional "forms," as Spalding's tender yet condescending language concerning ritual practice:

> We are, indeed, still subdued by the majesty of dimly lighted cathedrals, by solemn music and the various symbolism of the ritual, but we do not feel the deep awe of our fathers whose knees furrowed the pavement stones and whose burning lips kissed them smooth; and to blame ourselves for this would serve no purpose. To those who find no pleasure in sweet sounds, we pipe in vain, and argument to show that one ought to be moved by what leaves him cold, is meaningless.[26]

Because all of Spalding's tributes to modernity in the first half of his address assumed the superiority of American institutions, there could be no doubt that he and his fellow Americanists considered themselves not merely "included" in American society but fully certified spokesmen for it. Spalding assured his European brethren that the American way in religion, rooted in church-state separation and nonpreferential treatment for all faiths, "is the modern tendency and the position towards the Church which all the nations will sooner or later assume."[27]

John Ireland, archbishop of St. Paul, put the same case even more expansively, five years later, at a service celebrating the twenty-fifth anniversary of Cardinal Gibbons's consecration as a bishop. One of Ireland's biographers refers to him as "startlingly frank . . . a magnetic speaker, militant and yet conciliatory." What Ireland was willing to be frank and militant about in this sermon were his convictions that the Roman Catholic Church was out of tune with the times, and that its future welfare depended upon its willingness to undertake reforms based on American Catholic experience.

The watchword of humanity, Ireland argued, was "let all things be new." The church's mission, in that charged atmosphere, was what it had always been: to conquer the world for Christ; but the conquest of this rapidly changing world required that "the Church must herself be new, adapting herself in manner of life and in method of action to the conditions of the new order." Yet this renewal was not occurring. "The Church and the age are at war. I voice the fact with sorrow."[28]

Seemingly too excited to wait any longer, Ireland rose to his peroration in midspeech:

> What the Church at any time was, certain people hold she must ever remain. They do her much harm, making her rigid and unbending, incapable of adapting herself to new and changing surroundings. . . . What! The Church of the living God . . . the great, freedom-loving, truth-giving, civilizing Catholic Church—this Church of the nineteenth century afraid of any century! . . . I preach the new, the most glorious crusade. Church and age! Unite them in the name of humanity, in the name of God.[29]

Ireland closed with tributes to the two leaders "by whom salvation [would be] brought" to a worldwide Catholicism that had erred and strayed in its relations to modern society. One of these was the Pope himself, whose recent encyclical *Rerum Novarum* had convinced the Americanists that Rome was on their side: "Leo, I hail thee, pontiff of thy age, providential chieftain of the Church in a great crisis of her history!" The other, of course, was Cardinal Gibbons, who more than anyone else represented the dual sense that Catholic "inclusion" had become a reality and that the Americans had been divinely appointed to reform and modernize their church: "A special mission is reserved to the American Cardinal. In America, the Church and the age have fairest field to display their activities, and in America more speedily than elsewhere is the problem of their reconciliation to be solved. . . . My whole observation of the times . . . convinces me that the Church has now her season of grace in America."[30]

Cardinal Gibbons and President Taft, 1909. From Allen S. Will, *The Life of James Cardinal Gibbons*, 1911.

THE WORLD'S PARLIAMENT AS A SHOWCASE
FOR INCLUSION

To say that it was becoming standard practice by the late nineteenth century to embrace inclusiveness as an ideal is not, of course, to say that this ideal was regularly implemented, even under liberal religious auspices. The concrete gains for an inclusionary pluralism, moreover, though numerous, were usually incremental and not very dramatic: the achievement of ordination or other forms of recognition by women like Shaw; the hard-fought victories of Crummel and other black churchmen; the presence of Cardinal Gibbons on a reviewing stand, next to the president of the United States. Such gains were highly significant as building blocks for what was to come. The 1893 World's Parliament of Religions, however, offered more sweeping testimony to the progress of the inclusionary ideal, even though it also exhibited some of the problems with that ideal.

The Parliament was noteworthy, dramatically so, for domestic inclusiveness. No previous religious gathering of this magnitude had involved so many women speakers, and no meeting of any magnitude had brought

together Jews, Catholics, and Protestants. Its starting point and fundamental purpose, however, lay in the equally unprecedented project (unprecedented at least in modern Western history) of promoting understanding and mutual respect among all the "great religions."

Less than a century earlier, such an event could scarcely have been contemplated, at least by Americans or Europeans. Non-Western religions,
if not their adherents, had then been generally considered undeserving
of respect. In 1815, when the Reverend Samuel Worcester had preached
the annual sermon for the American Board of Commissioners for Foreign Missions (ABCFM), he had expressed attitudes much like the views
of Professor Wilkinson that I cited at the opening of this chapter; but, unlike Wilkinson in 1893, Worcester in 1815 had been reflecting an almost
unquestioned consensus. Although he had not suggested that Hinduism,
Islam, nature worship, or even irreligion deserved persecution, Worcester
in 1815 had averred that—as an Anglican in his place might have put it—
there was no health in any of these so-called religions. Those not reached
by Christianity, he said,

> have no good hope. . . . Their gods cannot save them; their wise men will not,
> cannot direct their feet into the way of peace; their religion does not satisfy
> the heart or the life; does not bring them to the blood which cleanseth from
> sin,—does not shew them a redeeming God, does not fit them for the mansions
> of immortal light and purity,—does not dissipate the darkness which heavily
> broods over them, thickening into the blackness of eternal night.[31]

Worcester was a staunchly conservative Congregationalist who just at
this time was involved in strenuous public disputes with William Ellery
Channing and other leaders of the emerging Unitarian movement. But
liberals could be nearly as dismissive about the religions of what Worcester called the "pagan world." When Hannah Adams, a distant cousin of
John Adams and like him a votary of the new liberal movement, had published the first edition (1784) of her own pioneering survey of the world's
religions, she had recognized Asian religions—as, indeed, the great theologian Jonathan Edwards had before her—but only in an appendix that
lumped them all together.[32] In her fourth edition, which appeared two
years after Worcester's sermon, Adams brought world religions into the
body of her encyclopedia, but this pioneer comparativist offered them

scant legitimacy. Her entries for non-Christian religions ended with an appraisal of Christian missionary efforts; and her accounts of such religions as Hinduism slipped easily into belittling phraseology: "They pretend that their legislator, Brama [sic], bequeathed to them a book, called the *vedas*, containing his doctrines and instructions." In other words, even Adams's treatment of most non-Christian peoples had carried the conviction, almost universal in her time and Worcester's, that these religions had no contributions to make to human welfare.

What made a project like the World's Parliament possible, some eighty years later, was a virtual sea change in this older conventional wisdom; customary ways of referring to non-Christian religions had shifted perceptibly. This change was very much in evidence when George A. Gordon, the liberal pastor of Old South Church (Congregational) in Boston, gave the ABCFM's annual sermon in 1895. Voicing the characteristic liberal disdain for the merely "transient" elements in a religion, Gordon urged the missionary movement to forget about formal creeds and institutions when attempting to convert the so-called heathen. The latter need our Christ, he told the ABCFM, but they do not need our formulas: "We are not under obligation to export our entire body of belief. . . . There is no particular call for our church polity, our special theology, or the traditions of our Christian life. These are not wanted; if sent, they would prove unsuitable." [33]

Gordon's biblical text was a telling one; it was Christ's assertion that "I am not come to destroy, but to fulfil." The religion Jesus had declined to destroy was of course Judaism, but Gordon was sure he would state his objective in the same way in relation to the religions of the modern world. Gordon expected Christianity to triumph over other religions, but it would do this by building on them, not by disrespecting and aiming to destroy them. Jesus, he said, "must prove Himself a better ruler to Japan, a nobler Confucius to China, a diviner Guatama to India; the whole sacred past must reappear in Him transfigured and carried utterly beyond itself. . . . He must come as the consummation of the ideals of every nation under heaven." [34]

Clearly this was inclusion on a worldwide scale. Given Gordon's convictions about Christianity's coming triumph, it was also, necessarily, inclusion on terms similar to those offered immigrants under the "melting pot" formula. Other religions were to be welcomed, but as junior partners or, perhaps better, as postulants. The ideals of Islam and Buddhism were to be honored, and even admitted to the sacred precincts, but these ideals could not be realized fully until those who held to them took the Christian vows. Islam and Buddhism could not be fulfilled until they became . . . something else.

This way of limiting one's respect for "the other" would come under attack during the next half-century, first in relation to the melting pot concept at home, then in attempts to bring further changes in missionary ideology and methods. In the 1890s, however, Westerners' objections to the Gordon approach came from the other direction—the Wilkinson direction. Gordon's detractors, and critics of the Parliament, were people who thought that any serious acknowledgment of the moral worth of other religions constituted a virtual sellout.

Even within the ABCFM and the Congregational churches, only a bare majority agreed with Gordon—just enough for him to become the much controverted choice for speaker of the year in 1895. Yet Gordon's address—and the board's decision to invite this leading liberal to give it—revealed that a great deal had changed over eight decades, not merely in academic circles or popular sentiment, but even within the missionary movement, an enterprise traditionally dedicated to the rooting-out and displacement of non-Christian religions.

The World's Parliament, in a dramatic realization of the newer attitudes, brought together as major participants roughly two hundred representatives of a dozen religions. Less spectacularly, but as an equally unprecedented feature of the event, it listed substantial numbers of Catholics, Jews, and women, most of them Americans, among its speakers. Even African-American participation, which was inadequate by any modern standard, constituted a breakthrough; although there were only two official delegates from the black churches, this was two more than had been included in any comparable gathering of a religious nature before the twentieth century. Among the 136 papers presented by Westerners at the Parliament, eighteen were offered by Catholics, eleven by Jews, and seventeen by such prominent women as Julia Ward Howe, Emma Willard, and Elizabeth Cady Stanton.

This, of course, meant that mainline Protestant bodies were substantially less dominant than usual. Those churches, bastions of the traditional establishment, could claim a plurality of delegates and papers; but what was entirely unusual for the time was the fact that this was merely a plurality, not even close to being a majority. The principal recent historian of the Parliament, Richard Seager, estimates the forces of the mainstream Protestant churches at just under 40 percent.[35] If we bring female delegates into the calculation, the hints of a realignment in the traditional male-dominated establishment are even more striking.

A cartoon drawn for an article in *Cosmopolitan* magazine depicted the new domestic inclusiveness with some statistical accuracy. The centerpiece in this drawing was an imagined structure consisting of vertical staves each of which represented a denomination or religious group—all held together by "the fatherhood of God, the brotherhood of man, and equal rights." Guarding this structure, one at each end of it, were two female figures that the artist may have felt stood for the outer limits of inclusion: to the viewer's right, a Roman Catholic nun; on the left, a woman in Salvation Army uniform. Of the thirteen religious groups named or depicted, only eight were mainstream Protestant—and that number was smaller if Quakers, Unitarians, or Universalists were not counted as "mainstream."

Front and center in this cartoon, an American eagle held in his beak a thoroughly dead snake labeled "Intolerance." The idea, one taken for granted at the Parliament and engraved on many of the structures of the Columbian Exposition, was that neither legal toleration nor social tolerance was any longer the issue; both could now be taken for granted as principles and celebrated as actual achievements. The exposition and the Parliament were making a pitch for something more—for the inclusiveness proclaimed in the motto *e pluribus unum*.

EARLY-TWENTIETH-CENTURY ADVANCES
TOWARD INCLUSION

After the turn of the century, gains for inclusionary pluralism became more visible and substantial. That was because, more often than in the past, they were collective in nature. It still mattered, of course, that out-

Religious pluralism in America, as depicted at the time of the Chicago Fair, from *Cosmopolitan*, March 1893.

standing individuals were fighting and sometimes winning battles against intolerance and exclusion; but larger-scale acts of inclusion said more about the advances those individuals had helped bring about.

Thus the Federal Council of Churches, at its founding in 1908, welcomed the major black denominations, none of which had been represented in the Evangelical Alliance, the FCC's nineteenth-century predecessor. Beginning in 1910 the powerful women's missionary societies were, one by one, merged into the various denominational structures, although some years passed before women assumed places as principal leaders in the mission boards of those denominations.[36]

A few years later, the participation of Catholics and Jews in a major war effort was not only more visible and acknowledged than in past instances; in practical and statistical terms it was much more of a reality. Catholics and Jews together constituted roughly a third of the total force of wartime chaplains. Equally unprecedented was the high degree of interreligious collaboration among such wartime agencies as the National Catholic War Council, the [Protestant] Wartime Commission of the Churches, the Jewish Welfare Board, and an impressive number of nondenominational or secular agencies in which members of the various faiths served together.

Despite the apparent gains for the ideal of inclusion, these collaborative ventures did not usually entail either equal treatment or the proportioning of "voice" to numbers. In the 1920s the notion that seventeen million Catholics should perhaps have as much influence on American public policy as was enjoyed by three-quarters of a million Congregationalists had scarcely been considered. With regard to the larger world scene, it was similarly difficult to find among Western Christians any notion that Buddhism or Islam might be entitled to as much deference as Christianity. Yet inclusion, wherever that much was achieved, did signify a new level of recognition for a broad range of religious outsiders in America and for "world religions" elsewhere.

More than that, as I shall show, inclusion was a Trojan horse. Whether in the boardrooms of the denominations or in cordial interfaith meetings like the one at the Columbian Exposition, it created settings in which the newly included were likely to speak out, and to act, in ways their cautious sponsors had not intended or expected.

6 Surviving a While Longer: The Establishment Under Stress in the Early Twentieth Century

In the 1880s, when Josiah Strong presented his mostly optimistic ideas about the future of "our country," neither he nor most of his readers felt any doubt about just who it was that *our* referred to. Whatever alien masses might now have to be counted in the census (and Strong, despite his worries about immigrants, was not for sending them back to Europe), America was the property, bought and paid for, of those popularly known as Anglo-Saxons—the people of northern European Protestant stock. And in spite of the serious threats Strong associated with Catholicism, Mormonism, alcohol, and tobacco, the society thus defined and directed held in its hands "the world's future." It was destined to extend to people everywhere, by entirely peaceful means, its own version of democratic and Christian idealism.[1]

Strong's book achieved its best-seller status because it set these themes in a compelling context of industrial-era challenges. But the themes themselves were venerable, and deeply ingrained. So it was especially noteworthy that a vocal minority were soon singing a different song.[2] William Graham Sumner, for example, who had never been either a super-optimist or a friend to Western imperialism, by the end of the century had become distinctly bearish about the future. In 1899, when others were taking to the streets to cheer America's multiple triumphs over the Spanish, Sumner was telling Yale Phi Betes about *The Conquest of the United States by Spain*. As most of his countrymen looked forward enthusiastically to peace and plenty in the dawning century, the old warhorse of free enterprise was referring darkly to a coming age of militarism and totalitarianism.[3] Strong himself, although he embraced the new imperialism and lauded his country's post-1898 decision to participate in it, had become more and more troubled about "cultural decline" in America and the West.[4] He was to become even more of a pessimist before his death in 1916, but in 1900 he was quoting the British historian Macaulay on the perils ahead. Macaulay, never much of a friend to democracy, had warned Americans that "either some Caesar or Napoleon will seize the reins of government . . . or your republic will be as fearfully plundered and laid waste by barbarians in the twentieth century as the Roman Empire was in the fifth." Strong, in at least partial agreement, now feared that the Anglo-Saxon Protestants might not make it after all.[5]

In 1900 such warnings were still minority expressions — little more than blips on the screen of American and Protestant triumphalism. Over the next several decades, however, a series of shocking, almost wholly unexpected events, both global and domestic, made the apprehensions voiced in 1900 read like prophetic utterances. America and the West were shaken by war, a devastating economic depression, and the rise of new totalitarian regimes. Partly because of these catastrophes, the religious liberalism that had become dominant within the Protestant establishment, and that had been a powerfully effective vehicle for the inclusionist version of pluralism, came under serious and increasing assault.

During these same years increasing numbers of social analysts became dissatisfied with the "melting pot" formula that governed most versions of inclusionary pluralism. Doubts about the melting pot — whether it worked, whether the kind of assimilation it implied had been a good idea in the first place — developed quite separately from doubts about liberal optimism, and I shall discuss the melting pot issue separately. What needs to be said here is that both of these forms of questioning, augmented and complicated by bitter liberal-conservative feuding within Protestantism, helped set the stage for changes that were to dominate discussions of American religion in the final decades of the twentieth century. They prepared the way, in other words, for a much-discussed "Protestant decline" that is more accurately understood as "the loss of the Protestant franchise" in American culture.[6] Over against that, they prefigured still another redefinition of pluralism — one that would regard both toleration and inclusion as necessary but insufficient responses to religious diversification.

BEFORE FUNDAMENTALISM: THE BUILDING OF A CONSERVATIVE OPPOSITION

For about three decades after 1890, liberalism was the most dynamic force in white Protestantism; and, despite persisting stereotypes that would suggest otherwise, it also made significant inroads in the black churches.[7] Liberal assumptions and theology managed to become the dominant mode in at least a third of the congregations, theological seminaries, and publications of the Protestant churches; and in roughly half of their denominational colleges and universities. Liberal infiltration of the mission boards was also substantial, although it was not as extensive as conservatives feared. (Their alarm on this point was a major spur to the rise of fundamentalism.)[8]

We might suppose that ordinary churchgoers would have been less attracted to liberal ideas than preachers and theologians were, but that seems not to have been the case. One testimony to this was the immense popularity of such religious best-sellers as *In His Steps*, James Lane Allen's *The Reign of Law*, and other novels sympathetic to the social gospel, science, and liberal theology. Another indicator was the surging growth of Lyman Abbott's newspaper, the *Outlook*, which was clearly a vehicle for the liberal movement. The *Outlook* in the 1870s (when it was still called the *Christian Union*) had boasted a readership of 15,000. By the early 1890s this figure had doubled, and in 1900 the *Outlook*'s circulation was 100,000— which may well have been the largest for a religious newspaper in either the United States or Europe.[9]

Because liberal movements had developed across the board on the American religious scene, not just within the Protestant churches, it is no surprise to find that a backlash, when it came, was evident in nearly all sectors of American religion. Reform Jewish leaders had barely made their way home from the landmark consultations in Pittsburgh, in fall 1885, before a conservative response appeared. Rabbis representing the older Sephardic Jewry, together with moderate Reform Jews for whom the

Pittsburgh Platform went too far, not only made themselves heard but before too long had formed a Jewish Theological Seminary Association that
began to sponsor instruction in 1887.

This conservative voice might have remained a soft and muted one without the megaphone effect of eastern European Jewish immigration. As it
was, the turn toward tradition qualified as a major movement. Although
many of the more traditional Jews aligned themselves not with Orthodoxy
but with a mediating position—called simply Conservatism—in which
some Reform principles lived on, Jewish liberalism had suffered a setback.
Sydney Ahlstrom's contention that Reform Judaism in the 1880s "had almost come to be American Judaism" is perhaps an exaggeration, but it is
clear that Jewish liberalism had declined in both numbers and dynamism
before the turn of the century.[10]

In the case of Catholics, reactions against the liberals, and against their
plainspoken enthusiasm for reforming the church along American lines,
came most powerfully and visibly from the Vatican. The progressive views
of Leo XIII on social questions had warmed the hearts of liberalizers in
Europe and America, but by the mid-nineties Leo was trying to disabuse
his flock about any wholesale, or even extensive, approval of American-
ist leanings toward political and cultural adaptation. In an encyclical of
1895 he warned that "it would be very erroneous to draw the conclusion
that in America is to be sought the type of the most desirable status of
the Church."[11] But the liberals—generally called modernists in Europe—
persisted in their advocacy, and many in the American contingent also
persisted in the happy notion that the Pope sympathized with them. At
the very end of the century, Leo set that part of the record straight by issu-
ing the encyclical *Testem Benevolentiae*—commonly known as the "Encyclical Against Americanism." After that pronouncement, which was sup-
plemented strongly by several condemnations of modernism in the early
years of the new century, Catholic liberalism for the most part was driven
underground. It did not reemerge until the time of the Second Vatican
Council in the 1960s.

Within the Protestant churches, conservative evangelicals responded
to the liberal advances either by simply reaffirming what they saw as the
orthodox faith or by going on the offensive—by lashing out vigorously,
and often bitterly, against liberalism and modernism. The most aggres-

sive reactions were marked by extreme biblical and creedal literalism, and by demands that liberals remove themselves, or suffer removal, from the denominations and the missionary movement; it was this sort of response that began around 1920 to be called fundamentalism. But in most of the white churches and nearly all of the black ones, a calmer, more taken-for-granted rejection of liberalism was equally common, especially before the acrimonious outbreak of the 1920s.

Dwight L. Moody, the leading evangelist of the late nineteenth century, showed little interest in formulated doctrine and even less interest in attacking or excluding anyone. Like Billy Graham, Jerry Falwell, and a number of other popular evangelists in the twentieth century, Moody was criticized by more militant conservatives for engaging in discussions with moderates and liberals instead of shunning them. For example, Moody's critics in the extremist wing of evangelicalism found fault with him for sharing speakers' platforms with champions of evolutionary theory.

There were also strong continuities, however, between the assumptions of noncombative evangelicals like Moody and the ideas of militant 1920s fundamentalists. Most significantly, they agreed about word-for-word adherence to Holy Scripture. Some passages in Moody's sermon on "The Inspiration of the Bible" (1894), in fact, suggest a kinship between Moody's biblicism and some of the best-known utterances of the statesman and religious fundamentalist William Jennings Bryan. In his testimony at the Scopes trial of 1925, Bryan asserted that seeming absurdities (such as Jonah's swallowing the whale instead of the reverse) would have to be accepted if the Bible recorded them; and when pressed about this he protested in exasperation that "I do not think about things I don't think about."[12] Moody in the 1890s had, less crudely, taken a similarly obscurantist position:

> People say, "What do you do with what you cannot understand?" "I don't do anything with it." "How do you understand it?" "I don't understand it." "Well, how do you interpret it?" "I don't interpret it." "What do you do with it?" "I don't do anything with it." "Don't do anything with it? Do you believe it?" "Yes, I believe it." Of course I do. I am glad that there is a height I know nothing about in the old book, a length and a breadth we know nothing about. It makes the book all the more fascinating. I thank God it is beyond me. It is a pretty good proof that it came from God, and not from the hand of man.[13]

Dwight L. Moody preaching in Agricultural Hall, London, 1875. From William R. Moody, *The Life of Dwight L. Moody*, 1900.

Ironically, this kind of simple, noncombative assertiveness also characterized the publications that gave a name to the fiercely combative fundamentalism of the 1920s. *The Fundamentals*, a series of ninety booklets published between 1910 and 1915, adhered generally to the promise conveyed in the series's subtitle: *A Testimony to the Truth*. The authors of these articles indulged in little direct assault on liberal positions and seldom attacked anyone by name. For a foretaste of the more confrontational brand of conservatism that was about to rear its head in the fundamentalist movement, one looks neither to evangelists like Moody nor to *The Fundamentals* but to the classrooms, theological journals, and occasional heresy trials of the major denominations.

Among the bastions of orthodoxy during the era of liberal ascendancy, none was more staunch than the principal Presbyterian seminary, Princeton, and its theological journal, *The Princeton Review*. The seminary and the *Review* had been guided to their prominence in orthodox circles by the theologian Charles Hodge, who had taught at Princeton from 1820 until his death in 1878.

Hodge had ranked as one of the most learned and prolific scholars of his time. He was also a warmhearted, kindly man and a superb teacher; yet in his controversial writings, and even in great tomes like his *System-*

atic Theology, he was fiercely and unsparingly contentious—about as different from the amiable Moody as one could imagine. In Hodge's most famous, or notorious, assault on the emerging liberal ideas, a short book called *What Is Darwinism?* (1874), his ringing answer to the title question had been, "It is atheism."[14]

Hodge also, at about this time, had uttered a boast that liberals then and since have never allowed him or his admirers to forget. At a celebratory occasion marking the fiftieth year of his teaching at Princeton, Hodge averred that he was "not afraid to say that a new idea never originated in this Seminary."[15] That perhaps unwise phrasing, although it has been ridiculed as the equivalent of Moody's obscurantism—or even Bryan's—in some respects was exactly the opposite: not "We won't think about it," but "We consider traditional doctrines unshakable, and we think and write about this issue all the time." Certainly that is what they did, as the Princeton professors, along with a large stable of colleagues and former students around the country, used the *Review* to spell out a carefully reasoned response to nearly every new idea (and some older ones) that liberals were promoting.

In the years after Hodge's death, as academic scientists came to accept the theory of evolution, Darwin ceased to be at the center of dispute, whether in seminaries like Princeton or in publications like *The Fundamentals*. In other respects, however, the *Review* maintained Hodge's legacy; its articles and reviews, mostly written by his former students and colleagues, reflected the master's erudition, his skilled combativeness, and his steadfastness in defense of biblical infallibility.

But they went still further, moving partway into a territory that, after 1930, would be dominated by the theological movement called neo-orthodoxy. This was a battleground on which the enemy was neither Darwinism nor advanced views of the Bible, but instead an alleged liberal capitulation to secular culture. One of the journal's editors, reviewing an 1897 book on *The Newer Religious Thinking*, complained that liberals had ceased to take the Bible as authoritative and instead were seeking guidance from "the Christian consciousness of the present age." This reliance on an allegedly converted secular culture was, he thought, misguided and dangerous. To assume that one lived in a happily christianized society, this writer thought, was to close one's eyes to the sinfulness rampant in that and every other society. More fundamentally, it was to ignore "the love in the heart for all within itself that is alien to the character of God, and that lies at the root of evil choices."[16]

A corollary of the liberals' casualness about essential doctrines, these traditionalists thought, was their equally misguided friendliness to non-Christian beliefs. The *Princeton Review* treated the World's Parliament with silence, but Benjamin Warfield, Charles Hodge's leading successor, spoke for most conservatives in reasserting what he took to be the biblical position: the "heathen religions" were "degrading to man and insulting to God," and their erring adherents were "without hope." Although Warfield made it clear that he agreed with the liberals about the universality of a religious sentiment, and was even able to acknowledge some beneficial features of non-Christian religions, he considered it folly to imply that religions are equally valid—or even approximately so. One passage, especially, set forth the stance of the more large-minded conservatives with great directness and considerable feeling. "Ah, brethren," he wrote, "let us avoid 'deisdaimonism' [by which he meant satisfaction with mere natural religiosity] in all its manifestations!"

> As you look out over the heathen world with its lords many and gods many, and see working in every form of faith the same religious impulses, producing in varying measure . . . the same civilizing and moralizing effects—are you perhaps tempted to pronounce it enough; possibly adding something about the adaptation of the several faiths to the several peoples, or even something about the essential truth underlying all religions? This is "deisdaimonism," and on its basis the whole missionary work of the Church is an impertinence, the whole history of the Church a gigantic error . . . a fool's errand, every step of which has dripped with wasted blood.[17]

This kind of plaintive exasperation became one trademark of the Princetonian protest against liberalism. Another was reflected in Warfield's contention—which to liberals and moderates seemed simply outrageous—that to question Christian exclusivism was to discard the entire structure and history of the religion Jesus taught. According to Warfield, one either accepts a defined set of doctrines or else forfeits the right to be called Christian. There could be no legitimate position in between.

This Princetonian emphasis on a clear, uncomplicated choice expressed, at a scholarly level, what Dwight Moody had meant when he told his thousands of hearers that Satan "has accomplished a great point" if he can get a Christian "to doubt just one thing" in the Bible. That one thing would of course lead to another, and before long the poor "believer" would be doubting nearly everything. To illustrate this, Moody had told about the parishioner who confronted his liberal pastor with what he called "The Minister's Bible." The man had snipped out everything that, over the years, the pastor had doubted. "He had got all of the book of Job cut out, all Revelations, the Song of Solomon, and about a third of the Bible was cut out. The minister said, 'I wish you would leave that Bible with me.' . . . But the man said, 'O, no! I have got the covers, and I am going to hold on to them.' And off he went with the covers. If you were to hear some men preach, you wouldn't have anything but the covers in a few months." [18]

The Princetonian argument was a more sophisticated version of the same plea: Doubts about biblical stories will lead to doubts about the miracles, which will raise questions about supernaturalism itself; and Christianity will fall like a house of cards. In 1897 the Reverend George Patton, son of a famous battler for orthodoxy who was then president of Princeton University, asked Christians to confront what he thought was the real choice:

> Let us be honest with ourselves. Let us face the question whether Christianity is a supernatural religion or not . . . [and if it is not] let us give up the old terminology and the old method of defending the faith. And when we have given up the God-man Christ Jesus, and the miracles He wrought, and His resurrection from the dead, and His atonement for sin, then at least, if not before, let us pause and ask . . . whether we are still Christians. [19]

The problem, as such conservatives saw it, was not merely that liberals slighted certain doctrines. The more basic fault was their disdain for doctrine itself. And behind that was a disinclination to make choices or accept definite commitments. The liberal's zeal for inclusivity—for bringing people and religious viewpoints together—was really an expression of this unwillingness to choose. Warfield cited what he saw as a weariness of "thinking, distinguishing, defending," and a resulting desire to combine all kinds of thought and belief into one "structureless, homogeneous mass." [20]

FRACTURED ESTABLISHMENT: THE
FUNDAMENTALIST-MODERNIST CONTROVERSY

By the 1920s, with conservatives feeling that things had simply gone too far, the all-or-nothing attitude was taking a different, considerably nastier, form; not "Let us all think what we are doing," but "These people are not really Christians, and they must be banished." Repeatedly, from the 1870s on, denominations and other bodies (such as the World's Christian Fundamentals Association, formed in 1920) had drawn up lists of essential doctrines—doctrines that effectively defined who deserved to be called a Christian and who did not. These lists varied in length, with the Presbyterian General Assembly in 1910 specifying five doctrines while others before and after insisted on as many as fourteen.

Discrepancies like that, with fundamentalists appearing to differ about what is fundamental, enabled amused opponents to question whether these conservatives agreed about anything at all. George Marsden is more on the mark, however, when he cites a short list of beliefs that nearly all shared: "the inerrancy of the Bible, the virgin birth of Jesus, the authenticity of the miracles, atonement for sin through the death of Christ, Jesus' resurrection, and his coming again." [21] And in any case, the fundamentalist-modernist dispute at its height was less a matter of particular doctrines than of the fundamentalists' winner-take-all mentality.

Fundamentalists could and did point out that their uncompromising attitudes had developed only because of the enormous challenges to traditional faith that a successful liberal movement had presented; and that any fracturing of the establishment was therefore the fault of the liberals. The first part of that plea, at least, was surely valid. Fundamentalism would have achieved little strength or visibility had it not been for the success and spread of liberalism. It seems equally true, however, that the militant us-or-them counterpunches of post-1915 fundamentalism were especially divisive and embittering.

J. Gresham Machen, a Princeton New Testament scholar of the generation following Warfield's, delivered the exclusivist message, with unprecedented clarity and force, in a 1923 volume called *Christianity and Liberalism*. Machen, a patrician from a prominent Baltimore family, brandished his stiletto in a velvet-gloved hand. He was too polite to name his book "Christianity *or* Liberalism," but that was the idea. These are two different religions, he argued, and everyone should simply choose between them. It is no disgrace to adhere to a non-Christian faith or ideology; both Socrates and Goethe did so, yet we respect and admire them. But it makes no sense to allow such people to call themselves Christians—especially given the conditions of the twentieth century. "The present time," Machen writes, "is a time of conflict; the great redemptive religion which has always been known as Christianity is battling against a totally diverse type of religious belief, which is only the more destructive of the Christian faith because it makes use of traditional Christian terminology. This modern non-redemptive religion is called 'modernism' or 'liberalism.'" [22]

Machen thought that the liberal, in a foolish effort to defend Christianity by removing everything that might clash with a scientific worldview, "has really abandoned what he started out to defend." The liberal's creed, like the "Minister's Bible" that Moody ridiculed, had a nice cover but was otherwise a thing of shreds and patches.

Machen may have respected his contemporary liberal enemies, just as he respected Socrates. But enemies they were, so long as they insisted on remaining in the churches. In the tradition that General Grant had helped embed in the American psyche, they could be offered no terms short of unconditional surrender: "There can be no 'peace without victory,'" Machen wrote; "one side or the other must win." [23]

The classic liberal protest against this exclusivist turn in conservatism came in a sermon preached in 1922, when Machen's book was in press. Harry Emerson Fosdick, a Baptist holding a Presbyterian pastorate in New York City, asked the question, "Shall the Fundamentalists Win?" His answer was that they must not be allowed to win. It was not just that they were wrong; their course of action was disruptive and destructive. Fosdick raised no objection to the fundamentalists' definition of Christianity, much as he disagreed with it. His plea, put forward in language about as strident as Machen's, was that professing Christians should be able to disagree about doctrines, or even about definitions, without ceasing to respect each other as Christians.

Fosdick had watched and listened in dismay as fundamentalists during the previous several years had sought to defeat or dampen liberal influence wherever it appeared—in churches and denominations, in the missionary movement, in public and private education, and elsewhere. The resulting conflict, he thought, was dividing the American churches not merely along fundamentalist-modernist lines, but also along the lines of difference between fundamentalists and other conservatives; while conservatives could often "give lessons to the liberals in true liberality of spirit," the fundamentalist program was "essentially illiberal and intolerant." And these multiple fractures were occurring at a time when the churches desperately needed to work and act together: "The present world situation smells to heaven! And now, in the face of colossal problems, which must be solved in Christ's name and for Christ's sake, the Fundamentalists propose to drive out from the Christian churches all the consecrated souls who do not agree with their theory of inspiration. What immeasurable folly! . . . Well, they are not going to do it." [24]

That last impassioned prediction proved accurate. Fundamentalists did not disappear after the battles of the 1920s (most elite observers thought they had, and thus were bewildered by their prominence in the public life of the 1970s and after); but they did fail, spectacularly, in their efforts to gain control of mainline institutional Protestantism. Their defeat in the Scopes trial (John Scopes was ordered to pay a one dollar fine; and even that conviction was reversed on appeal) was only the most visible of a series of episodes in which liberals and moderate evangelicals collaborated to prevent the purging of nonfundamentalists from the denominations, the schools, and the international missionary and ecumenical movements.

WHAT THE WAR DID TO THEIR MINDS

The conflict between fundamentalists and their opponents had thus been resolved, at least for the time being. That conflict had taken its toll, and had highlighted a large and very troubled area of intra-Protestant conflict. But an establishment infused with liberal ideology was even more affected by the doubts that domestic and world events were raising about liberalism's relatively optimistic worldview. The first really overt and orchestrated challenge to that outlook came in connection with the so-called Great War of 1914–18.

When the *Christian Century* ran a retrospective series in 1928 under the general heading "What the War Did to My Mind," the religious intellectuals surveyed were just that: religious intellectuals—the kind of people whose minds had been sharply changed by the war and the flawed Versailles settlement. Common stereotypes of the 1920s could lead us to assume that nearly all Americans shared their disillusionment, and that a large number became hedonists or flappers or bemused members of a "lost generation." That was not the case, nor did all Americans succumb to the grossly materialist ethic that seemed to have spread through the upper echelons of the business world. Real changes in the intellectual climate had occurred and, as I shall try to show, were affecting a broad population; but a great many Americans, perhaps most, lived their daily lives about as they had before 1914, and pursued personal aims with something like the old mix of idealism and self-interest.

For a host of social critics, religious and secular, this seeming obliviousness about the true state of the world was a large part of the problem. They were appalled that so many minds had not been changed by the failure of the Great Crusade. What President Harding celebrated as a "return to normalcy" seemed to them an unprecedented rise in complacency and status quo thinking. From their point of view, which they wished more of their contemporaries would take seriously, the experiences associated with the Great War had thoroughly discredited formerly taken-for-granted assumptions about human goodness and the steady, God-ordained progress of human societies.

Paul Fussell, in a celebrated study of The Great War and Modern Memory, calls World War I "a hideous embarrassment" to the prevailing belief in a natural upward tendency in human development. The realities of the war not only refuted this belief; they held it up to scorn and humiliation. The black humor—as we would now call it—that was common in England during the worst days of the war was really, in the words of a British writer whom Fussell quotes, "the laughter of mortals at the trick which had been played on them by an ironical fate. They had been taught to believe that the whole object of life was to reach out to beauty and love, and that mankind, in its progress to perfection, had killed the . . . savage law of survival by tooth and claw. . . . All poetry, all art, all religion had preached this gospel and this promise. Now that ideal was broken like a china vase dashed to the ground."[25]

Americans, most of whom had neither lost loved ones in the war nor seen comrades shot down beside them, found it hard to connect with bitterness and black humor, even in literary discourse. Still, because idealistic optimism had reached such unusual heights in the prewar United States, the gap between older and newer sensibilities could be considerable. In America, as in Britain and on the Continent, terms like *valor*, *comrade*, and *gallant* had, for many, come to seem quaint and nearly unusable—redolent of an earlier generation's "daydream during a brief spell of exceptionally fine weather." [26] In Ernest Hemingway's *A Farewell to Arms* (1929), the protagonist professes to have become embarrassed by "abstract words such as glory, honor, courage or hallow." To anyone experiencing the war at first hand, such words seemed "obscene beside the concrete names of villages, the numbers of roads, the names of rivers, the numbers of regiments and the dates." As Fussell remarks, if Hemingway had penned such ideas during the famously glorious summer of 1914, instead of some years after the conflict, "no one would have understood what on earth he was talking about." [27]

A year before *A Farewell to Arms*, Reinhold Niebuhr expressed something close to Hemingway's insight as he offered his own recollections about what the war had done to his mind: "When the war started I was a young man trying to be an optimist without falling into sentimentality. When it ended and the full tragedy of its fratricides had been revealed, I had become a realist trying to save myself from cynicism." [28]

This kind of sharp disillusionment, although we normally associate it with youthful segments of the American population, also found expression among older writers and intellectuals. Some of the realistic and pessimistic writers who captured public attention in the 1920s were just starting out, but others, relative old-timers, were just starting to gain a substantial hearing. Hemingway, John Dos Passos, and F. Scott Fitzgerald were all in their twenties. Sinclair Lewis, whose five novels of the decade, quite unlike the five he published before 1920, were all best-sellers, was in his thirties (as was Reinhold Niebuhr). But Theodore Dreiser, nearly fifty years old when his *An American Tragedy* appeared in 1925, is an even better example of a writer whose pessimistic (indeed fatalistic) point of view enjoyed more resonance in the twenties than in the prewar period.

In Dreiser's *An American Tragedy*, as in Horatio Alger's *Ragged Dick*, the pivotal dramatic event is a boating accident. In Dreiser's story, however, the interplay of fate and human intent leads to the protagonist's downfall and death, not to fame and fortune.

Clyde Griffiths has risen in the world much as had Ragged Dick and Mark the Match Boy. Like them, he has been driven by the lure of the American success story. But in Clyde's case these drives lead him not just to excel, and learn to write, and clean up his language; in his case the self-help ideology induces a fatal mistake: Clyde plans the drowning of a girl, Roberta, whom he has loved but who also has become a liability in his rise beyond the stockroom.

Clyde takes Roberta out in the boat; but his hesitancies and fears get the better of him, and he does not move to do away with her. At that point, however, fate intervenes. Roberta *does* make a move that causes the boat to tip, and she drowns by accident. Not having murdered Roberta, Clyde is executed for seeming to have done so.[29]

Presumably Alger would have said that Clyde's encounter with fate had ended differently from Ragged Dick's because of obvious flaws in Clyde's character. Dreiser's view, however—and presumably that of a good many of his readers—was that the laws of the universe are not necessarily on the side of those who work hard and who either make virtuous choices or repent their dubious ones.

Insofar as fate or chance does conspire against us, moreover, the new realists questioned whether we can do much about it. "The essential tragedy of life," Dreiser wrote, is that man is "a waif and interloper in Nature," and that the individual has "no power to make his own way." Clyde Griffiths's defense attorney, as part of a desperate strategy to save the young man's life, calls him a mental and moral coward, but adds: "Not that I am condemning you for anything you cannot help. After all, you didn't make yourself, did you?" As Scott Fitzgerald wrote in the famous closing line of The Great Gatsby—which also appeared in 1925—we are all "boats against the current."[30]

Dreiser, along with other naturalist writers like Stephen Crane, had begun well before the war to question the cheerful individualist assumptions that had pervaded the Alger stories and Russell Conwell's famous oration. Dreiser's character Sister Carrie, in the novel of that name published in 1900, had been treated almost as cruelly by the fates as was Clyde

Clyde and Roberta. Grant Reynard illustration for *An American Tragedy*, 1948 edition.

Griffiths; but it was *An American Tragedy*, the 1920s novel, not *Sister Carrie* or any other of his earlier books, that made Dreiser well and widely known.[31] The war experience, like that of Darwinism around 1870, had intensified currents of change already existent in American life and thought, and had caused these currents to flow more broadly throughout the culture.

FAREWELL TO REFORM: JESUS CHRIST AS CEO

Another social reality, one often taken as the defining reality in the post-war United States, was the increasing power and prestige of free enterprise capitalism. At the least, the climate of acceptance for business and for overtly materialist values seemed to have changed. Long before this, of course, the assumptions of a ruthless free enterprise system had been known to seduce upwardly mobile young Clydes and energize social reformers. The difference now, at least as disillusioned intellectuals saw it, was that the corrective reform spirit had lost its power to correct — that bottom-line business values were now virtually unopposed.[32] Reinhold Niebuhr and other postwar social critics agreed with Fosdick that the world situation smelled to heaven. Many of them thought that, closer to home, laissez-faire capitalism and the general cultural situation smelled just as rotten.

The year 1925 was a remarkable one for books that, directly or otherwise, expressed misgivings about American culture. It was the year not only of *An American Tragedy* and *The Great Gatsby* but also of Lewis's *Arrowsmith*, Dos Passos's *Manhattan Transfer*, and Hemingway's *In Our Time* stories. But the number one best-seller of that year, and the next, was a book written from a very different perspective: Bruce Barton's *The Man Nobody Knows*. This was a work of nonfiction (although many found it supremely fictional) that purported to explain who Jesus really was and what Christianity is all about.

The book's epigraph, blaring forth from an otherwise blank page, conveyed Barton's answer. It was Jesus' well known rebuke, "Wist ye not that I must be about my Father's *business*?" (emphasis Barton's). For the more jaded social critics, especially those within the churches, such renditions of the Gospel, together with the book's enormous success, confirmed that materialist values were rushing into the vacuum produced by postwar disillusionment.

Barton was an advertising executive, a founder of the pioneering firm that still bears his name. He had been a journalist and later, as a two-term congressman, became especially well known as a vigorous battler against Franklin D. Roosevelt and the New Deal. In *The Man Nobody Knows* and Barton's other popular works on religion, Jesus was portrayed as a prototype for the successful modern business executive.

Although the author asserted Christ's divinity, that acknowledgment merely hovered in the background. In the foreground was the Christ whose humanity was so much emphasized in liberal theology and in popular literature. Barton's Jesus, however, was very different from the social outcast portrayed in social gospel novels, and also quite unlike the mild, pale, judgmental young man children learned about in Sunday school.

Jesus, Barton wrote, was neither a weakling, nor a killjoy, nor a failure: "A kill-joy! He was the most popular dinner guest in Jerusalem. . . . A failure! He picked up twelve men from the bottom ranks of business and forged them into an organization that conquered the world."[33]

One of Jesus' greatest gifts, Barton wrote, was this ability to recognize talent. People had been shocked by his choice of disciples, but Jesus had known exactly what he was doing: "What a list! Not a single well-known person on it . . . a haphazard collection of fishermen and small businessmen, and one tax collector. . . . What a crowd! Nowhere is there such a startling example of executive success as the way that organization was brought together."

Barton made special mention of the incident, in the gospels of Matthew and Luke, in which a Roman centurion expressed a confident sense of his own authority. When the centurion boasted that "I say to this man 'go,' and he goeth, and to another 'come,' and he cometh," Jesus understood. Both were take-charge executives, and they talked the same language.

Nor did Barton the business leader shy away from the story of Jesus' harsh dealings with the money changers plying their trade in the temple. He explained that these were the *bad* kind of businessmen; Barton admired Jesus for overturning their tables and driving them out. But again he objected to depictions that showed Jesus carrying out this operation while looking weak and wearing a halo. Barton was quite sure that "as [Jesus'] right arm rose and fell . . . the sleeve dropped back to reveal muscles hard as iron."

Jesus also followed good public relations practice in being unpredictable. He kept the reporters (the scribes) guessing. And when he did something in public, he made sure it was worthy of what we would now call headlines. Barton illustrated this by letting his imagination run to first-century Jerusalem newspapers:

PALSIED MAN HEALED
PROMINENT SCRIBES OBJECT
"BLASPHEMOUS," SAYS LEADING CITIZEN
BUT ANYWAY I CAN WALK, HEALED MAN RETORTS

and:

PROMINENT TAX COLLECTOR JOINS NAZARETH FORCES

MATTHEW ABANDONS BUSINESS TO PROMOTE NEW CULT

GIVES LARGE LUNCHEON

The parables were great, too. They were succinct and peppy. They exemplified "all the principles on which advertising textbooks are written. Always a picture in the very first sentence: 'Ten virgins went forth to meet a bridegroom'—a striking picture and a striking headline." Jesus had not originated the advertising business; that, according to Barton, had happened much earlier when God said, "Let there be light!" (The stars, he pointed out, had been the first and greatest electric signs.)

In other words, Jesus, if living in the 1920s, would be an advertising man. The business philosophy he would advocate was evident in the principles he had stated during his life on Earth. Barton, putting his own entrepreneurial twist on familiar biblical passages, represented Jesus as teaching that whoever wishes to "find himself at the top must be willing to lose himself at the bottom," and that those who travel the second, undemanded mile will achieve "the big rewards."[34]

FROM GREECE TO JUDEA: THE GREAT TREK
TO RELIGIOUS REALISM

As I have suggested, Bruce Barton's readings of biblical faith and American values were not necessarily those of most Americans. Yet for at least two years in the mid-1920s his evocation and sacralizing of the business culture displaced Sheldon's mildly reformist novel at the top of the bestseller list. It is probably fair to say that Barton's book and its popularity testified to a veneration of business values not seen before and not equaled since—even, I would argue, in the supposedly greedy climate of the 1980s and 1990s.

In any case, many at the time thought Barton had reached a kind of limit, that the receptiveness to his ideas signaled not merely the impoverishment of American mainline religion but also the tragic upending of a prophetic tradition. Winfred Garrison, an editor of the *Christian Century*, expressed positive embarrassment. In *The Man Nobody Knows*, Garrison thought, "amateurism rises to its maximum. If even seven weeks of historical study went into it, there is no evidence of the fact. . . . It [describes] an efficiency expert's Jesus, a super-Babbitt, who projected a long-term selling campaign, kept down his production costs, and built a successful organization. How the foreign critics will chuckle and chortle over this Americanized Jesus, if they see the book—which heaven grant they may not."[35]

The young Reinhold Niebuhr, who still, in the mid-1920s, ministered to a working-class parish in Detroit, conveyed similar reactions by way of a 1926 *Christian Century* article called "The Reverend Doctor Silke." Here the focus of objections and satire was not so much the Bartons of the American scene, although Niebuhr was at least as scornful of Barton as Garrison was.[36] Niebuhr's critique was directed at an age-old target, the pulpiteer who comforts some of the afflicted but never afflicts the comfortable. In the updated version of that complaint, however, Dr. Silke represented a liberalized, thoroughly upbeat form of Christianity that Niebuhr saw as unequipped to relate prophetically either to the materialistic excesses of post-Versailles America or to its deeper experience of broken dreams.

Niebuhr's fictitious Dr. Orlando Silke, pastor in the equally fictitious and aptly named midwestern city of Richway, is not only a smoothly satisfying preacher; he is a very liberal one. His parishioners know that they need not believe in a Jonah-swallowing whale, let alone a Devil. What they are urged to believe is that God is in the sunshine, the flowers, the Declaration of Independence, and the local community fund—that "God is in fact everywhere." Beyond that, they are given every reason to believe "that the world is good and that men are good and that evil is gradually overcome by enlightenment and progress. Of course, there are such unlovely facts as war, but now we have the league of nations . . ." When Dr. Silke goes out on the circuit, his two main addresses are "The Glory of America" and "The Right to Be an Optimist." In other words, "hearing Dr. Silke is a cure for the blues."[37]

The famed preacher and lecturer is also renowned for the business-like way in which he runs his parish. Ministerial groups call upon him to tell them about "The Efficient Church," and back home, the businessman who chairs the church board never tires of remarking that "if I had him in my organization he would [be earning] twice what we are paying him.

. . . Dr. Silke is, in short, a Success." Not surprisingly, "Roads to Success" is another of the good doctor's most popular sermons.[38]

It is at this point, the point of connection between virtue and success, that Niebuhr's critique most resonates with that of Dreiser and the naturalists. Dr. Silke, like Conwell and Alger, is sure that honesty, thrift, temperance, and prudence are paths to success. Niebuhr, in contrast, sees those paths as strewn with obstacles, and most of the obstacles have to do with evil propensities in individuals and societies. Human nature, he suggests, may or may not be as bad as the Freudians and some Marxians believe,

> but they have certainly proven that virtue has a more difficult battle in the soul and in the world than our traditional modernism has assumed. What these modern scientists are talking about is strangely akin to the mysteries of evil which the ancient church tried vainly to apprehend in its dogmas of total depravity and original sin. They introduce us to forces so vast and so stubborn in defying and corrupting human virtue that we have a new understanding of our fathers' faith in the devil.[39]

For Niebuhr and other critics of the prevailing liberalism, a renewed interest in traditional doctrines of the fall and original sin involved neither slavish adherence to the words of Scripture nor reverence for doctrine per se. They were resorting to Genesis and John Calvin because they considered liberal (and Enlightenment) confidence in human nature a poor starting point for dealing with modern social problems.

This sort of revisionism was not original with young rebels like Niebuhr —although the latter, in the heat of their exasperation with the liberal outlook, often made it sound that way. It had been at least a minor theme, before the war, in the writings of some liberals, and had become a rather prominent liberal theme just afterward. In 1921 Dean Willard Sperry of the Harvard Divinity School had proclaimed the need for "a modern doctrine of original sin." A year later, Fosdick, staunch liberal though he was, had branded ideas of inevitable human progress "amiable idiocies" and had called for "a fresh sense of personal and social sin."[40]

What was happening in the late 1920s was that the demand for renewed ethical realism was becoming more intense. In the hands of younger critics of the theological status quo, it was becoming a much broader indictment of the Western capitalistic culture and, at home, of a Protestant establishment that appeared to have become subservient to that culture.

CLOSING TIME IN THE GARDENS OF THE WEST: TILLICH AND THE NIEBUHRS ON THE RELIGIOUS SITUATION

As often as not, new religious movements acquire names that were not of their own choosing. That had been true of the Quakers and Methodists, and it was true of the "neo-orthodox" movement that arose in the United States around 1930. To promoters of this revisionary approach, the word *orthodox* had a certain ring to it, but it was a ring they didn't care for. Even with *neo* in front of it, the term could easily suggest not only that they were traditionalists but also that they were planted solidly in the mainstream culture; and that was not at all the way they thought of themselves. They preferred terms like *religious realism*.

By midcentury, neo-orthodoxy had achieved considerable public resonance, particularly because it had helped bring more "realism" to the conduct of international affairs. As a result, many by then had come to think of it as mainstream—in fact as the ethical voice of a Protestantism that could still claim preeminent cultural authority. In most of its early expressions, however, the movement was stridently countercultural. To the question posed in the title of Reinhold Niebuhr's first book, *Does Civilization Need Religion?* (1927), the answer of these young revisionists was that it does—badly—but that civilization would not be saved by a religion as complacently conformed to its surrounding culture as was America's dominant Protestant faith. What Niebuhr called "modern churches" (by which he really meant the churches of white middle-class Protestantism) "are not acutely conscious of any serious defects in contemporary civilization. If they do recognize limitations in the social order, they give themselves to the pleasant hope that time and natural progress will bring inevitable triumph to every virtuous enterprise. . . . Life, according to their gospel, goes automatically from grace to grace and from strength to strength."[41]

Such indictments carried with them a high potential for the further fracturing and weakening of the Protestant establishment. The fundamentalist critique had targeted liberal theologians, preachers, and mission executives, but this one seemed to be directed against nearly everyone in the churches, not excluding the conservatives, and quite definitely including those complacent people in the pews. This time, furthermore, the indictment was framed more broadly than the complaints of the fundamentalists had been. Revisionists like Niebuhr, although they hammered away at such specific points as the alleged liberal naïveté about human nature, were saying that the Protestant churches generally, but especially the liberal ones, had lost their prophetic edge.

This new round of criticism, however, would obviously have little effect, either divisive or renovating, unless someone was listening. And in the late 1920s that was questionable; young critics like Reinhold Niebuhr and his younger brother H. Richard Niebuhr were being accorded only the sort of polite, limited response that had greeted the liberal self-criticism of Sperry and Fosdick earlier in the decade.

By the early 1930s, however, that situation was changing. Social and theological critics like the Niebuhrs, along with several of the European thinkers to whom they were indebted, *were* being read and heard. They had become well known not only to other theologians but to thousands of pastors, professors, and students, and to the large readership of journals like *Christian Century*. The new trends were becoming broad enough that a professor at Yale Divinity School, Halford Luccock, later likened the change of mood to a Great Trek "from Greece to Judea"—from the confident rationalism that people display in times of prosperity to the Judeo-Christian awareness of sin that overtakes them in times of adversity.[42] The new critique of the Protestant establishment—which was also a reaction against most other establishments and forms of conventional wisdom in American society—was catching on.

Why? Contemporaries thought they knew. In 1939 the *Christian Century* published a kind of sequel to the 1928 series on "What the War Did to My Mind." This one was more extensive; thirty-five religious thinkers, nearly all nonfundamentalist Protestants, recorded their reflections on "How My Mind Has Changed in This Decade." A great majority of them noted what they perceived as a widespread shift to a more "realistic" theology, and most pointed to the terrible post-1929 economic depression as the immediate cause of this shift. Luccock put the case graphically:

On October 29, 1929,

> The king was in his counting house
>   Counting out his money.
> The queen was in the parlor
>   Eating bread and honey.

Then the paper boy delivered the evening paper telling about a momentous stock slump. . . . The jazz party of the 20's, paralleled by the optimistic trust in automatic progress, broke up; the sound of revelry by night was interrupted by the subterranean rumble of an earthquake. The elevator loaded with humanity, due to shoot upwards to some sixty-fifth story of a skyscraper of man's own construction, jammed at about the tenth floor and then dropped. In that drop it was not only General Motors and A. T. and T. and other hopes of salvation that were deflated, but faiths as well.[43]

Contributors to the *Christian Century* series, however, were not inclined to isolate economic catastrophe as the sole explanation for the Great Trek. Luccock himself warned against the simplistic idea that when the flow of dividends is dammed "theology follows the advice of Paul and turns 'from these vain things to the living God.'" One needed to look not only beyond economics but well beyond the American scene. The breakup of America's "jazz party" was one incident in the broader and more gradual estrangement from a relatively carefree pre-1914 world. It was a premonition of what another writer, perhaps with happy Montmartre café scenes in his mind, depicted poignantly as "closing time in the gardens of the West."[44]

The European thinker who, beginning in about 1925, best articulated the challenges to Protestantism in global terms of this kind was the German theologian Paul Tillich. Just a few months after the Crash, the Niebuhr brothers, traveling in Europe, had begun to take serious notice of Tillich, and when Tillich was suspended from his university post in 1933, his American champions grasped the opportunity to bring him to the United States; the members of the faculty at Union Theological Seminary in New York donated 5 percent of their salaries to make this possible.[45] Richard Niebuhr, at about the same time, introduced the expatriate to Americans by producing an English-language edition of Tillich's little book on "the contemporary religious situation."

Back of Tillich's analysis, as Niebuhr explained in the translator's preface, lay "the conviction that modern civilization is not only on trial but that it has been judged and found wanting." A further Tillichian premise, as Niebuhr wrote, was that these radical deficiencies would require radical responses. More was at stake than "the discovery of new political and economic organizations which will enable the West or humanity . . . to survive a while longer."[46]

The challenge of the time, as Tillich outlined it in this book and continued to express it in the 1930s, was that the capitalist culture, and Protestantism with it, had broken down. The basic tenet of this culture, its implicit trust in human nature and human initiatives, had at one time been liberating and necessary, but had gradually become oppressive. The capitalist spirit of "self-sufficient this-worldliness" had spawned a culture that "no longer possessed any symbols by which it could point beyond itself." The resulting unchecked exaggeration of human powers had not only ratified human freedom; it had left humans free to oppress each other.[47]

So Western societies now had a clear choice. On one hand, they could opt for some form of totalitarianism, political or religious. (Tillich considered even Catholicism and Calvinism totalitarian. Though far more benign than fascism or communism, both were closed, dogmatic systems not open to criticism.) On the other hand—and Tillich considered this the only real path to salvation—the West could choose to be guided by what he called the Protestant principle, the great central idea that the sixteenth-century reformers had proclaimed and that their successors had too regularly forgotten. According to this principle, God alone is sovereign. All human institutions, quite definitely including the Church, are under divine judgment. All must be revised and corrected constantly in the light of an absolute standard.

Up to this point, Tillich's ideas resonated with those of the Swiss theologian Karl Barth and the other European "crisis theologians" who had flourished since the beginning of the First World War. Like these theologians, Tillich was warning that nothing in human culture can be absolutized. Like them, and in reaction against the reigning liberalism, he was calling for a renewed emphasis on divine transcendence—on the idea that God stands above all human cultures and endeavors, guiding and judging

Paul Tillich, early 1920s. Courtesy Tillich Papers, Andover-Harvard Theological Library, Harvard Divinity School.

them. Tillich, however, from an American point of view was vastly preferable to the Barthians because he represented those for whom a theology of transcendence allowed for social involvement—not only allowed for it, but actually demanded it. In Tillich's thinking as in that of the Americans, God's "otherness" relativizes all things human and earthly; but this in no way diminishes the importance of "distinctions between the relatively good and the relatively evil," nor lessens the imperative to work for an improved social order.[48]

Nearly all the crisis theologians had begun as religious socialists, but Tillich criticized the Barthians for, in effect, having become supporters of things as they are—not because Barthians considered the existing situation a good one, but because they saw human schemes of reform as equally "under judgment." Tillich took them to be insisting, dangerously and perhaps fatally, that the church must remain aloof from the world. Under the influence of that idea, their radical theological position had been transformed into "an actual reenforcement of the spirit of capitalist society"—a way of encouraging the secular order to proceed on its own Godless course. The church must instead be involved in culture and attempt to transform it.[49]

Socialism, like the liberal culture in which it had arisen, lacked any symbols pointing beyond itself. As a result, socialists too were allowing certain absolutized doctrines to organize and rule them. Tillich's version of religious socialism, for which he thought no organization or party yet existed, would recombine the socialist and Protestant principles. The result would be a fusion between the political movement, socialism, that was most devoted to justice and equality, and the religious ideal that would enable socialism continuously to correct itself. Tillich held that the "Protestant principle" — self-correction guided by an absolute standard — must in fact infuse all the institutions of Western society. If it did not, both the Protestant era and Western culture could expect a rendezvous with irrelevance and, quite possibly, with extinction.[50]

NEO-ORTHODOXY AND THE FATE OF THE ESTABLISHMENT

Ralph Waldo Emerson, in his best-known essay, asserted that "an institution is the lengthened shadow of one man"; and American neo-orthodoxy, which did become institutionalized in the 1930s and after, is frequently depicted as the lengthened shadow of Reinhold Niebuhr. Niebuhr was modest enough, genuinely so, to protest this idea, but he was also combative enough to give it plausibility. Among any top ten or twenty leading spokespersons, no one, not even Tillich, rivaled the older Niebuhr brother as "point man" for the movement.

Thus it was Reinhold Niebuhr, more than anyone else, whose pronouncements and actions in the 1930s defined what neo-orthodoxy was all about. By the same token, he and his antagonists, between them, defined the principal differences and animosities that had developed within the liberal wing of American Protestantism. The three books Niebuhr published between 1929 and 1934 provoked respectful but often severely negative reactions from old-line liberals, and the beleaguered young theologian was not shy about responding in kind. The same was true at such other defining moments as Niebuhr's partial withdrawal in 1934 from the pacifist Fellowship of Reconciliation and his founding of *Christianity and Crisis*, a neo-orthodox alternative to the liberal and pacifist *Christian Century*, in early 1941.

Moral Man and Immoral Society, finished just before Niebuhr's 1932 run

Young Reinhold Niebuhr. Photo by Lilo Kaskell. Courtesy Estate of Reinhold Niebuhr.

for Congress on the Socialist ticket (he lost decisively), has been called "the most disruptive religio-ethical bombshell . . . to be dropped during the entire interwar period."[51] Certainly the controversy stirred by the book revealed with considerable clarity the newest fissures in the establishment.

The title of *Moral Man and Immoral Society* put succinctly what the book was about. It was about the difficulty—in fact, the near impossibility—of making individual morality effective in social groups and institutions. Some liberals interpreted this as rank heresy, or at least as "throwing in the towel" on the potential christianizing of society. Yet it was not really a new idea, having appeared prominently in the writings of Walter Rauschenbusch and other leaders of the social gospel. Niebuhr was only underlining and intensifying the theme. Civilization, he wrote, had become an agency "for delegating the vices of individuals to larger and larger communities."[52]

Niebuhr at this time accepted the Marxian analysis of society's ills, and embraced some elements of a Marxian solution. Society was immoral in that it was geared to the preservation of power for those who rule—that is, for the bourgeoisie. Conflict and struggle were therefore inevitable; and so was some form of revolution. This last point, which implied acquiescence in a violent outcome, was one element in the book's "bombshell" effect. Niebuhr himself discounted the supposed differences between the violence of revolution on one hand and, on the other, the brutalities and life-killing inner violence of the existing class situation. Most of his fellow pacifists, however, insisted that there was a difference, a vital and defining one. Norman Thomas, while he applauded Niebuhr for "challenging some of the easy assumptions of superficial pacifism," thought the younger man was giving aid and comfort to a much more dangerous tendency. This was, in Thomas's words, "the easy acceptance of the inevitability of wholesale violence."[53]

Other criticisms, both of *Moral Man* and of Niebuhr's subsequent writings during the early 1930s, showed that the divisions within the liberal establishment were even broader and deeper than the wrenching disagreements about pacifism. Many liberals assailed the new realists for allowing themselves—illogically and ironically—to be swayed unduly, just as they thought the old-line liberals had been, by the circumstances of an immediate domestic and international situation. Niebuhr, one of them wrote, had "looked upon certain evils in the social order so intently that desperation has gripped his soul." These detractors thought that the resulting pessimism—about human nature, about the possibilities for applying a Christian ethic to social problems—would actually bring mainstream Protestantism perilously close to conservative rationales for inaction. The critics charged that the new realists, in their impatience with the inadequacies in social gospel programs, were threatening to throw away "the only tools by which human society can ultimately be redeemed."[54]

Debates and recriminations of this kind, having begun in the 1920s, became increasingly bitter in the new decade of domestic and international crises. And those twenty years, roughly 1920 to 1940, are also the ones in which historians have located a "second disestablishment" of American Protestantism.[55] What we need to ask here is how much, if at all, the falling-out among liberals contributed to the relative decline (many would call it the ending) of Protestant hegemony in American culture.

Despite the cautious disclaimers of leaders like H. Richard Niebuhr, the revisions in outlook fostered by neo-orthodoxy were in some ways positive for the establishment; they did help it "survive a while longer."

By the late 1940s, the movement was generally seen as a matter of "re-newal" rather than of dismantling; and those leading it, or heavily in-debted to it, by that time had become at least as prominent on the national scene as were evangelists like the young Billy Graham. In the mid-1950s, *Newsweek* lauded Tillich not merely as "the idol of thousands of think-ing ministers" but as someone who could claim a similar status well be-yond that circle. A *Time* writer, concurring, thought Tillich was "perhaps alone in commanding among his fellow intellectuals something that ap-proaches awe." And when it came to political influence, Reinhold Niebuhr by then seemed no less awesome; a secular historian and political activist, Arthur Schlesinger, Jr., testified in 1956 that Niebuhr had "helped accom-plish in a single generation a revolution in the bases of American political thought."[56]

Neo-orthodoxy's relation to the Protestant establishment can be as-sessed in at least two ways. The numerous signs of public adulation and influence can be read as signaling a mere changing of the guard within a still hegemonic mainline Protestantism. It is equally valid, however, to view neo-orthodoxy as promotive—and very willingly so—of the so-called second disestablishment of American Protestantism. Obviously, the realists wanted Protestantism to survive, and they were more than happy to exert influence if they could; but they also thought that survival and influence, as Tillich had been trying to persuade everyone back in the Twenties, would be merited only if Protestantism renewed itself as a prophetic movement. Establishments, which by contrast involved ac-commodation more than prophecy, remained noxious to them, and they worried when they themselves seemed entangled in the power structure. Words like *Christendom* that struck most people as quite harmless were to them more than a little dubious. Such stock terms stood for Christian and, worse, Western pretensions to a worldwide political and cultural au-thority—a global "establishment"—in which they could have little or no interest.

All this, of course, was theology and theory. But the division created by the rise of neo-orthodoxy was also visible at a practical and personal level. Although it may be true that "the people in the pews" were scarcely aware of any intraliberal feuding, still the falling-out among their leaders—among those who ran their denominations and agencies, and who trained their pastors—did affect them. It influenced what was said and done in their own churches. And with respect to such issues as pacifism and intervention, this falling-out was frequently bitter, and surprisingly personal.

In 1934 John Haynes Holmes, the influential pastor of the liberal Community Church in New York City, unleashed an assault on Niebuhr's *Reflections on the End of an Era*, but in personal correspondence assured the author that they could still be friends. Niebuhr, who had called Holmes's review "monstrous," was having none of it; the friendship was over. Seven years later, after a long period of worsening relations with his early sponsor C. C. Morison—editor of *Christian Century*—Niebuhr rejected a similar gesture by telling Morison that "you can get no moral advantage of me by generously claiming to be my friend. . . . This whole business of covering up ugly realities with words is of no avail."[57] These are extreme examples of more widespread coolings and estrangements within the establishment. Yet because that establishment was, as much as anything else, a personal network of lay and clerical leadership, personal estrangements and vendettas took their toll.[58]

Finally, although Protestant churches and their leaders were exceedingly prominent in the "return to religion" that manifested itself after the end of World War II, Catholics and Jews by that time had achieved something close to parity with the Protestants in a "new mainstream." They had been accorded nearly equal legitimacy despite a continuing wide disparity in numbers. The sociologist Will Herberg wrote in the mid-1950s that the melting pot had become segmented into three parts—Protestant, Catholic, and Jewish. Among other things, this meant that the Protestant establishment of old was sharing its mainstream status with the other two major faiths. The neo-orthodox movement had, on the whole, done far more to promote this sort of outcome than to champion the continuance of an exclusively Protestant hegemony.

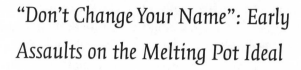

"Don't Change Your Name": Early Assaults on the Melting Pot Ideal

Shelley Berman, like Bill Cosby and other standup comics who flourished after the Second World War, frequently used autobiographical humor to make serious points. One of Berman's monologues in the 1950s reproduced, in slightly altered form, his immigrant father's reaction when young Shelley, years before, had telephoned across Chicago to ask for some parental funding. The younger man wanted to go east to drama school; and he had telephoned, rather than paying a visit, because he feared the reaction would be near-violent. It was. As far as his father was concerned, Shelley's priorities were all wrong, and the hardworking Berman *père* was not about to throw good money at loony ideas.

"Would I refuse you one dollah," the father asks plaintively (and in a heavy accent that Berman mimics), "to go to learn something in a collich?—to be a doctah, a lawyah, *a* CPA? Would you hang on your door a shingle, 'ACTAH'? Eh? What's the matter with you, Sheldon?"

After a good deal more of such ranting ("I'll tell you the truth, Sheldon, the honest-to-God truth. . . . I do not like the show people. . . . They all need a haircut, and they all got pimples, and I don't want them in my house"), Berman's father relents and agrees to send the money. Speaking in a low, feeling, voice, he assures his son that if things should not work out at acting school, "you wouldn't stahve. You are not alone in the world. . . . In Chicagah there is some-body. Know what I'm talking? Yeh, you know what I'm talk-ing." The call concludes with an immigrant father's plea that would scarcely have been necessary if this conversation had occurred after mid-century: "Uh, Sheldon? Sheldon?—Don't change your name."[1]

The simple admonition "Don't change your name" is one motto that could be inscribed over an imagined gateway into the multiethnic America of the late twentieth century. But one would need to understand its broader meaning: the point is not just that Jewish and Slavic celebrities or businessmen would feel less and less pressure to Anglicize their names; and not just that women by the 1970s would feel comfortable about keeping the names they were born with. The point, just as much, is that if they wished, Native and African Americans could *change* the names imposed generations earlier by European masters. The fundamental idea is neither the freedom to change one's name nor the acceptability of keeping it; the important message is that "it's up to you." A good many Americans, by the late decades of the century, came to believe that many modes of naming and living—not merely those of the traditional "mainstream"—are legitimate and serviceable in their society.

Although this sort of revision (or rejection) of the hallowed melting pot ideal became visible after World War II, especially in the tumultuous sixties, a number of its elements had been in place long before. As the inclusionary ideal expanded during the first two decades of the century, some of the included raised new questions, or revived older ones, about the reigning myths and conventional assumptions embedded in American culture. Most notably, perhaps, they contributed to a growing discomfort with the premises of an assimilative definition of pluralism.

OUR OLYMPICS: THE FAIR, THE PARLIAMENT, AND THE LIMITS OF INCLUSION

In this as in so many other respects, the events of summer 1893 in Chicago offer an important and revealing backdrop. The World's Parliament, and the Columbian Exposition as a whole, provided superb models of the new inclusionary pluralism. They also, however, illustrated very well what later critics (and a few at the time) identified as the inadequacies in that form of pluralism.

The Parliament, though it offered unprecedented recognition of the "great" religions, gave none at all to so-called primitive ones; and thus,

"Uncle Sam's Show." Drawing by F. B. Opper, 1893. Prints and Photographs Division, Library of Congress (LC-USZ62-91168).

especially from a later perspective, was simply not inclusive enough. Other parts of the Columbian Exposition, although they reached farther into the world of indigenous cultures, did so in an entirely assimilationist fashion. Both Parliament and Fair, unlike the modern Olympic Games instituted in the same decade, invited nearly everyone to participate. But there was no question—none at all—about who was supposed to win the gold medals.

This "we're number one" confidence was more blatantly evident in the fair as a whole than in the Parliament of Religions. In its format and architecture, and in every other way, the Columbian Exposition qualified its welcome to the world's diverse peoples with constant reminders that the West, and the host nation in particular, represented the evolutionary endpoint toward which all human societies were moving. In Lord Tennyson's words, which were frequently quoted in publicity surrounding the exposition, Chicago prefigured "the Parliament of mankind, the Federation of the world." But it also projected a Tennysonian faith in the Christian West as "the heir of all the ages in the foremost files of time."[2]

Because the magnificent, if mostly temporary, central buildings of the fair displayed Classical Revival motifs, they were nicknamed, collectively, the White City. When Katherine Lee Bates later that summer composed "America the Beautiful," she was enjoying the spacious skies of Colorado; but her reference to "alabaster cities" that "gleam undimmed by human tears" owed a good deal to her recent visit to the Columbian extravaganza. Many other visitors, including magazine artists of an ethereal bent and both the author and the illustrator of *The Wonderful Wizard of Oz* (1900), similarly romanticized the fair and the messages it conveyed about the glories of American and Western civilization.[3] A writer for the Chicago *Inter-Ocean*, identifying the fair as "The New Jerusalem," rhapsodized about

The city so holy and clean,
No sorrow can breathe in the air;
No gloom of affliction or sin,
No shadow of evil is there.[4]

Those messages were also carved into the exposition's various structures, and widely publicized in the press. In the White City itself, scarcely a building or archway or statue failed to proclaim the intrepidity, triumphs, and superiority of the Euro-Americans. Above the Peristyle, a row of columns flanking a central archway, one could read not only the names of the states and quotations from Abraham Lincoln and the Bible, but also lengthy tributes to "the pioneers of civil and religious liberty . . . who first off-cast their moorings from the habitable past and ventured chartless on the sea of storm-engendering liberty." Another inscription, reflecting the common belief that the American continent had lain unexplored and uncivilized until the Europeans conquered it, quoted Isaiah 35 ("The wilderness and the solitary place shall be glad for them") and lauded "the bold men . . . who first explored through dangers manifold the shores, lakes, rivers, mountains, and plains of the New World."

It would be nearly a century before American museums and historical exhibits began to acknowledge darker elements in the westward movement; as late as the 1990s, in fact, that sort of realism would rouse major controversies.[5] As for Bates's trouble-free (or at least stain-free) "alabaster cities" and the many millions who sang about them lustily and proudly,

The White City: Looking West from the Peristyle. From *Official Views of the World's Columbian Exposition*, 1893.

one can make allowances for poetic license and for the tendency in all of us to blur the lines between reality and aspiration. That said, we must note that the fair's designers were inclined to be quite realistic about conditions in non-Western societies, and that the horrendous slums and ghettoes of the Western world were not available for viewing. It was as though Jacob Riis had never written a word, and Charles Dickens had never lived.

Down on the Midway Plaisance, adjacent to the White City, visitors could experience some of the realities of life in a Javan village or a teeming Cairo street. They could view near-naked Samoans and read signs like the one next to their encampment—"Do not mention cannibalism to these people as it annoys them."[6] What they would not find were inscriptions quoting the sacred books of the world's various non-Christian cultures, or artistic displays conveying the nobler ideals and happier realities of those cultures.

Nor could visitors gain any sense at all of the conditions of life on New York's Lower East Side, in London's East End, or in the capital of the United States. (In Washington, D.C., America's only real-life white city, the figures for poverty, crime, vagrancy, and corruption were notoriously

The Peristyle and (in the center) the Quadriga. From *Official Views.*

high—enough so that citizens around the country were pressuring their congressmen to withhold funding for the District.[7]) And no one was reminded of the human tears shed, almost within hearing distance of the exposition, during the recent Haymarket Riots.

The message of social-evolutionary development was made more explicit in the arrangement of the various displays that represented the world's peoples. To stroll from the White City through the Midway Plaisance was, according to one observer, to plunge downward along "a sliding scale of humanity."[8] First, nearest to the White City, one encountered the Teutonic and Celtic "races" as represented in reconstructed German and Irish villages; then on through the Islamic and Asian worlds to the sites of the Africans and the American Indians—those whom the same prominent writer (the literary critic Denton J. Snider) referred to cheerfully as "the lowest specimens of humanity."

Or, as Snider himself advised, one could travel in the opposite direction and gain a sense not of declension but of the glorious upward movement of humanity. In the unlikely event that some fairgoer remained unclear about the precise ideal types toward which humanity was striving, he or she could check out the indoor ethnological displays, one of which settled

Cairo street scene as reconstructed on the Midway Plaisance. From J. W. Buel, *The Magic City*, 1894.

that issue with significantly placed statues of two college students, one from Harvard and one from Radcliffe.[9]

From a privileged later perspective we may be tempted to dismiss the intercultural attitudes of the fair's sponsors as simply the ignorance and cultural insensitivity of the time. To do so, however, would be to show our own insensitivity to a powerful belief that most of us no longer hold—at least not with anything like the tenacity and enthusiasm of the 1890s. This was the belief—not subscribed to by everyone, but quite definitely informing the thought of the fair's planners—in a benevolent and nearly inexorable process of social evolution. As a later ditty put it, whimsically, "Oh evolu-, oh evolu-, there is nothing in this world you cannot do." The process that had led from protozoa to the apes, and from apes to Andrew Carnegie, could surely lead from cannibalism to "civilization," and from dark hovels to Fair Harvard.

That the newly "included" could become properly assimilated to the norms of Western culture was seen not as a certainty but, at most, as a desperate hope. What was certain was their ineligibility, should they not rise to that challenge, for the benefits of full respect and equal treatment. A guidebook note on the Bedouin encampment remarked that "these strange people," these "gypsies of the Orient," had refused "to yield to the onward march of progressive civilization, preferring their tents"; but it also ventured that "time may accomplish what the government has failed to do—civilize these semi-barbarians."[10]

If the fair proclaimed American and Western superiority by recalling Western culture's classical and biblical origins, it expressed this same confidence by celebrating modern technology. Although classical architects like Daniel Burnham and Richard Morris Hunt dictated the fair's general decor and designed most of its structures, Louis Sullivan's state-of-the-art Transportation Building was also a major showpiece. So were a number of more spectacular and crowd-pleasing tributes to technological modernity—one of them a wondrous "moving sidewalk" on a long pier, just off the Midway, that stretched out into Lake Michigan.

Such displays and gimmicks advertised future technological possibilities but also, of course, provided for amusement in the here and now. The very terminology of midway suggested a carnival or circus; and the aura of an amusement park (if not a red-light district) was intensified by such

Bedouins on the Midway. From *The Columbian Gallery*, 1894.

concessions as a World's Congress of Beauty that contributed to the running controversy about whether or not the fair should be kept open on Sundays. (It was.)

The Midway displays also introduced visitors to artifacts of societies generally considered civilized (a German village, for example) or nearly civilized (reconstructions of Blarney Castle and of the Blarney Stone). Yet the fact that Ferris wheels and other amusement-park entertainments held joint tenancy, on the Midway, with tepees and totem poles must at least give us pause. The inference that non-Western cultures, and some Western ones, were seen as belonging in a carnival sideshow is an uncomfortable but inevitable one.

That point is reinforced in some lines of a popular song, "After the Fair," that Charles Harris set to the tune of the Gay Nineties favorite "After the Ball":

> Oh, what a picnic this fair will be,
> What wondrous people at it we'll see,
> Indians from Indianapolis, Japs from Japan,

The Great Moving Sidewalk. From *Official Views.*

Mr. Joe Bunko and the three-card-Monte man,
Buffalo Bill and his great Wild West show;
Things will be lively, money to spare,
But oh, what a diff'rence after the Fair.

After the fair is over, what will Chicago do? . . .[11]

These elements of cultural condescension and Western triumphalism were somewhat less evident—less on the surface—in the proceedings of the World's Parliament than they were in the exposition as a whole. They would have been more evident had Hindu and Buddhist temples been constructed out on the Midway, where they would have been assigned their evolutionary slots somewhere between Penobscot tepees and Japanese teahouses. As it was, the predominating attitude among Westerners in the Parliament—the view that Christianity "fulfills" and "completes" all other religions—was at least a first cousin to the kind of evolutionary inclusionism so loudly proclaimed in the White City and on the Midway. The premises of an assimilative pluralism, if less crudely set forth, were very much in place.

World Congress of Beauty. From *Official Views*.

To say that there was a predominating attitude—call it friendly assimilationism—among the Western delegates is not to say that liberals and moderates all embraced this attitude in the same way. When Barrows spoke of "meeting together in loving conference," or when he and others used terms like *inclusion*, they had varying scenarios in mind.[12] For a few, togetherness and respectful inclusion were little more than new strategies for Christian missions; if you could get the world's spiritual leaders into interfaith discussions, especially in an impressive Western setting, you would move them to that inevitable next step into the true faith. For a somewhat larger group at the other end of the spectrum—for example, Unitarians, Quakers, and liberal Congregationalists—inclusion implied a disdain for any form of proselytizing, especially in a setting like the one in Chicago. And there were other permutations of the "fulfill, not destroy" formula. But nearly all, in spite of such differences, shared a confidence in the eventual triumph, one way or another, of Christianity and the Christian West. A large majority among the Westerners (and not just the Protestant Westerners) identified the shimmering White City with some kind of Kingdom on Earth, and were yearning to lead the Bedouins and Penobscots upward into that light.

Vivekananda. From John Henry Barrows, ed., *The World's Parliament of Religions*, 1893.

In other words, the Parliament stood for a form of pluralism that went beyond mere toleration, that welcomed and respected difference, but that was also triumphalist and ultimately assimilative. In the worldwide melting pot of religions and cultures, as in the domestic melting pot of which Americans were so proud, difference and strangeness were valued. But there was an implicit, quite crucial condition: You must, eventually at least, become less different, less strange, more "like us."

Diversity, in other words, was valued; but this was diversity as seen in a rearview mirror, not as an accompaniment or goal for the journey ahead.

TROJAN HORSES

Swami Vivekananda, the young reform-minded Hindu leader who later founded the Vedanta Society in the United States, gave an address toward the end of the World's Parliament that, according to the Reverend Mr. Barrows, dismayed Western delegates. Barrows reported that although Vivekananda "was always heard with interest . . . very little approval was shown to some of the sentiments expressed" in this closing speech.[13]

What upset Barrows and others were Vivekananda's polite warnings about the conceptions of religious "unity" that he thought were held by too many of the Western delegates. "If anyone here," he said, "hopes that this unity would come by the triumph of any one of these religions and the destruction of the others, to him I say, 'Brother, yours is an impossible hope.'" Ought anyone to wish that Christians would become Hindus, or that Hindus and Buddhists might become Christians? "God forbid," the swami exclaimed. Surely the Parliament had "proved to the world that holiness, purity, and charity are not the exclusive possessions of any church in the world." If, in the face of such evidence, someone still thinks one religion will triumph over the rest, "I pity him from the bottom of my heart."[14]

Among the approximately forty non-Christians who gave papers at the Parliament, few others issued so direct a rebuke to the assimilationist agenda of the Western Christians. But they did not need to. There was more than one way to wheel a Trojan Horse of difference or dissent through the gate that inclusionary practice left ajar. The rhetoric of Vivekananda and others constituted radical questioning of fundamental Western assumptions and structures. Just as important, however, especially in the long run, were the ideas and activities of a far larger number who fought for inclusion, domestically or internationally, without seeking to restructure the institutions from which they were demanding recognition.

It is difficult, perhaps impossible, to say which kind of activism was more effective in nudging the churches and American society toward more appreciative responses to diversity. What we do know, however, is that for every Henry McNeal Turner—a leading bishop of the African Methodist Episcopal (AME) Church who by the 1890s had become a strident back-to-Africa radical—there were scores of more moderate black churchmen who labored effectively to lessen discrimination in religious and other institutions. Similarly, in the fight for women's recognition, Elizabeth Cady Stanton's 1895 *Woman's Bible* was clearly radical in its presentation of an alternative vision that contradicted a great deal in Judaism and Christianity besides their scriptural expressions.[15] Yet for every Stanton who spoke uncomfortably to the dominant Zion there were many persevering women like Anna Howard Shaw who saw themselves not as religious or political innovators but simply as battlers for women's place in the existing system.

Among those who took advantage of their partial inclusion by daring

Elizabeth Cady Stanton. Courtesy Archives, Seneca Falls Historical Society.

to pose alternative visions of their society and its deepest certitudes was the great African-American leader W. E. B. Du Bois. Du Bois, holder of three Harvard degrees and widely acclaimed for his *The Souls of Black Folk* (1903) and other writings, published an article in 1911 that raised a very quizzical eyebrow about Charles Sheldon's America. In Sheldon's all-time best-seller, as in the many contemporaneous variants on the same basic tale, the mysterious figure who appears in the midst of erring moderns and tries to save them is an indigent or at least ordinary white man. In Du Bois's "Jesus Christ in Georgia," the Christ figure is an equally mysterious and unexpected visitor who, the townspeople murmur, "must be a foreigner," because he has long hair and an olive complexion; "the man [is] a mulatto, surely." The stranger's presence unsettles the townspeople about as much as the vagrant in Sheldon's story upset the good people of Henry Maxwell's congregation; but these same Georgians, Du Bois makes clear, are not disturbed when a black man, a desperate escaping convict, is hunted down by bloodhounds and hanged from a tree limb. In this and numerous other writings, Du Bois was calling attention to an

Theophilus Gould Steward, c. 1891. Courtesy
Photographs and Prints Division, Schomburg
Center for Research in Black Culture, New York
Public Library, Astor, Lenox and Tilden Foun-
dations.

America from which, in his view, even the social gospelers were averting
their eyes.[16]

A more extensive and explicit example of an alternative vision appeared
in the writings of Theophilus Gould Steward (1843–1924), a controversial but highly respected black churchman and educator. (A biographer
calls him "one of the leading thinkers in African Methodism" and "one
of the most prominent African Americans of his generation."[17]) In 1888,
just a few years after the appearance of Josiah Strong's *Our Country*, Steward published a book called *The End of the World* that, among other things,
asserted that Strong had got it all backward — that he had utterly mis-

read the divine plan. The so-called Anglo-Saxons were supreme only in the sense that the Roman Empire had appeared supreme just before its fall. In the endtimes that Steward believed were imminent, those scheduled for divine favor were the oppressed peoples of what would later be called the Third World.

Steward was born and brought up in Gouldtown, a community of freed blacks in New Jersey. A prodigious reader and linguist with little formal training, he became an AME minister at age eighteen and, after the Civil War, played an active role in both religious and political reconstruction in the South. During the 1870s, while serving a pastorate in Philadelphia, he entered the Episcopal seminary there and promptly rose to the top of a mostly white class.[18] Steward then followed multiple callings—first as a preacher and author, then as an administrator at Wilberforce University in Ohio. He also, repeatedly, served as a chaplain in and between America's wars.

Steward's various writings in support of America's military ventures confirm that he was not an out-and-out radical. He is better understood as an enormously talented black leader whose nurturing and self-education had produced the kind of result slaveholders had had in mind when they tried to keep blacks uneducated: he was in a position to speak his mind with confidence and, as necessary, to question his society's most sacred myths and shibboleths.

In his opening references to Josiah Strong, Steward credited the publicist of Anglo-Saxonism as "a writer of great theoretical power" and "a man of great ability as a collator of the signs of the times." The problem was that Strong suffered from "a singular obtuseness in the matter of reading those signs." The biblical prophecies that Steward had cited in earlier chapters of his book made it clear "that the age which is to reach its end involves the fate of particular nations, and not of the whole world." The losers in the final great battle would be the Europeans and Americans on whom Strong had cast such a rapt and admiring gaze— "the bloody-knife men" currently preoccupied with their great campaigns of "acquisition and conquest, subjugation [and] extermination." The very "impatience, energy, and momentum" of these marauders could only be read as the desperation of an inwardly decaying civilization hastening to its end.[19]

But what about those great beneficent principles that the Anglo-Saxon civilization was so intent on offering to the rest of the world? Unfortunately, Steward asserted, while these were always touted as gifts for the world's people, they had been such only "in the dreams and fancies of self-applauding men." Throughout most of modern history, the principle of civil liberty championed by the Anglo-Saxons had invariably been "for us," while the lot of everyone else had been "subjugation, slavery, and death." And to the extent that such fetters had been removed, "Christian Saxons" had not always been foremost in removing them.[20]

As for the noble aim of spreading abroad a "pure spiritual Christianity," in the hands of the so-called Anglo-Saxons this had too often served as a rationale for the project of ensuring that "the contemned, despised, hated, darker races [are] civilized off the face of the earth." Even in more benign applications, the offer of an allegedly spiritual Christianity had amounted to an invitation to the darker races to throw themselves into the "seething cauldron" of a worldwide melting pot. If the darker races were to allow themselves to be "Christianized" by those who were currently betraying Christ's teachings, "their moral and intellectual identity, if not their physical," would be suppressed and lost. The real prospect, however, was that the new heavens and new earth contemplated in Scripture would come about not because of any triumph of the Anglo-Saxons but because at long last the biblical prophecy would be fulfilled in its true meaning: the princes of the new age would indeed "come out of Egypt," and Ethiopia would "stretch out her hands unto God."[21]

In their own time, Steward and most other outsiders who hoped to rattle the cages of mainstream America attracted little attention outside their own communities. Only Du Bois and a few others were able to reach beyond that. But Steward's kind of alternative reading—of America, Christianity, and the world—could and did reach thousands of educated blacks—could and did plant the seeds for later, wider, forms of empowerment.

CULTURAL PLURALISM TAKES SHAPE

Among innumerable instances of the Trojan Horse phenomenon, the most articulate and impressive, by far, were those that appeared as Judaism and Jewish thinkers gained significant inclusion on the American scene. Fear about overassimilation had always constituted at least a minor theme—more regularly than in any other ethnic community—in Jewish reflections about their own experience in America. It was only in the period around 1900, however—the heyday of evolutionary notions about human development and the heyday of enthusiasm for the melting pot ideal—that the doubts about both began to gain serious attention. Once again, the events and displays at the Columbian Exposition play a part in the story.

Six years before the Chicago fair, a Jewish anthropologist named Franz Boas, recently arrived from Germany, had raised serious questions about the evolutionary approach to world cultures that ruled the exhibits at the U.S. National Museum in Washington.[22] His complaint at that time had taken the form of a letter in the journal *Science*, for which the young immigrant had just become an assistant editor. Neither in this letter nor in later writings did Boas attack the melting pot idea directly. In fact, much of his early reputation as a pioneer in the field of anthropology was to rest upon a landmark study, published in connection with the U.S. census of 1910, that undercut the racists and nativists by demonstrating the immigrant's ability to adapt to the dominant culture.[23] Yet Boas also, in these years, was planting some potent seeds for later revisions of the melting pot construct. He was formulating the idea that a culture should be thought of as an integrated whole, an entity that must be understood in its own terms and that should not be—probably cannot be—induced to surrender its identity and become melted into something radically different.

Boas reiterated and expanded his doubts about the evolutionary approach after several years' experience on the staff of Frederic W. Putnam, the Harvard scholar who organized the ethnological displays at the Chicago fair and then at the American Museum of Natural History in New York. At Chicago, as in New York and at Harvard's Peabody Museum, the exhibits related given cultural artifacts *not* to other traits and characteristics of that same culture but rather to supposed gradations in the evolution of humankind. A certain kind of hammer, for example, whether it had been unearthed in Africa or Europe or South America, was thought to be representative of an identifiable stage in social evolution, and so was displayed next to similar-looking implements from other places. Boas,

Franz Boas in 1887. Courtesy American Philosophical Society (B/B61/#49).

however, even though he honored Putnam and could work with him, was on record as believing that such displays were just not enough. As he had written in 1887, the ethnologist should also show how the hammer relates to the history, artifacts, and day-to-day realities of those who produced and used it.

> By regarding a single implement outside of its surroundings, outside of other inventions of the people to whom it belongs, and outside of other phenomena affecting that people and its productions, we cannot understand its meaning. . . . We want [in addition] a collection arranged according to tribes, in order to teach the peculiar style of each group. The art and characteristic style of a people can be understood only by studying its productions as a whole.[24]

This "culture concept," under Boas's influence and that of his students, was to become one of the most important in the twentieth-century development of anthropology. And one of the most controversial: The culture concept dictated that a people's practices and characteristics must be understood within their immediate context; and one did not have to be some kind of conservative to experience difficulties with the resulting cultural relativism. Those intensely concerned about human rights, for example, would face a dilemma, because a "liberal" respect for the integrity of a given human society could mean that an outsider cannot criticize such practices as infanticide or torture. Critics of the culture concept could also portray it as leading, within a national entity such as the United States, to a dangerously fragmented society.

Those dangers were real enough, and still are. But in any of the more measured, moderate forms of the culture concept—the forms anthropologists and others usually promoted—it provided support and a new visibility for long-simmering concerns about melting pot inclusiveness.

Throughout the nineteenth century, and well into the twentieth, this sort of objection to the melting pot had been most evident in the observations of Europeans about what they thought was happening to their particular group in America. The complaint of British Reform Jews cited earlier—that their overseas cousins were interested only in "assimilation to Americanism"—was typical of the objections from many religious and ethnic groups throughout the history of migrations to the New World. During the early years of the twentieth century, as immigrant numbers rose to about a million per year, enthusiasm for the melting pot idea grew commensurately. But so did the various kinds of resistance to that idea.

The familiar "nativist" form of resistance was voiced, at this time, in a widely read book of 1916 that warned, in grandly melodramatic style, about an imminent *Passing of the Great Race*. The author, a New York lawyer and amateur naturalist named Madison Grant, thought that the American's insistence on "import[ing] serfs to do manual labor for him" was "the prelude to his extinction." Grant thought a bloodless takeover was under way. The immigrant laborers, who were unassimilable and could never become real Americans, were "breeding out their masters and killing by filth and by crowding as effectively as by the sword."[25]

In the same period, however, came new and stronger objections from the other side—from those who considered assimilation very much a reality but deplored what it was doing to ethnic communities. This sort of dissent was evident in negative reactions to the celebrated literary work that brought the melting pot terminology into common usage. This was a play with that title by the British writer Israel Zangwill.

In Zangwill's *The Melting Pot*, which opened in Washington in October 1908, the principal message—certainly the message everyone noticed and remembered—was a rousing endorsement of the success and future possibilities of the assimilative process. Some of Zangwill's predecessors in the marketing of similar metaphors—Crèvecoeur, Emerson, Melville— had been more accomplished and more renowned, but none had reached Zangwill's level of enthusiasm (more precisely, the level reached by the play's young hero, a composer named David Quixano). Emerson had written in 1845 that the American "asylum of all nations" had produced a "new race" just as the "smelting pot of the Dark Ages" had brought forth a new and vigorous modern Europe. And young Wellingborough Redburn, in the novel that Melville published four years later, had likened "American blood" to "the flood of the Amazon . . . a thousand noble currents all pouring into one." ("You can not spill a drop of American blood," Melville wrote, "without spilling the blood of the whole world.") But Zangwill's David outdid both of them, and most others, with a rhapsodic enthusiasm for the melting pot and what it was bringing forth.[26]

In the first act David explains to Vera (the play's female protagonist), that the "American symphony" he is composing has been inspired by "the seething of the Crucible." When Vera responds, innocently enough, that she does not understand what that means, David expresses shock: "Not understand! . . . Not understand that America is God's Crucible, the great Melting-Pot where all the races of Europe are melting and re-forming!"

And he goes on. Although the people streaming in through Ellis Island speak fifty languages and harbor fifty blood hatreds and rivalries, David is sure that all that will end: "You won't be long like that, brothers, for these are the fires of God you've come to—these are the fires of God. . . . Into the Crucible with you all! God is making the American." [27]

At the end of the play, despite some two hours' worth of discouraging experiences that would convince most people of the illusory nature of the melting pot, David remains undaunted: "East and West, and North and South, the palm and the pine, the pole and the equator, the crescent and the cross—how the great Alchemist melts and fuses them with his purging flame! Here shall they all unite to build the Republic of Man and the Kingdom of God. Ah . . . what is the glory of Rome and Jerusalem . . . compared with the glory of America!" [28]

It would be unfair to write Zangwill off as an uncritical enthusiast for the melting pot ideal. The playwright was a good deal more skeptical than the hero of his play. Had he not been, he would have been driven to second

Walker Whiteside as David Quixano. Harris and Ewing photo. Courtesy Harvard Theater Collection, Houghton Library.

thoughts by some of the adverse reviews that came along with numerous rave notices. Teddy Roosevelt, who attended the play's opening, thought it a bully production, and said so to the delighted author. But the reviewer for the *Times* of London sniffed that it was all "romantic claptrap, this rhapsodising over music and crucibles and statues of Liberty."[29]

More tellingly, some Jewish leaders and journalists took umbrage. This was not so much because the play exaggerated the success of the melting pot, though certainly they thought it did that; their problem was with the ideal itself. "The older generation of immigrants," as one of Zangwill's biographers put it, ignored the play's summons to them "to be melted in the American pot." To be sure, the next generation, as the same author tells us, "indulg[ed] in a wild flight from Jewishness"; but that only increased the stridency of those determined to perpetuate Jewishness. Judah Magnes, a Conservative leader who had left Reform precisely because of its overaccommodation to the mainstream culture, wrote later that the accommodationists in and beyond Judaism had misunderstood what America is about: "[It] is not the melting pot. It is not a Moloch demanding the sacrifice of national individuality."[30]

Zangwill, always highly sensitive to criticism, protested that he had been misunderstood. In his view, as he insisted in 1914, "the process of American amalgamation is not assimilation or simple surrender to the dominant type . . . but an all-round give-and-take by which the final type may be enriched or impoverished." Taking the case further, he suggested that his Jewish critics, with all their apprehensions about loss of identity, were underestimating their own people: "The Jewish immigrant is . . . the toughest of all the white elements that have been poured into the American crucible." Jews over the centuries had developed a protective "asbestoid fibre" that had been "made even more fireproof by the anti-Semitism of American uncivilization."[31]

Just where Zangwill's asbestos metaphor left "the fires of God" may be a little unclear. His 1915 apologia for *The Melting Pot*, however, made him a forerunner for Michael Novak and others who, a half-century later, would call attention to the "unmeltable ethnics."[32]

The most cogent and forceful early assault on the melting pot ideal, however, was one that appeared that year in the form of two articles for the *Nation*. Called "Democracy *versus* the Melting Pot," this long essay was the work of a young academic named Horace Kallen, who was then teaching psychology and philosophy at the University of Wisconsin. Three years later he was forced to leave Wisconsin after he had defended the pacifist position. Kallen spent the rest of a long and illustrious career at the New School for Social Research in New York City.

Born in Germany, the son of a rabbi against whose religion he rebelled with some ferocity, Kallen was educated at Harvard, where he earned a Ph.D. in philosophy in 1908. He was "an extraordinarily wise and compassionate" man, but also an unusually vigorous one—intellectually and physically. As one of his students remembered, "He lived his days with the desperate eagerness of a man destined to die young." And he displayed that kind of intensity until the day when he did die, at age ninety-one![33]

Kallen's 1915 articles echoed David Quixano in likening the diverse American society to a symphony; the metaphor was almost as important to Kallen as it was to Zangwill's fictional character. But the two usages

Young Horace Kallen. Courtesy American Jewish Archives, Hebrew Union College–Jewish Institute of Religion, Cincinnati.

differed significantly. David's symphony was meant to evoke a seething cauldron in which ethnic differences are melted away. In Kallen's orchestra, by contrast, nothing was fused or melted—neither performers nor instruments nor music. To the extent that Americans resolve to respect and nurture what each ethnic group has to contribute, "the outlines of a possible great and truly democratic commonwealth [will] become discernible." The form of this commonwealth, he wrote, "will be that of the federal republic; its substance a democracy of nationalities."[34]

To those who might think that Kallen's vision, if ever realized, would break America apart, he offered various forms of reassurance. Unity would not be imposed from above; that, he wrote, almost never works. Instead, his democracy of nationalities would cooperate "voluntarily and autonomously through common institutions." More than that, "the common language of the commonwealth, the language of its great tradition, would be English," even though each nationality "would have for its own emotional and involuntary life . . . its own esthetic and intellectual forms." The political and economic life of the commonwealth would be "a single unit," serving as the foundation for the pooling of group resources "in a harmony above them all." He foresaw "a multiplicity in a unity, an orchestration of mankind": "As in an orchestra every type of instrument has its special *timbre* and *tonality*, founded in its substance and form; as every type has its appropriate theme and melody in the whole symphony, so in society, each ethnic group may be the natural instrument, its temper and culture may be its theme and melody and the harmony and dissonances and discords of them all may make the symphony of civilization."[35]

Was this a new conception of America prompted by the post-1880 "new immigration"? In Kallen's view it was not new at all. What could be more American, he asked rhetorically, than a "harmony" within which individual and group contributions retain their integrity? From the colonial period onward, this sort of cultural pluralism (as he began to call it in the mid-1920s) had been essential to the developing American democratic tradition.

President Franklin Roosevelt, just over two decades later, startled the ladies of the Daughters of the American Revolution by asking them to "remember, remember always that all of us, and you and I especially, are descended from immigrants and revolutionists." Kallen (as Roosevelt well knew) had pressed the same debating point. Most modern ethnic groups had been solidified, if not defined, by the exclusion or persecution they had experienced in European societies — or at least by an intentional separation from those societies. Well, Kallen asked, had that not been the case with the Pilgrims? the Puritans? most other Anglo-Saxon and western European immigrants? Of course it had been. Recent immigrants might be "hyphenated Americans," as the first President Roosevelt had called them, disapprovingly; but were they really any more so than the early and later British-Americans? All newcomers, from the Virginia colonists and the Pilgrims to the latest immigrants, had maintained vital elements of their ethnic heritage. These elements included their religion and, often, their language. They also included forms of group consciousness that were deeper and less open to eradication, such as the "group self-respect" engendered by their having survived persecution and exclusion.[36]

More broadly, group identity was rooted in the "psycho-physical inheritance" of the various peoples. Melville's enthusiasm for racial melting had led him to contend that most Americans cannot tell you where they came from. "Our ancestry," he had announced grandly, "is lost in the Universal paternity." [37] Kallen disagreed. He was not at all sure the British-Americans had forgotten where they came from; certainly the Irish and countless others had not forgotten.

Even if they had, an unconscious inheritance was still there. People, he insisted, can change "their clothes, their politics, their wives, their religions, their philosophies, to a greater or lesser extent; [but] they cannot change their grandfathers. . . . The selfhood which is inalienable in them, and for the realization of which they require 'inalienable' liberty, is ancestrally determined." [38]

Kallen's revised definition of pluralism did not attract widespread attention, even among professional analysts of American society, until several decades later. What we might call a "ripple effect," however, was evident well before that. Leading intellectuals such as Randolph Bourne, John Dewey, and Bertrand Russell applauded Kallen's articles. Bourne shocked his Brahmin editor at the *Atlantic Monthly*, Ellery Sedgwick, by seconding Kallen's protest against the "tasteless, colorless fluid of uniformity." Dewey was a bit more cautious; he wanted to be sure that "we really get a symphony and not a lot of different instruments playing simultaneously." But he told Kallen that "the theory of the Melting Pot always gave me a pang" and that "I quite agree with your orchestra idea." [39]

When formulations like Kallen's did begin to catch on in the 1950s, most of those who offered them were aware, or became aware, that the New School philosopher had planted the seeds. Nathan Glazer, several years before he and Daniel Moynihan produced a landmark study called *Beyond the Melting Pot* (1963), told Kallen that he had just reread *Culture and Democracy*. "I was amazed," Glazer wrote, "to discover how much that I and others had thought and written [on the subject of immigrant groups] had been written by you a long time ago." [40] But of course there were many reasons, in addition to direct and indirect intellectual influence, for the reemergence of Kallen-like ideas after the middle of the century. The most prominent and readily verifiable reasons had to do with the continuing improvement—however slow and maddeningly imperfect—in the relations among America's three most prominent religious groups.

Protestant-Catholic-Jew: New Mainstream, Gropings Toward a New Pluralism

In many areas of American intellectual and theological history, World War I looks very much like a watershed. From the firing of the guns of August in 1914 to the machinations of Versailles five years later, the war experience awakened, shocked, and terrified. It changed minds and hearts. With respect to interreligious relations, however, this profound national experience was not so much a watershed as a window. That is, the impressive joint efforts of Protestants, Catholics, and Jews during the war years displayed what had been happening, over a number of decades, to intergroup relations and the traditional Protestant hegemony. During the war years it became evident to anyone who was paying attention (not many were) that the traditional religious mainstream was widening into a triple mainstream.

Given this show of wartime collaboration, the mixed situation of the 1920s was something of a disappointment for interfaith enthusiasts; organized intolerance displayed itself in the Ku Klux Klan and in the unprecedented success of anti-immigrant legislation. On the other side, however, were such vigorous and equally well-organized efforts of reconciliation as the Goodwill Movement—an initiative of the Federal Council of Churches.[1] Toward the end of the decade, moreover, and into the thirties, one can cite the progress represented by the founding in 1928 of the National Council of Christians and Jews, and by the instituting of National Brotherhood Week in 1934. In the foreign missions movement, which provides a different sort of window on interfaith attitudes, the mainline Protestant churches (to the immense dismay and disapproval of religious conservatives) devoted themselves increasingly to education, healing, and social service—discreetly leaving evangelism to native pastors.[2]

The Second World War, like the First, made visible the gains in interfaith relations that had been hammered out in preceding decades. This time, however, the gains were consolidated and advanced by perceived societal needs. More specifically, interfaith advances in the 1940s were spurred by urgent calls for a common spiritual front against "godless Fascism"—later rechristened "godless Communism." During National Brotherhood Week in February of 1942, the National Conference of Christians and Jews released "in hundreds of communities" what its publicists called "a stirring declaration of fundamental religious beliefs held in common by Protestants, Catholics, and Jews."

Among the more revealing affirmations in this five-hundred-word statement were the following:

> We, the undersigned individuals of the Protestant, Catholic, and Jewish faiths, viewing the present catastrophic results of the Godlessness in the world . . . realize the necessity for stressing those spiritual truths which we hold in common. . . .
>
> We believe in one God . . .
>
> We believe that the mind of man reflects, though imperfectly, the mind of God, and we reject, as a betrayal of human dignity, all attempts to explain man in merely material terms. . . .
>
> We reject all deterministic interpretations of man and all reduction of his moral duties to mere custom or social adjustment. . . .
>
> We believe that God's fatherly providence extends equally to every human being. We reject theories of race which affirm the essential superiority of one racial strain over another. . . .
>
> We believe the republican form of government to be the most desirable for our nation and for countries of similarly democratic traditions. Any political forms, however, can bring liberty and happiness to a society only when moral and religious principles are accepted and practiced.
>
> We believe, with the founders of this republic, that individual rights are an endowment from God. . . .[3]

In these same wartime years the term *Judeo-Christian* came to be used for a purpose that, at that time, was significantly new. In the past, the term had usually reflected the kind of evolutionary thinking dominant among the Christians at the World's Parliament; that is, it had carried an implication that Christianity had retained some elements of Judaism but also had "fulfilled" and in effect replaced it. In the 1940s, however, *Judeo-Christian* became a shorthand term for a worldview, and a set of beliefs, that Jews and Christians held in common.[4]

A wartime incident that achieved legendary status as an expression of this new interfaith solidarity was the martyrdom of the "four chaplains" in 1944. When the troop ship *Dorchester* was sinking in the North Atlantic, these chaplains—one Jewish, one Catholic, two Protestant—had given away their life preservers to save others. Standing shoulder to shoulder, praying and singing together, they had gone down with the ship.

Over and over during the next decade, their story was told and pictured. In a typical assertion, the head of the army's Corps of Chaplains remarked that "men of all faiths can be proud that these men of different faiths died together."[5] In 1951 a mural depicting the chaplains' last moments was dedicated at Faith Baptist Temple in Philadelphia.

The artwork was less than adequate, in both conception and execution. The symbolism was powerful.

MIDCENTURY: RELIGIOUS REVIVAL AND THE ISSUE OF INCLUSION

The Four Chaplains story and mural were icons of a popular ideology of religious inclusiveness that had grown steadily in the wartime years. They were also symbols of a "no atheists in foxholes" mentality that helped produce an astonishing and variegated "return to religion" in the immediate postwar period.

President-elect Dwight Eisenhower told a *New York Times* reporter in 1952 that "our government makes no sense unless it is founded in a deeply felt religious faith—and I don't care what it is." Such utterances were pounced upon by detractors (both of the new religiosity and of President Ike) as confirming that the revival was inclusive only in a vague lowest-common-denominator fashion—that "down deep it was shallow." But this kind of indiscriminate piety was only one among many postwar indications of renewed religious interest and commitment, and of a readiness to include religion in public discourse.[6]

Nils Hogner, *The Four Chaplains*. Courtesy Chapel of the Four Chaplains, Philadelphia.

Forms of revival traversed a wide spectrum. At one extreme, indeed, were notorious Ike-like expressions of a religiosity that seemed nominal at best. Most of those who told pollsters that they believed in the absolute truth of the Christian Scriptures could not name any of the four Gospels; and critics both religious and nonreligious ridiculed "celebrity religion," "piety on the Potomac," and the widespread enthusiasm for an undemanding feel-good faith. As Will Herberg and other critics complained in the mid-1950s, a number of politicians seemed to be getting religion just in time to get elected, while screen idols were urging their fans to cozy up to a nice Man Upstairs whom Jane Russell called "a livin' doll."[7]

In 1960 advertisements for a book on weight reduction showed the kind of before-and-after photographs common in the genre. Below the book's title, I Prayed Myself Slim, the ad writer promised that "you can too!" By following Deborah Pierce's prayerful regimen, anyone who bought the book could reduce and stay reduced "regardless of age or religious belief," and without exercise or harmful drugs. "All you need is faith!" the ad proclaimed. (Just in case, however, it added something that churches and the purveyors of religious nostrums are usually too stingy to offer: a money-back guarantee.) The book would be mailed in a plain wrapper.[8]

Very little in such religious puffery could be called new in a society famous or notorious for its Conwells and Bartons and "Dr. Silkes." But the cascading expressions of popular religiosity after 1945 did seem startling to those who had experienced the relative religious depression of the prewar years. As a result, popular piety of all sorts got more than its share of attention in the press and from various social analysts.

At the other end of the postwar revival spectrum, however, were more persuasive evidences of maturing attitudes concerning religion, and of a rather impressive increase in religious commitment. It was becoming possible for Americans, in and out of the churches, to discern and accept a distinction between religion as dogma and religion as a matter of serious intellectual and social concern; and one result of this was that the study of religion flourished in colleges and universities where, during much of the twentieth century, such pursuits had been considered suspect. In the same period, theological discussion groups were being generated by the laity in churches and synagogues; and secular publications, in some cases explicitly reversing earlier antireligious stands, ran symposia like the one on "Religion and the Intellectuals" that stretched over four issues of *Partisan Review* in 1950.[9]

Between the two extremes were more standard, but at least equally convincing, indications that churches and synagogues were flourishing. Americans' participation in religious bodies, which had declined in the 1920s and 1930s, rose by more than 20 percentage points (roughly, 42 percent to 63 percent) between 1940 and the early 1960s. Other indexes, such as the sale of bibles and the amounts spent on church construction, rose even more impressively.[10]

At the same time, under the leadership of Billy Graham, traditional sawdust-trail revivalism gained a wider appeal and a much better press than it had been accorded in the days of Billy Sunday. The old problems with mass evangelism, going back not just to Sunday but to Moody and his predecessors, were still evident. For example, people already attached to churches accounted for most of the attendance at Graham revivals, and also for most of the "decisions for Christ" generated there; so it is not easy to gauge the effect in numerical terms of revivalism's return to respectability. Without question, though, Graham and other conservative Christian leaders who distanced themselves from prewar fundamentalism changed public perceptions of evangelical Protestantism in ways that were to prove highly important to American society and politics over the next half-century.[11]

Because the postwar "upswing in religion" (Herberg's phrase) took so many differing forms, it is no surprise to find that it accommodated differing and even contradictory attitudes about religious diversity and how to deal with it. Herberg's *Protestant-Catholic-Jew*, which in the mid-1950s was the most comprehensive and widely read analysis of the new religious situation, highlighted a number of these differences. On one hand, it documented a restructuring of American religion along lines that Kallen's symphonic model had laid down forty years earlier: It appeared that descendants of turn-of-the-century immigrants were picking up the violins and horns and drums of their grandparents' religious identity. To that extent at least, they and other Americans were dealing with diversity by electing to preserve it—by not acquiescing in the older assimilative process.

But Herberg's data and analyses also raised major questions about this perhaps-promising new pluralism. Had it really escaped the bonds of the older assimilative model? Even if it had, was its vaunted "inclusiveness" really inclusive enough? Herberg himself voiced major misgivings on the first of these points. As to the second, a number of his critics saw problems that they thought he was ignoring or explaining away.

"IT'S ALL RIGHT TO BE DIFFERENT": PLURALIST ELEMENTS IN THE NEW CONFIGURATION

Herberg, a man of immense intellectual and physical energy — "quite literally a movable seminar," as a former student put it — had been born in Russia in 1901 and brought to the United States in early childhood. In the 1920s he had worked and written for the Communist Party's Young Workers League, and he had remained a Communist (though of the "right deviationist" variety) through the following decade. In these roles, and in his labor union activities of the 1940s, Herberg displayed such an intellectual and pedagogical bent that fellow activists called him "rabbi." In his later years (he died in 1977) he would become, if not a rabbi, certainly something of a theologian; and in his political leanings he would be one of the numerous former radicals who graced the pages of the conservative *National Review.* In between, as Nathan Glazer remarked just after Herberg's death, the Drew University professor "became, for a time, a sociologist" — in fact one of the most discerning and widely read sociologists of his generation.[12]*

Herberg believed that religious and cultural pluralism in America was moving, slowly but also powerfully, beyond mere undifferentiated inclusion. His position concerning the melting pot was that such a thing still existed, but not in its old form. Ethnic groups were still becoming fused

---

*Although Herberg pretended otherwise, his educational preparation for these varied careers was mostly informal. For reasons that may never be entirely clear, he felt it necessary not only to list academic degrees he had not received but to alter his birth date (probably because he dreaded retirement) and to record New York City as his place of birth. Herberg's erudition and scholarly scrupulosity were such that even his colleagues at Drew were unaware of these deceptions until the time of his last illness. Ralph Luker, entry for Herberg in *American National Biography,* ed. John A. Garraty and Mark C. Carnes (New York: Oxford University Press, 1999), 10: 634–35.

together, but they were doing so in three vessels rather than one. The sociological evidence for this had emerged in studies that showed high rates of intermarriage not (as yet) across the lines separating Protestants, Catholics, and Jews, but *within* each of those three faith communities. People of the same faith but of different ethnic stock—Italians and Irish, Germans and central Europeans—were intermarrying with a good deal more frequency than in the past.[13]

These studies had not pretended to be definitive, and before long even their raw data were brought into question. But Herberg, who was not the number-crunching type of sociologist in any case, relied on several other kinds of evidence and social analysis to support his conclusion that a triple melting pot had indeed come into being.

In 1938 a historian of immigration named Marcus Hansen had identified a pattern of sharply differing generational attitudes about a given group's assimilation within the dominant culture. Hansen found that the children of immigrants, to the dismay of their elders, had commonly sloughed off as much of the ethnic heritage as they could—changing their names and discarding most of the ancestral traits and folkways. But their children, feeling more secure within American society, had been ready to return to some of the traits and ways of their grandparents. "What the son wishes to forget," Hansen had written, "the grandson wishes to remember."[14]

By the 1950s, this theory had become almost the conventional wisdom, enough so that it was commonly referred to as Hansen's Law; and Herberg, although he thought both Kallen and Hansen had overstated the case somewhat, believed it was being vindicated in startling ways in the milieu of the postwar religious revival. The grandchildren of the great turn-of-the-century surge in immigration were not just rejecting parental preferences; they were participating in a religious revival that was raising adherence and attendance, in each of these sectors of American religion, to rather startling new levels. Largely as a result of these third-generational tendencies, there had come to be three socially approved ways of being an American, rather than just one. With respect especially to religion, the older melting pot was very nearly out of business.

Herberg's findings were focused on religion not, allegedly, because religion was his particular interest but because the studies lying behind his analysis showed that religion was one of the few elements in an ethnic or racial heritage that individuals and groups could recapture. The heirs of the 1880–1914 immigrations were worshiping like their grandparents but not, in general, dressing or talking like them. Still, if the scope of the third generation's "return" was limited, the implications were immense. Even if talk of a New Mainstream referred to nothing broader or more differentiated than "Protestant-Catholic-Jew," this was still a very different entity from what had preceded it. The fundamental message, one that gained greater resonance and breadth in the 1960s and after, was that "it's all right to be different."

Herberg's was the most important examination of the specifically religious contours of the new mainstream; but other sociologists and social ethicists over the next two decades elaborated the Hansen-Herberg distinction among ethnic generations. Michael Novak's *Rise of the Unmeltable Ethnics* (1971) put the case with special eloquence:

> Millions of Americans, who for a long time tried desperately even if unconsciously to become "Americanized," are delighted to discover that they no longer have to pay that price; are grateful that they were born among the people destiny placed them in; are pleased to discover the possibilities and the limits inherent in being who they are; and are openly happy about what heretofore they had disguised in silence.[15]

Still other social analysts, without disagreeing entirely, went a step further and questioned whether white ethnics, to say nothing of nonwhites, had ever "melted" in the first place. In *Beyond the Melting Pot* (1963), a study of New York City that implied wider geographic applications, Glazer and Moynihan acknowledged that some ethnic groups—Germans, for example—had "disappeared." On the whole, however, "the point about the melting pot . . . is that it did not happen." It had not happened in New York and, even if one took into account the special circumstances elsewhere, the alleged assimilation had not, and they thought would not, occur "in those parts of America which resemble New York."[16] Even though it had been "all right," in 1890 or 1930, to dive into David Quixano's Great Crucible, a good many in the second generation, as well as the first, had quietly refused. Group identity had not merely experienced a postwar revival; it had been a persistent feature, all along, in immigrant and post-immigration communities.

ROCKS IN THE NEW MAINSTREAM

As Herberg had stressed, however, one simply could not sustain the happy notion that these distinctive subgroups were ready to stand together, arms linked, singing "We'll all go together when we go." Some commentators, in fact, thought it was premature to take for granted the achievement of intergroup tolerance, to say nothing of inclusion. As one Jewish scholar, Herberg, was touring the country, in the late 1950s, with his mixed outlook on Judeo-Christian pluralism, another—a young mathematician named Tom Lehrer—was reaching wider audiences with satirical assaults on this and most other public pieties of the time. During fifty-one weeks of the year, as Lehrer sang to his own rollicking pianistic accompaniment,

> The Protestants hate the Catholics
> And the Catholics hate the Protestants,
> And the Hindus hate the Moslems,
> And ev'rybody hates the Jews . . .

But all this, he suggested, becomes utterly untrue for seven precious days each year:

> During National Brotherhood Week,
> National Brotherhood Week,
> National Everyone-Smile-at-One-Anotherhood Week . . .
> Step up and shake the hand
> Of someone you can't stand;
> You can tolerate him if you try.[17]

Lehrer was far from alone in looking askance at postwar euphoria about the new Judeo-Christian mainstream. Nor was he the earliest to rain on that parade. At the end of the 1940s, the lyricist Oscar Hammerstein II had delighted *South Pacific* audiences with what one of his characters called "happy talk," then startled them with bitter gibes at the way intolerance is passed along from one generation to another. The children in the story are told that hatred toward others is something that requires careful nurturing:

> You've got to be taught before it's too late,
> Before you are six or seven or eight,

To hate all the people your relatives hate;
You've got to be carefully taught.[18]

Lehrer's lyrical observation that "the Catholics hate the Protestants," and vice versa, struck most people in the 1950s as a bit of humorous exaggeration. By that time it seemed obvious that old-style fear and loathing of Catholics had, outside of Klan enclaves, either disappeared entirely or shriveled to fear and loathing of the Vatican's alleged global designs. Sadly, however, his observation that "ev'rybody hates the Jews" was not far off the mark.

Clearly, anti-Catholicism in its venerable anti-Vatican shape had not evaporated. The controversy over Paul Blanshard's *American Freedom and Catholic Power* (1949) may not have been, as one writer claimed in a Blanshard obituary, the most heated since the controversy over *Uncle Tom's Cabin*.[19] But it did, at the least, tell a good deal about the state of play in the years before John Kennedy's presidential campaign.

Blanshard was a shy and soft-spoken man who by the late 1940s had pursued careers as minister, lawyer, author, and crusader for socialism and civil liberties. He deserved to be believed, or at least given the benefit of the doubt, when he insisted in his 1949 book that he was hostile not to Catholics, nor even to most elements of Catholic faith, but solely to Catholicism as a world power with headquarters in Rome. Blanshard was careful to laud the "mighty achievements" of the Roman Catholicism of past ages, and he expressed respect for those who valued the modern Church, despite its undemocratic elements, as an indispensable bulwark against Communism. Yet he rejected any notion that "fear of one authoritarian power justifies compromise with another, especially when the compromise may be used to strengthen clerical fascism in many countries." Good Catholics in the United States, he insisted, were in the grip of an American hierarchy "that is becoming more and more aggressive in extending the frontiers of Catholic authority into the fields of medicine, education, and foreign policy, [and that] uses the political power of some twenty-six million official American Catholics to bring American foreign policy into line with Vatican temporal interests."[20]

Blanshard saw "no alternative for champions of traditional American democracy but to build a resistance movement." This movement would offer no support to "those who would curtail the rights of the Catholic Church as a *religious* institution. Its sole purpose should be to resist the anti-democratic social policies of the hierarchy." The intent, like that of the American Revolution, would be to throw off "an alien system of control."[21]

Blanshard's plea to non-Catholics—that they should detest Rome but love and try to rescue their Catholic neighbors—obviously inspired a wide popular response; his book stayed on the best-seller lists for seven months and continued selling long after that. Religious and secular journals that were zealous about church-state separation welcomed the book enthusiastically. An editor of *Christian Century* saw it as striking "valiant blows in defense of that heritage of liberty which belongs both to American Catholics and to American Protestants."[22]

From other quarters, however, especially but not solely Catholic ones, came charges that Blanshard was not merely prejudiced but, despite his evident concern for accuracy and his heavy reliance on Catholic sources, profoundly uninformed. Father John Courtney Murray, a staunch advocate both of democratic values and of the Catholic Church's adherence to them, wrote that "Mr. Blanshard has about done it. . . . That is, he has given what is to date the most complete statement of the New Nativism. In the cold, cultured manner of its utterance it is unlike the ranting, redfaced mid nineteenth century nativism. . . . [But] despite the intellectualization, it is pretty much the same old article."[23]

A reviewer for *Commonweal*, the left-leaning Catholic weekly, called Blanshard "both immensely informed about the Church and immensely ignorant of it." The reviewer added that he had "never come across an author who knew so many details about his subject, and yet so consistently missed the point." A writer for the secular journal *Social Forces* thought that, although the topic of Catholic political power deserved solid scientific analysis, this was not what had emerged from Blanshard's "hostile, antagonistic, and belligerent approach."[24]

Ironically, Blanshard's polemic and the storm it aroused may have aided John F. Kennedy in his pursuit of the presidency. Kennedy could and did say that if that was all the anti-Catholics were worried about, he could reassure them: he would never take orders from the Vatican. On the other hand, as Kennedy must have known, Catholic leaders had been offering that same assurance at least since Bishop England's speech to Congress in 1826 ("I would not allow to the Pope . . . the smallest interference with the humblest vote at our most insignificant ballot box").[25] Catholic-baiters had not listened to such assurances before, and might well not listen now. In that respect, at least, anti-Catholicism was still alive and well.

Nonetheless, anti-Semitism in the immediate postwar period seemed a substantially more serious problem than the lingering intolerance toward Catholicism. Anti-Catholicism did at least appear to be waning; Blanshard himself was guessing, by 1960, that Americans were ready to elect a Catholic president.[26] Jews, on the other hand, were being subjected to personalized attacks and exclusions that were more reminiscent of old-style nativism than anything coming out of the Blanshard camp. The editor of the *Nation*, Carey McWilliams, had documented this in a 1948 book called *A Mask for Privilege*; and Hollywood had drawn shocked (often defensive) attention to it a year earlier in two movies that constituted the first full-scale cinematic treatments of anti-Semitism: Elia Kazan's *Gentleman's Agreement* and Edward Dmytryk's *Crossfire*.

McWilliams wrote that anti-Semitism in the United States had "entered a new and decisive phase" in the postwar period. The WASPs in upper economic echelons were finding increasingly subtle ways to exclude Jews from social, political, and educational institutions, and from positions of control in business and industry. Not sheerly by coincidence, all this was happening at the very moment when the State of Israel was being founded as a refuge for world Jewry. Americans of goodwill, he thought, would need not merely to fight the various manifestations of anti-Semitism; they would have to attack it at its sources by reforming the economic system, and by paying much closer attention to the signals sent out through religion and education. To rid their society of anti-Semitism, Americans would need to "drain the swamps of our social life where the Anopheles of antisemitism breed."[27]

Another kind of reservation about the new mainstream echoed earlier complaints about the lack of mutuality in the fabled melting pot process. Herberg himself, however pleased he often sounded about increased respect for Catholic and Jewish identity, agreed emphatically that the melting process had generally been a one-way proposition. Picking up a term coined, about a year earlier, by a writer named George Stewart, Herberg suggested that the melting pot had really been a "transmuting pot."[28]

He acknowledged mockingly that in some respects Americans had achieved the "genuine blending of cultures" anticipated by melting pot idealists: Spaghetti, frankfurters, borscht, and gefilte fish had been accorded "a perfect equality with fried chicken, ham and eggs, and pork and beans." Although it was supposed to follow, as the night the day, that the average American thinks of him- or herself as a melding of disparate ethnic elements, that, Herberg thought, was not the case. "The American's image of himself is still the Anglo-American ideal that it was at the beginning of our independent existence."[29]

Herberg's most original contribution at this point was his introduction of a middle term—the recognition of a particular kind of civil religion—into discussions of the flawed melting process. Often enough, he wrote, outsiders to the Anglo-Saxon Protestant mainstream had felt pressure to conform to such overtly Protestant or Christian practices as Sunday worship. Even more often, however, they had been pressed toward an essentially secular religion of "the American Way of Life" that was really a sociopolitical surrogate for the principal ideologies of Protestant America. From the very beginning, this common civic faith had been "shaped by the contours of American Protestantism; it may, indeed, best be understood as a kind of secularized Puritanism."[30]

THE PARKAY EFFECT

A television advertisement in the early years of the medium featured a bar of margarine that diners insisted must be butter but that kept speaking up for itself, magically and whimsically. Each time a diner said "butter," a polite little voice responded, "PARKAY!" When politicians and others boasted about a new, more inclusive religious mainstream, anyone paying attention was likely to hear a disembodied but distinct rejoinder: "PROTESTANT!"

Among the more visible evidences that Protestantism retained its privileged position within the new tripartite mainstream, one of the most striking was the conception and layout of the religiously inclusive chapel at the Air Force Academy in Colorado Springs.

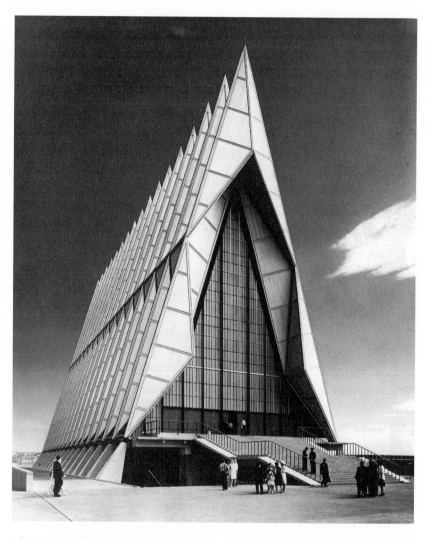

Air Force Academy Chapel, Colorado Springs. Photo © Korab. Courtesy Skidmore, Owings, and Merrill LLP.

This building, completed in 1962, was touted as a magnificent modern tribute to American religious pluralism. The intention of the architects (the noted firm of Skidmore, Owings, and Merrill) and of the federal government had been to fashion "a unique expression of the democratic ethos accommodating Protestant, Roman Catholic, and Jew within a single enclosure."[31]

Catholic Chapel entrance. W. R. Hutchison photo.

As far as it went, that boast clearly was justified. In preceding years, interfaith religious spaces had been provided, often out of sheer necessity, in various military and naval settings; and the celebrated Four Chaplains mural graced an "all faiths" chapel in Philadelphia that had been opened in 1951. It would be some years, however, before such venues for worship would be a common feature in educational institutions of any sort.[32] In that perspective, the Academy Chapel was indeed a cutting-edge venture. The completed building offered facilities not only for adherents of the three dominant faiths but, minimally at least, for "others" as well.

In the arrangement of these facilities, however, the chapel managed to offer a powerful statement, indeed a blatant one, in support of a Protestant hegemony that the planners seem to have thought would be as enduring as the building itself. If this determinedly interfaith building had featured a common space adaptable in its furnishings to the requirements of different religious groups, that would not have been an entirely unprecedented move; Eero Saarinen's chapel at the Massachusetts Institute of Technology, completed in 1954, was only the most celebrated of several such facilities that by this time had appeared in airports and hospitals

Jewish Chapel entrance. W. R. Hutchison photo.

as well as military bases, and that were rather well known among the architects, religious leaders, and chaplains who were decision makers or consultants for the Academy Chapel project.[33]

The fact that multifaith spaces already existed elsewhere contributed, undoubtedly, to the widespread concern about the way the interfaith idea was being implemented in Colorado Springs.[34] Each faith or group of faiths was awarded its own space, with square footage and seating capacities in the three main sanctuaries keyed to 1955 estimates of the relative representation of Protestants (66 percent), Catholics (29 percent), and Jews (5 percent) in the American military. The problem, however, as critics saw it, was one not of square footage but of the total volume of the various spaces. The planners and architects had managed to allot roughly 80 percent of the building's cubic footage to a soaring Protestant sanctuary—one hundred feet from floor to peak—that could seat 900 cadets and was later reconfigured to accommodate 1,200.

Beneath the Protestant chapel (indeed somewhat below ground level) the building's designers provided elegant but much smaller, lower-ceilinged spaces for Catholics (500) and Jews (100). A "meeting room" that with some difficulty could seat 25 worshipers and that could be adapted to the needs of Muslims, Buddhists, and others occupied the rest of this partially underground space.

Although proponents of the newer pluralism could approve an arrangement that affirmed the distinctive identity of Jews and Catholics, they could also wish that other ways had been found to embody this affirmation. As it was, a number of the chapel's structural features and accoutrements fell short (however unintentionally) even of the old "separate but equal" standard that the Supreme Court had rejected in another context in 1954. The Protestant cadets not only worshiped in an ampler, more elevated space; they were privileged to enter their soaring cathedral by way of a grand outer stairway. All others were asked to reach their below-ground spiritual quarters through portals whose positioning, if not their design, could make one think of tradesmen's entrances.*

The Air Force Academy Chapel was not an aberration. It was a symbol of its own transitional times—just one among many, even if it was much more "national," visible, and therefore controversial than most. In its interfaith identity it looked to the future. In its extraordinary (even for that time) privileging of one element in the much advertised "new religious mainstream," it was an atavism, an evocation of times gone by.

NOT SO FAST: NON-PROTESTANTS QUESTION INCLUSIVENESS

Again, as so often in the past, some within the Catholic and Jewish communities found fault with what most of their coreligionists welcomed as a new and promising stage of inclusiveness. To interfaith enthusiasts, the Four Chaplains depiction in Philadelphia meant that "we're all in this together"—in spiritual respects as well as in battles against totalitarianism. But the Catholic hierarchy's response was, in effect, "Not so fast. There are limits." The family of John P. Washington, the priest who had gone down with the *Dorchester*, was not allowed to attend the dedication of

---

*By the turn of the century, marriages and other gatherings too large for the Catholic or Jewish spaces could be held in the Protestant chapel. Furnishings in the latter, however—in particular, the forty-six-foot aluminum cross—could not, as a practical matter, be altered or covered on such occasions.

the mural. The reason for this was that the ceremony was held, and that the mural resided, in an interfaith chapel.[35]

Even John Courtney Murray, whom a recent writer depicts as Catholicism's "lonely champion of religious pluralism" in the pre–Vatican II period, begged fellow pluralists to stop lumping everyone together. Protestantism, Catholicism, and Judaism, he reminded them, are "radically different" styles of belief, none of which is reducible, "or perhaps even comparable," to the others.[36]

Within the Jewish community as well, a few prominent scholars and leaders mounted resistance, on grounds much like Murray's, to the popular idea of a "common faith" within which theological differences are nonexistent or unimportant. Robert Gordis protested that some Jews were justifying ideological ties to Christian neo-orthodoxy "by constructing a cloudy, blurred image of an imaginary 'Judeo-Christian world view.'" And Alexander Burnstein expressed the view that Niebuhr's emphasis on man's "frightening iniquity" was fundamentally at odds with normative Jewish views of human capacities. Burnstein also chided Tillich for not honoring, perhaps not grasping, fundamental differences between Christian devotion to Christ and Jewish devotion to Torah.[37]

With newly anointed participants in the religious mainstream expressing reservations, it is no surprise to find more intense forms of questioning arising among some of those who thought that they were still being treated as outsiders—that the membership roster had been expanded and they were not on it.

To inveigh against early analysts of the new mainstream for ignoring women and minorities would be less than fair, and also less than accurate. Herberg, for example, alluded specifically to blacks and black churches more often than he referred to Italians. But, in accordance with the sensibilities of the 1950s, which were not those of the 1970s, he found it natural, especially in a book about religion, to deal with women, African and Native Americans, Hispanics, and a number of other distinct groups as members—albeit, in some cases, sadly or criminally subordinated members—of the three major faiths.

Clearly, though, many were coming to see that way of understanding American society and religion as, at best, insufficiently nuanced. Black

Protestants and Catholics, for example, could and did question whether their theoretical inclusion in subsections of the triple melting pot was anything more than theoretical. And after 1965 liberalized immigration laws began to swell the ranks of Muslims and others who could not claim—and in some cases did not covet—inclusion in the new mainstream.

"WHO YOU ARE": PERSONAL IDENTITY AND GROUP IDENTITY

Tom Lehrer's jabs at current hypocrisies were especially acerbic when they referred to racial intolerance. His 1965 song depicted Sheriff Clark (bigot-in-chief during the recent confrontations at Selma, Alabama) as "dancing cheek to cheek" with Lena Horne, the black singer, during National Brotherhood Week. Over the rest of the year, however, "the white folks hate the black folks, and the black folks hate the white folks." And if, as this suggested, pluralism as tolerance was still a problem, surely pluralism as inclusion was more so: "It's fun to eulogize the people you despise . . . As long as you don't let 'em in your school."[38]

As Lehrer would surely have agreed, however, the issues for nearly all minorities were not simply the straightforward matters of intolerance and exclusion. They were more complex than that; and the principal complexity related to what W. E. B. Du Bois, much earlier, had called "twoness." Blacks and, to one degree or another, the members of any group treated as outsiders lived their lives in the consciousness of "two souls, two thoughts, two unreconciled strivings; two warring ideals." In the somewhat changed atmosphere of the mid-twentieth century, no one expressed this complex fate more poignantly, or analyzed it more perceptively, than the novelist James Baldwin. Baldwin, in an especially noteworthy conversation of 1962 with the journalist Studs Terkel, explained that a large part of the problem is that blacks *are* so enmeshed in the so-called mainstream culture—that in so many ways they *have* been thrown, willy nilly, into the great cauldron: "One is born in a white country, in a white Protestant Puritan country. . . . You go to white movies, and like everybody else you fall in love with Joan Crawford and you root for the Good Guys who are killing off the Indians."[39]

"It comes as a great psychological collision," Baldwin added, "when you begin to realize all these things are really metaphors for your oppression, and will lead into a kind of psychological warfare in which you may perish."[40] In Baldwin's own case, which in such respects he considered entirely typical, cultural assimilation within the great seething melting pot had entailed the suppressing of almost every form of personal or group expression that the dominant society saw as stereotypically "black." As a young writer he had been stymied by the fact that he was "ashamed of where I came from and where I had been," ashamed of his father's black pentecostal church and ashamed of his father. It went much farther; he had been "ashamed of the Blues, ashamed of Jazz, and, of course, ashamed of watermelon. . . . Well, I was afraid of all that; and I ran from it. . . . I had acquired so many affectations, had told myself so many lies, that I really had buried myself beneath a whole fantastic image of myself which wasn't mine, but white people's image of me."[41]

Baldwin explained that he had been unable to become a writer at all, let alone a successful one, until he found a way to shake off the identity imposed upon him by others—to find out who he really was. As he put it to Terkel, he had found that if one is to become a writer—indeed, if one is to survive at all—

> you have to really dig down into yourself and re-create yourself . . .
> according to no image which yet exists in America. . . . You have to
> *decide* who you are, and force the world to deal with you, not with
> its *idea* of you.
> TERKEL: You have to decide who you are, whether you are black or white.
> BALDWIN: Yes, who you are. Then the question of being black or white is
> robbed of its power. . . . The social menace does not lessen. The
> world perhaps can destroy you physically. The danger of your de-
> stroying yourself does not vanish, but it is minimized.[42]

Baldwin in many other contexts, but especially in his *Notes of a Native Son* (1955), had made it clear that he saw his own way of coping with this dilemma as an enactment of the process that Kallen and others had described and celebrated. A James Baldwin, if he did choose to help compose and perform the symphony of American culture, would not play someone else's instrument or mimic someone else's sounds: "When I followed the line of my past I did not find myself in Europe but in Africa. And this meant that in some subtle way, in a really profound way, I brought to Shakespeare, Bach, Rembrandt, to the stones of Paris, to the cathedral at Chartres, and to the Empire State Building a special attitude. These were not really my creations, they did not contain my history."[43]

Yet this *was* his orchestra, and his symphony, if only by default. Though French cathedrals and New York skyscrapers were not Baldwin's heritage, neither, really, were the folkways and artifacts of Africa; the dilemma of two-ness could not be solved by choosing one and rejecting the other: "I had no [non-European] heritage which I could possibly hope to use—I had certainly been unfitted for the jungle or the tribe. I would have to appropriate these white centuries, I would have to make them mine—I would have to accept my special attitude, my special place in this scheme."[44]

In more specifically religious terms, we can paraphrase Baldwin's message to mainstream contemporaries in about the following terms: Although I was reared in an American Christian church, and thus share "your" religious tradition, my history is not the suburban or small-town church, nor even the urban church. It is the balcony where the slaves sat. It is the secret place in the woods where the slaves met to pray their own prayers. And I must be allowed to emphasize and honor my own history.

BEYOND INCLUSION

For some participants, black or otherwise, in the emerging campaigns for recognition of special group identities, Baldwin's kind of resolution seemed not merely "subtle," as he called it, but too compliant—too much infected by a persisting, deeply ingrained Eurocentrism. Similarly, his later enigmatic phrasing for the dilemmas of two-ness—"nobody knows my name"—was not assertive enough for more radical spirits who insisted that names and other markers of Anglo-Saxonism deserved, quite simply, to be expunged.[45] Yet it is probably fair to say that Baldwin's mature positions, subtleties and all, spoke for most of those who were seeking to move beyond the older assimilative pluralism. These positions were also, on the whole, concentric with an emerging public policy—

Supreme Court decisions, civil rights and voting rights legislation, and much else—that was bolstering group identities in the course of outlawing group disabilities.

One further way of understanding what was going on in the Baldwin-like analyses that became common in the 1960s is to view them as seconding, but also greatly broadening, Herberg's observations of a decade earlier. This was evident in at least two respects. Most obviously, it was clear that public pleas for genuine recognition of group identity were expanding beyond the Herbergean preoccupation with immigrant ethnic groups to women, blacks, American Indians, and others. Secondly, actual claims and advocacies concerning group identity were reaching beyond a few items like religion; by the early 1960s they were taking in a whole range of cultural practices (our own holidays, not yours—or as well as yours; our own music, along with yours).

Baldwin, in the Terkel interview and elsewhere, had given a stunning literary endorsement to the broadened "group identity" element in the new pluralism, and also to its other most distinctive feature: the insistence that inclusion in itself is not enough. But here the plot thickened in some important ways. When Baldwin chose to keep an Anglo-Saxon name and to continue cheering for Shakespeare and Rembrandt (if not Joan Crawford and Gary Cooper), this was only in part because he, unlike so many others, felt unable to connect extensively or deeply with Africa. It was, on Baldwin's part, a more positive and assertive move than that.

When Baldwin decided that "I would have to appropriate these white centuries, I would have to make them mine," he was, obviously, opting for inclusion in the American and Western cultures. He was also, however, asserting his right to what members of the various white subcultures had generally been able to take for granted—the right to bring a "special attitude" to bear, to claim a "special place in this scheme."

The special attitudes of former outsiders, moreover, would gain expression through genuine participation, just as they always had for insiders. Baldwin was claiming for his own and other "minorities" not just a place at the table but a right to speak and be heard, and a right to help formulate the agenda.

Whose America Is It Anyway?
The Sixties and After

At an open meeting of President Bill Clinton's Advisory Council on Race, held in Annandale, Virginia, in December 1997, the discussion, according to a *Washington Post* writer, suddenly "turned raw." A man named Robert Hoy grabbed the microphone to complain that "there's no one up there [in Washington] that's talking about the white people. We don't want to be a minority IN OUR OWN COUNTRY." (I've added the emphasis, but quite possibly it was present in the spoken form.) During a further shouting match after Hoy had been ousted from the meeting, he defended his intervention by warning that whites were in danger of losing "our homeland."[1]

Hoy may have felt especially aggrieved and isolated because other white Virginians, at least those quoted in the newspapers, insisted that his views were not representative; and Mr. Hoy, allegedly an ally of the white supremacist David Duke, almost certainly was speaking for a smaller and more despised minority than he imagined. But he was also articulating in extreme form a resistance to pluralism that others were expressing in more rational and sensitive terminology. The unitive or counterpluralist impulse, in fact, remained alive and vigorous in the final decades of the twentieth century not because of extremists like David Duke and Robert Hoy—who captured attention but probably harmed their own cause—but because of a larger "religious right" that was predominantly white and Protestant. And this wider phenomenon of religiously based antipluralism gained support at some crucial points from at least two other important sources. One of these involved a sort of cobelligerency (rather than alliance) with social scientists who were generally quite unfriendly to the programs of the far religious right, but who tended to agree with the latter about the alleged dangers that a pluralistic ideology poses to the system of common values on which a society depends. Another source of partial or selective support consisted of moderate Protestant evangelicals who drew the line at forms of inclusion that implied equality between "Christian truth" and the beliefs of non-Christians.

Although these more moderate, rational forms of resistance were more effective than the impassioned pleas of the berserkers—the wild ones— on both sides of the cultural divide, I am not in the least suggesting that the latter can be ignored. Extremists on the pluralist fringe were inclined to argue that European and Judeo-Christian traditions, especially as per- petuated in the utterances of dead white males, were now to be regarded as of virtually no importance. At the other end of the spectrum, some anti- pluralists considered it perilous for the society if little black children were taught about their African roots. Extreme advocacies of these kinds— there were quite a few more—had important effects, and not always dele- terious ones. (Gadflies perform a vital function.) I simply contend that moderate, thoughtful, go-slow positions regarding pluralism were more widespread, and relatively more persuasive.

The most common reasoning among moderate foes of the newer plu- ralism proceeded as follows: Of course there are many in our society whose past is different, and whose present group identity is distinctive. But when push comes to shove—when the question is what kinds of prayers are to be offered in Congress, or allowed in prisons and public ceremonies—then we must tell all these nice other people that this is a Christian country. It was all decided two hundred or more years ago, in spite of technicalities about church-state separation.

But then, what to do about the guests?—the invited and the uninvited, the Indians whose pesky ancestors claimed the land before "we" arrived, and the "different" who have come along since then. This had been the question animating Josiah Strong's significantly titled *Our Country* in the 1880s. And clearly it was one of the motivating questions—the princi- pal one—driving the objections and cautions that arose after the series of solid gains that the newer pluralism achieved beginning in the mid-1950s.

WHO WRITES THE AGENDA?

During the tumultuous era commonly called the sixties but best understood as including a few years before and after that decade, "agenda questions" began to be asked. In particular: Who controls the social agenda? and: Who ought to control it?

Here again, pluralist rhetoric should be understood as having been affected but not controlled by the gadflies and extremists. Ordinarily, in other words, the raising of agenda questions did not imply that Catholics or Jews or blacks or women should have the right, unilaterally, to take over or dictate the society's agenda. Admittedly, it often seemed otherwise in the heat of battle or amid the pressures of public advocacy. And occasionally an advocate did in fact mean that a given group or subculture can be trusted to run the society. But for most card-carrying practitioners of the newest form of pluralism it was precisely *not* that any one definable subculture should run everything; we had had quite enough of that.

The demand, for the most part, was not that formerly suppressed or subordinated outsiders should take over. It was that they should take part, often for the first time. Like the farming constituency that had fueled populist crusades, or the laborers who had sought and gained recognition over the preceding one hundred years, women and minorities were asking for something like a proportional voice in the management of American society.

Why did so many differing expressions of the newer pluralist ideology converge in the sixties? Some explanations, such as the horrendous disruptions and divisions occasioned by American involvement in Vietnam, have received extensive, almost routine, recognition. Of nearly equal importance, however, were processes set in motion in the early 1950s and, in some cases, long before. Catholic, Jewish, and African-American advances toward full inclusion, even though halting and imperfect, not only had provided models for imitation; they had initiated a logical process that other minorities could apply in their own situation—"Don't change your name." Decide "who you are." "It's okay to be different."—and that growing segments of mainstream America also found compelling. Two changes in public policy in the early 1950s, moreover, bolstered the foundation on which further pluralist advances were to be built.

One of these landmarks of the 1950s was the inclusion in an otherwise xenophobic piece of legislation, the McCarran-Walter Act of 1952, of a provision ending the long-standing ban on immigration from Asia and the Pacific. The other, far more sweeping, was the Supreme Court's 1954 decision in *Brown v. Board of Education*, which (to put it in the wording most relevant to this discussion) had implanted the principle that "inclusion" is not a sufficient answer if offered on terms that are inherently demeaning to the included.

In the social and theological movements that for most people, whether adherents or bitter opponents, came to characterize the sixties, the agenda question held a central position. The campaigns for civil rights and the proclamations of black, feminist, and Native American theologies all embodied demands for group as well as individual empowerment; and public policy initiatives, most prominently the federal civil rights and voting rights acts of the mid-sixties, sought to ensure that pluralism, henceforth, would mean participation rather than mere toleration or mere inclusion.

At the same time, liberal and radical initiatives within the Christian churches and their theologies provided powerful support—sometimes indirect, often very direct—for the new pluralism. Among Catholics, the fundamental change of attitude endorsed by the Second Vatican Council (1962–65) expressed itself through liturgical reforms that validated diverse languages, cultures, and theological forms (for example, the liberation theologies emerging especially in Hispanic settings); and that promoted an unprecedented openness to both interfaith dialogue and religious-secular dialogue. In Western Protestantism, most prominently that of Americans, radical or "death of God" theologies registered a protest not, generally, against theism itself, but (very much in the neo-orthodox terms made familiar in the preceding era) against forms of belief that, the radicals thought, made God a mere agent of the dominant Western culture. That culturally constructed God was the one the radicals believed was dying a slow and painful death.

Once again, however, as so often in the past, new initiatives in theology were gaining their clearest—and for traditionalists their most alarming—expressions in the context of overseas missions, where questions about Christianity's relation to other religions could not be avoided or papered over with ambiguities. A generation or so earlier, in the years around 1920, conservatives had been scandalized by the evident tendency of liberally inclined missionaries to emphasize collaboration with people of other faiths—often, it seemed, to the exclusion of serious attempts to make Christian converts; such collaborationist attitudes had been a major provocation for the rise and spread of fundamentalism. In the sixties the same interfaith inclinations produced a more explicit questioning of the traditional assimilative aims of Christianity, and of "Christian civilization."

This sort of radical innovation in missionary thinking arose even among Catholics in the post–Vatican II era. In 1967 a professor of missiology at the Catholic University of America, Ronan Hoffman, responded affirmatively to the question "Are conversion missions outmoded?" After pointing out that Judaism "remains firm" after centuries of Christian evangelization, Hoffman asked rhetorically whether this might be so "precisely because Almighty God, for his own reasons, wishes [Judaism] to continue?" Christians, Hoffman suggested, might well find themselves opposing God himself "if we were to try in the future to overthrow Judaism or any other non-Christian religion."[2]

By the late 1960s, similar challenges in Protestant precincts to traditional missionary assumptions—assumptions that even liberals like George Gordon had retained—had become much more than the utterances of a few lonely voices. In fact, in the ecumenical gatherings and writings of the time they appeared to have become the conventional wisdom. In such venues and writings, the church's mission was being redefined as "Christian presence," while "conversion" referred at least as much to the radical remaking of social structures as to the results that this kind of Christian witness might produce in individual lives. Whether operating overseas or working in ghettoes at home, the witnessing Christian must not seek to impose some ready-made program, however firmly she or he might believe it to be God's program. In taking up the concerns of others, one was to discern and honor "their issues and their structures."

In these and numerous other ways, as one observer wrote after the 1968 meeting of the World Council of Churches in Uppsala, Sweden, "the world was writing the agenda." The right of "the world" to do this was taken for granted. "Uppsala," he wrote, "tried to read the writing, understand it and respond to it."[3]

Interwoven in all these advances, intellectual and activist, toward a non-assimilative definition of pluralism was the burgeoning interest in Asian and other non-Christian religions. Many of the landmarks of this interest were in place by the mid-sixties. Alan Watts's *Way of Zen* and Jack Kerouac's *Dharma Bums* were both published in the late 1950s. The International Society for Krishna Consciousness (Hare Krishna) appeared in 1965. In the longer run, however, the most important contribution to this interest in non-Western religions was the Immigration and Nationality Act of 1965, which finally abolished the quota system that had kept immigration from Asia to a minimum.

In the wake of that epochal change in immigration policy, the numbers of Hindus and Buddhists from Asian countries rose, in the quarter-century after 1965, from a few thousand of each to a half million of each. By the 1990s "American religion" included far more Hindus than Quakers, far more Buddhists than Unitarians. And the Hispanic population grew, in these years, to nearly twenty-five million.

The steepest and most dramatic growth, however, was that of Islam. Here good estimates were even harder to achieve than they had always been for other religious groups. According to some attempted counts (and these were not the highest), Islam in the United States matched or nearly matched the Jewish community (six million) in size. Even according to the most conservative estimates, which ran from below two million to just under four million, the Muslim population had become comparable in size to that of such old-line Protestant denominations as the Presbyterians or the Episcopalians.[4]

WHOSE AMERICA? VOICES FROM THE RIGHT AND CENTER

In early January, 1980, Pete Seeger, the eminent and reform-minded folk singer, surprised an audience at Harvard's Sanders Theatre by announcing that he would offer a tribute to "that old time religion." He began with the traditional refrain — "Give me that old time religion; it's good enough for me" — but the verses were anything but traditional:

We will pray with Aphrodite;
We will pray with Aphrodite;
She wears that see-through nightie,
And it's good enough for me.

We will pray with Zarathustra;
We'll pray just like we useter;
I'm a Zarathustra booster,
And it's good enough for me.

We will pray with those old Druids;
They drink fermented fluids,
Waltzing naked through the woo-ids,
And it's good enough for me.

I'll arise at early morning,
When my Lord gives me the warning
That the solar age is dawning;
And that's good enough for me.[5]

Just joking? Perhaps. But Seeger over a long period had been one of the most effective of American social critics and social activists; and it is equally likely that he meant to make some serious points. He was passing along the idea (Seeger said that he did not write the song) that for many millions of Americans the old-time religion is something other than revivalist Christianity. Whether or not they pray to Aphrodite, Americans pray to or meditate upon many deities other than the Christian God. And he was hinting—at least this is a reading that I would give to Seeger's song—that Christian and even Judaic conceptions owe more than they usually acknowledge to a large number of ancient and/or primitive worldviews.

The sellout crowd in Sanders Theatre greeted the song (especially that last ecologically tuned verse) with screams and wild applause. It is safe to surmise, nonetheless, that out in the real world, beyond Harvard and other liberal venues, many of those who heard Seeger's song did assume that he must be joking. It is also likely that they didn't think it was a bit funny.

Even less amusing, for those provoked to what the sociologist Peter Berger called a "counterpluralist animus," were the heresies that pluralists seemed to be uttering about who is supposed to run America.[6] Almost no one, least of all a new-style pluralist, could be found denying that white Protestant Christians had been running things for several centuries; but certainly it had become common to question whether this was "so stated in the bond"—that is, whether the founding settlers and, especially, the "Founding Fathers" of the revolutionary era had settled the question for all time.

To a counterpluralist, the fact that minorities were growing and new religions proliferating was troubling enough. But the idea that the people of the putative mainstream might be losing control of "our own country" was, for many of them, truly frightening. Those most alarmed by the new pluralism therefore resorted, almost as a matter of course, to arguments based on what constitutional scholars call "original intent." This is a Christian country, they asserted—and some still meant by that a Protestant country—not simply because of nineteenth-century historical developments but because the early settlers and Founders had established a Christian country; and because these Founders, in doing so, had been implementing God's own intentions. A typical statement of that point of view—but one of the most detailed and breathless—appeared in 1977 in a book called *The Light and the Glory.*

This book was the work of two former Yale students, Peter Marshall and David Manuel, who as collegians had been hostile or indifferent to religion. (Marshall had been in revolt against his parents, both of whom were best-selling Christian writers.) Later, after they had become converts to evangelical Protestantism, the authors had been stunned—and they were quite sure others would be—to learn that key figures in the early American past had, allegedly, not only professed personal allegiance to Christianity but also seen the establishment of the American republic as a Christian enterprise.

It had all started with Columbus, but no one, they thought, at least in twentieth-century America, had even suspected this. "All we had ever read or been taught," they insisted, "had indicated that Columbus had discovered the New World by accident. . . . No mention had ever been made of his faith . . . nor had we suspected that he felt called to bear the Light of Christ to undiscovered lands in fulfillment of biblical prophecy."[7]

And so it went. "The people who first came here knew that they were being led here by the Lord Jesus Christ, to found a nation where men, women, and children were to live in obedience to Him." In the revolutionary struggle it was God who "forged an army out of a disintegrating band of independent individuals." The authors quoted Ethan Allen's challenge to the British at Ticonderoga "in the name of the great Jehovah," but neglected to mention Allen's long career as an opponent of Christianity. And Thomas Paine, hero both of the Revolution and of American deism, was named only once—as a nasty little man who criticized George Washington because the latter had not chosen him as postmaster general. According to Marshall and Manuel, most of those who wrote the founding documents of the American polity—except for villains like Jefferson, the crypto-Unitarian—knew that national morality would depend upon national adherence to Christianity. And they thought that the Constitution, given its Madisonian distrust of human nature, was clearly based upon Christian, especially Calvinist Christian, theological traditions.[8]

The few historians and religion scholars who reviewed this widely read book found in its excited revelations little that was new, and still less that could be called "stunning."[9] (Had the authors perhaps slept through their American history or literature classes at Yale?) But Marshall and Manuel were far from alone in using an original-intent argument to prove that the United States had been chartered, in perpetuity, as the domain of Protestant Christians.

The Reverend Jerry Falwell, for example, founder and principal spokesman of the religious right's Moral Majority organization, took virtually the same stance, though much more cautiously, in his manifesto of 1980, *Listen, America!* Because Falwell was intent on building a movement inclusive of Catholic, Jewish, and secular conservatives, he avoided any overt proposals about returning to an earlier Protestant hegemony. (This was one of a number of points at which more rigid fundamentalists found him deficient.) Yet even Falwell, when he listed the heroes of the American and European religious past, found it unnecessary to mention any non-Protestant contributors.[10]

Among those who were most disturbed by this original-intent argument, and by its corollary, the idea that God has chosen America for a unique, world-hegemonic mission, were scholars and others in the large nonfundamentalist wing of Protestant evangelicalism. In the early 1980s, with the Moral Majority and the new religious right in full cry, three leading historians, all committed evangelicals, issued a stinging, detailed refutation of "the distorted and overinflated view of America as a distinctively Christian nation." Their book, called *The Search for Christian America*, argued with some acerbity that any such search is far more problematic than these fellow evangelicals appeared to believe. "When we look at the Puritans of the 1600s," they asked, "do we emphasize only their sincere desire to establish Christian colonies? . . . Or do we focus rather on the stealing of Indian land, and their habit of displacing and murdering these Indians whenever it was convenient?" As for the revolutionary leaders, they were by and large "genuinely religious but not specifically Christian. . . . The God of the founding fathers was a benevolent deity, not far removed from the God of eighteenth-century Deists or nineteenth-century Unitarians." Both the Declaration of Independence and the Constitution, they declared, were deistic in character.[11]

As for the idea of America's "chosen" status, the authors stood with Roger Williams in asserting "that no nation since the coming of Christ has been uniquely God's chosen people." To imagine otherwise, they said, "leads to idolatry . . . and an irresistible temptation to national self-righteousness." Although they took pains to acknowledge the sounder elements in a "Christian nation" discourse, their book on the whole was a careful dissection of such advocacies. One reviewer, perhaps indulging a bit of wishful thinking, speculated that it might leave Christian-nation enthusiasts "red-faced with embarrassment."[12]

This is not to suggest that evangelical moderates necessarily felt comfortable with the new pluralism. That was, and still is, far from true. In a widely used textbook published in 1990, George Marsden, a coauthor of the *Search* critique, continued to insist that, given the crucial roles played by such leaders as Paine or Jefferson, "clearly the nation could not officially claim a Christian sanction"; but Marsden by that time had become highly critical of what he thought were excesses in practical applications of the new pluralism. He thought, for example, that religion departments in universities were devoting far too much of their attention and resources to nontraditional forms of faith, to the virtual exclusion of Christianity— especially the Christianity of Protestant evangelicals.[13]

Objections to alleged pluralist excesses arose in liberal contexts as well. The United Church of Christ, though polyglot in origins, could be ranked, overall, just behind the Unitarian-Universalists and the Quakers as the most liberal of America's major denominations; so it was no surprise when the UCC, in 1995, published a *New Century Hymnbook* that set off a firestorm of negative reactions. This revisionist hymnbook, more radically than nearly all others of the time, excluded racist, sexist, and militarist or superpatriotic language. (In its pages, "Christian soldiers marching as to war" were nowhere to be found.) On the positive side, the book gave unprecedented attention to the hymnology of formerly ignored minorities.[14]

Some critics, within and outside the denomination, dismissed the whole effort as mere "political correctness"—in other words, with an increasingly common but peculiarly insulting form of putdown that implied a lack of genuine conviction in those they were criticizing. But other detractors of the new hymnbook, perhaps the majority, were simply voicing concerns about the elimination of long-treasured hymns or about the many alterations in language. Some 30 percent of UCC congregations—about the usual proportion for a new hymnbook—adopted the *New Century* during the first years after its appearance, but those who objected were unusually upset and unusually vocal. Entire books were devoted mainly to their objections and the responses these elicited.[15]

Still other forms of discomfiture, most of them paralleling objections being raised elsewhere in public discourse, were grounded neither in a desired return to "Protestant America" nor in accusations about an abject surrender to "political correctness." Instead, as so often in the past, they invoked a unitive principle in support of highly traditional concerns about social cohesion. Peter Berger, the eminent sociologist of religion, warned that religious pluralism, which he had always favored, had ceased to be undergirded by the moral consensus that in the past had made it workable. He wrote in 1983 that "until very recently most, if not all, the religious groups coexisting in America have shared a broadly common morality." But in the new climate, he thought, agreements about right and wrong had given way to a kind of individualism that exalted or permitted mere "preferences" in matters vital to a sane and orderly society. As he saw it, one could now voice a preference for a particular faith such as Catholicism, but also a moral preference for almost anything. The idea that one might champion the use of arson in labor disputes, or remark that "I happen to be a rapist"—and not be sent to jail or a mental institution—was, he thought, not so far-fetched as it might sound. We had to worry, Berger wrote, about the very survival of a society beset with such fundamental moral divisions.[16]

Although Berger, along with a host of social analysts in the early 1980s who shared his concern, harbored no illusions about a return to some pristine "religious America," let alone a Protestant America, some found this warning about moral decline unduly nostalgic. One of his critics pointed out that "the evidence for old-time sanctity comes from suspect sources such as hagiography, panegyrics, and sermons," and that a closer look even at those sources shows ministers of the Gospel "upbraiding the mass of ordinary people for lack of faith." It would appear that "the gift of which, we are told, modernity has deprived us was always rather the exception."[17] Another, responding to Berger's own assumptions about past moral unity, reminded him that "we are talking about a past American society that, for example, either approved lynchings or did nothing about them—or was morally confused about them." As for labor disputes, even if we were to concede "the relative benignity of the railroad strike of 1877 (in which arson was a preferred method) . . . we would still have to talk about expressed moral preferences . . . for burning convents, burning villages and cities, and burning negroes."[18] Yet Berger and others, minus the nostalgia and the attendant illusions about moral declension, were voicing a valid concern about the divisive potential in a new pluralism that seemed to leave little room for the forms of moral consensus that hold a society together.

THE MIXED FORTUNES OF THE RELIGIOUS RIGHT

Through and beyond the 1980s, the political initiatives of the "new religious right" succeeded often enough, especially at the local level, to keep the media in a frenzy and—not coincidentally—to keep nonrightists severely frightened. As calmer observers tried to point out, however, failures and disillusionment had overtaken the conservative campaigns almost as rapidly as their hopes and reputed numbers had risen at the outset. For reasons that seemed a good deal more political than religious, the new Christian right had turned up its collective nose at the presidential candidacies in 1980 of two lifelong evangelicals, Jimmy Carter and John Anderson, and had placed its trust in Ronald Reagan. But once it became clear, as Richard Pierard puts it, "that the New Christian Right had not been the decisive influence in his election," Reagan seemingly lost interest in the religious right's social program (for example, "pro-life" initiatives, school prayer, and tuition tax credits).

Thus Reagan, along with others whom the religious right had supported, set up a dynamic, one not very friendly to ultraconservatism, that persisted through the presidency of the first George Bush: Politicians who had vied for this support turned out to be listening to other constituencies besides the reputed millions on the religious right's mailing lists; and judicial appointees — most egregiously, Supreme Court appointees — failed repeatedly to deliver as extreme conservatives had expected. To make matters worse for the far right, such campaigns as those promoting the inclusion of creationism in public school curricula were enjoying limited success with the textbook companies and almost none at all in courts and legislatures.

It was a sign of the times when Jerry Falwell, after every one of his candidates lost in Virginia in 1985, began dismantling the Moral Majority the following year—first retreating to a bunker called the Liberty Federation, and then withdrawing more fully to pursue his ministry and run his Liberty University. Subsequently, the Pat Robertson candidacy for the presidential nomination in 1988 elicited enough support to affect the policies of Bush and the Republican Party, especially with respect to Supreme Court appointments that at least seemed promising. Yet the failure of Robertson's bid was still a serious blow from the far right's point of view.

How did all this happen? Those who knew something about the similar experiences, throughout American history, of left-wing as well as right-wing radicalism, found it unsurprising that voters and politicians had again cheered extremism-in-general and then, in voting booths and legislatures, opted for moderation-in-particular. More specifically, however, it seemed clear that the new Christian right had suffered loss or decline with respect to both of the advantages that a radical or extremist movement must hold if it is to be effectual. Such movements must maintain a high degree of unity and, in addition, forge alliances with those moderates who lean in their direction. But the religious right in the second half of the 1980s was finding it impossible to paper over its bitter internal divisions, and also was suffering from the unreliability of wider constituencies whose support had never, evidently, been more than partial and selective.

The climactic moment was the Republican National Convention of 1992. Although salient points on the agenda of the religious right had been written into the party's platform, Jerry Falwell was not invited to speak. Pat Robertson, supremely the preacher in politics, spoke but made little impression. So it was up to Patrick Buchanan, the layman, to sound a trumpet blast that might rally the faithful. Appealing especially to conservative disdain for gay rights legislation, Buchanan referred to the recent Democratic convention as "that giant masquerade ball . . . where 20,000 radicals and liberals came dressed up as moderates and centrists in the greatest single exhibition of cross-dressing in American political history." The agenda that he attributed to Bill and Hillary Clinton — "abortion on demand, a litmus test for the Supreme Court, homosexual rights, discrimination against religious schools, women in combat" — would bring change; but, said Buchanan, "it is not the kind of change we can tolerate in a nation that we can still call God's country." [19]

This was indeed a mighty blast, but the negative response, first among mainstream Republicans and then in the electorate, was even more deafening. Scandals involving some of the most prominent television evangelists discredited the movement further, particularly in the broad and essential community of mainstream evangelicals; and these scandals also exacerbated tensions within the card-carrying religious right.

With respect to internal divisions, recent history repeated itself. Hardline fundamentalists for years had excoriated Billy Graham for his moderation. In the 1980s they were blasting Falwell for something even worse: unlike the Graham of recent years, Falwell dared to style himself a true fundamentalist.

Although this political and social movement did not and will not disappear, between 1980 and the elections of 1992 it had run through a cycle of political involvement and high visibility and had reverted to something close to its position of the early 1970s. For the time being, at least, the religious right had had to settle for being just another voice.

UNITY AND/OR PLURALISM: CURRENT OPTIONS

For those who had seen the right-wing extremism of the early 1980s as a kind of disease, reversion of the disease, by the end of the decade, from an acute to a chronic state offered only limited reassurance. The hard religious right had suffered defeats and disappointments, and would continue to do so. But it had not expired, any more than (despite real and imaginary death rattles) fundamentalism had expired after the Scopes trial of the 1920s.

And sure enough, by the mid-1990s it seemed evident that the religious right not only lived on in relation to perennial issues like abortion; it had also regrouped, with a somewhat changed set of moderate and secular allies, for an assault on pluralism itself. The backlash against "multiculturalism" and other forms of recognition for group identity led some liberals and moderates to fear that pluralist advances of the late twentieth century might now be reversed definitively. Although I do not share that apprehension, I do believe that the struggle will be difficult and confused until the rationales for the newer forms of pluralism are clarified—historically, philosophically, and, in the case of religious pluralism, theologically.

First, however, what are the options? They would seem to be, at one extreme, acceptance of pluralism itself as the only remaining common value for the society at large; and at the other, a return to the kind of unitive ideal that, even in expanded form, would repristinate and reimpose the common values of an older Protestant America.

The first of these polar solutions, a thoroughgoing, unqualified pluralism bereft of any concern about common values, has been cited frequently as a fear or accusation but almost never promoted as either a desideratum or a practical possibility. With regard to the second option, a somewhat more plausible one, Professor Marsden in 1990 stated his reservations as I believe most of his fellow evangelicals, as well as virtually all liberals, would now state them: "What is needed in America today is recognition by both religious and nonreligious peoples that the days are past when any one group, whether religious or nonreligious, can dictate a comprehensive public philosophy that will prevail for the whole of the people."[20]

The median position that seemingly, in the early years of the new century, can claim majority support both in religious bodies and in the society at large is that we should accept pluralism as a primary value, but that we must also deal seriously and studiously with pleas concerning social and moral cohesion.

The question, of course, is how to make that sort of stance into something more than a plausible but empty formula; more specifically, how to achieve a new symbiosis between pluralism and unity without returning to the traditional melting pot formula—a celebration of past but not present diversities—that by now has been so widely discredited. On what basis (or bases) can a new, truly inclusive social covenant be formed and maintained?

Robert Bellah, the prominent sociologist of religion at Berkeley, in the 1970s made a gallant start toward new formulas that might hold up as more than hopeful rhetoric. In a somewhat despairing book called *The Broken Covenant*, Bellah expressed some agreement with those who portrayed the original American nation as having formulated a covenant— with God, and among its own peoples. But unlike those on the nostalgic religious right, Bellah was not referring to a pristine moment of American history when God was in his heaven and all was right with an egalitarian polity. There had been no such time. Americans had broken the covenant even as it was being drawn up—for example, by condoning and perpetuating human slavery. Thus a renewed covenant, or "civil religion," was necessary—one that, this time, would spell out just what it means, and truly mean what it proclaims, about such matters as human equality.[21]

Many who agreed with that initial prescription remained chary, especially through the decade of the 1980s, about including pluralism, at least in its more advanced forms, as a primary value in any revised social covenant. My own view, which I still hold, was that a renewed civil religion cannot be constructed without a frank and strong affirmation of pluralism as a major principle, even if it is not the only principle involved.

I would argue this, first of all, because it seems to me that commitments to pluralism as tolerance and pluralism as inclusivity have by now, after long struggles, become intrinsic to the social covenant; there can be no turning back. Beyond that, I would argue that the logical arguments in favor of a pluralism that goes beyond inclusivity, that is mutually respectful and nonpatronizing, are compelling if one wishes to contemplate any civil religion at all.

Pluralism under this newer definition, as under previous ones, rests upon a two-way logic. The better-known way, almost a truism, dictates that as long as the members of culturally dominant groups continue to demand respect (not just tolerance) for their own firmly held religious and other commitments, they will have to respect those of others. In its less-familiar reverse form, this same logic is proving to be compelling because it undercuts the most common objections raised against advanced forms of pluralism—especially in the sphere of religion. It is a logic that deprives the culturally dominant, or those who aspire to such status, of one of the most common excuses for resisting the pluralist principle.

That is, this reverse form of the logic makes nonsense of the idea that a fully respectful pluralism means that one does not really hold to his or her own convictions. I call this nonsense because, if I do concede your right to hold firmly to your beliefs, it makes no sense at all for me to deny or compromise that same right in relation to myself. Pluralism in its leading contemporary meaning—support for group identity and the integrity of competing beliefs—emphatically does not imply "lack of all conviction," either for historically dominant American faiths and their adherents or for the society at large.

One can also hold that this advanced form of pluralism, like its predecessors, has become sufficiently embedded in the public mind and public policy that there can be no turning back. I think Nathan Glazer was correct (despite some self-acknowledged rhetorical excess) when he asserted in 1997 that "we are all multiculturalists now"—that this part of the future has also arrived. Glazer then predicted that, in some institutional settings at least, the newer definitions of pluralism are going to survive the current vigorous attempts to outlaw them. Turning to a principal site of such attempts, he asserted that "those few who want to return American education to a period in which the various subcultures were ignored, and in which America was presented as the peak and end-product of civilization, cannot expect to make any progress in the schools."[22]

Finally, the newer definition of pluralism will continue to advance because, unless its meaning is willfully or thoughtlessly distorted, it is not inimical to those elements in historic social and religious covenants that are commonly considered unifying. It in fact presupposes and, at its best, strengthens most of these other values. If pluralism has seemed inadequate as a unifying ideal, that may be because our civic and religious rhetoric has proclaimed it so inadequately—so thinly and defensively—when the pluralist ideal has been proclaimed at all.

Pluralism, not always but far too often, has been defended as little more than a practical necessity, a prudent stance taken because of the pressures of diversity and the demands voiced by the American Civil Liberties Union, or the Anti-Defamation League, or a liberal judiciary. It deserves a more positive kind of advocacy, both as a leading element in democratic ideology and as an allowable, perhaps a necessary, element in theistic religion.

PLURALISM, DEMOCRATIC TRADITIONS, AND THEISM

The symphonic pluralism that asserted itself in the second half of the twentieth century can fairly be seen as a modern recycling of democratic ideals that, historically, have been considered unifying. Present-day programs of affirmative action, for example, derive in part from the historic agreement that our society, although it cannot ensure equality of achievement, can and must ensure equality of access—coming in at the same entrance. Similarly, the modern insight that "inclusion" must not mean simply inclusion on someone else's terms draws on very traditional American ideals of religious freedom and other First Amendment civil rights. Finally, the idea that a pluralist society should involve virtually all of its members in the writing and management of a social agenda seems, at the least, a highly respectable idea in the American democratic setting.

Advocates of religious pluralism can also rely, much more than they customarily do, on the argument that such a stance is mandated—not merely permitted—by any thoroughgoing theism. Those who confer God-like status on particular institutions or scriptures may well disagree, but the pluralist is on firm ground in pointing out that in the Judaic, Christian, and other traditions "only God is God"; all apart from God is penultimate—less than absolute. Given that theological stance, neither "we" nor "others" can claim that our institutions embody final truth.

In one of the many expressions of this, the Judaic God reminded Israel, via the prophet Amos, that they were *goy b'goyim*—a people among peoples.[23] And early modern theological formulations recognized and reflected the penultimacy, the derivative or secondary status, of religious and civic covenants. Anglo-American forms of Puritanism were built upon belief both in an overarching Covenant of Grace, and in derivative covenants that were subordinate to this but nonetheless strong, specific, and firmly held.

A similar pattern of belief in the contemporary world dictates that group loyalties—religious loyalties as well as racial, ethnic, and national ones—can be accorded full credence and at the same time understood as secondary. That is part of the covenantal agreement: that they are secondary.

Given such an understanding, even such now-suspect ideas as national chosenness can be honored. Although those ideas can no longer be considered acceptable if they mean that "we're chosen and you're not," a pluralist view of the world provides ample space for the conception that every people is chosen for a particular task or tasks.

Sadly, however, other traditions and experiences—particularly those that are by-products of the rise of the West since the early modern era—have made it hard for Westerners to accept what some Reform Jews in the nineteenth century called "the chosenness of all peoples." In the course of such twentieth-century happenings as the decline of imperialism, we have seen just how difficult it is to divest ourselves of ideas that we are God's chosen instruments and that others cannot be.

For America, in fact, and particularly for its traditional Protestant culture, the process of cleansing ourselves of such hubristic ideas has perhaps been even more wrenching than it has been for once-dominant nations that held, then lost, large numbers of colonized areas. Americans, despite the lateness (compared with most European powers) and the material meagerness of their experience with overseas conquest, did hitch their wagons to the star of what some mission leaders promoted as the "true imperialism" inherent in Christianity.[24] In a real sense, the world was their colony. For a people to suffer the loss, or even the decline, of that sort of cosmic self-assurance can easily be more deeply traumatic than the mere loss of an Algeria or an India.

It is therefore not surprising that the propensity to identify "our country" with "God's country" survives in American thinking to a significantly greater extent than in other nations of the once-superconfident Western world. Englishmen a century ago boasted that the sun never set on their empire. They and other Europeans, to say nothing of Asians and Africans, are both amused and appalled that American intentions, whether admirable or otherwise, so often come clothed in a similar rhetoric.

All of which provides additional reasons for acknowledging that pluralism remains a work in progress. It must contend not only with persisting strains of intolerance, exclusion, and nationalistic hubris, but also with world-hegemonic aspirations that live on in American religious discourse despite the best efforts of those who revise hymnbooks and prayerbooks.

THROUGH A GLASS, DARKLY: THE PROSPECTS FOR FURTHER REDEFINITION

Any historian of an ideal like pluralism, especially if he or she tries to describe how definitions have changed in the past, is certain to be asked what might be in store for the future. If pluralism is a work in progress, should we expect further changes in what it means to accept and celebrate diversity?

The historian's usual first response to such a question is to explain patiently that he or she is not competent in the science of futurology—perhaps adding that no one else really is either. In the present instance, however, changes in definition seem already under way. The most prominent of these is a form of revision that calls attention to the increased salience of personal choice in the formation and sustaining of religious and ethnic communities.

In the 1990s most analysts and policymakers were, quite understandably, preoccupied with the sharply increased emphasis on group identity—some welcoming this emphasis as the shape of a glorious future, others deploring it as the end of civilization as we supposedly had known it. But in those same years a few strong voices were raised in anticipation of what the historian David Hollinger called a "post-ethnic America." This would be, and perhaps already was, an American society in which the boundaries defining ethnic groups, and even those defining "races," would become less rigid—more permeable.[25] No one (as far as I know) predicted that racial distinctions, or even intraracial ethnic distinctions, would disappear entirely; and very few took the position that such an outcome would be desirable. The point about postethnicity, as Hollinger put it in 1995, is that it "prefers voluntary to prescribed affiliations, appreciates multiple identities, pushes for communities of wide scope, recognizes the constructed character of ethno-racial groups, and accepts the formation of new groups as a part of the normal life of a democratic society."[26]

As Hollinger recognized fully, and as Nathan Glazer argued more despairingly two years later, the invitation to choose one's community has, in general, been extended to African Americans and other nonwhites in peripheral ways but almost never in fundamental ways; and, as Glazer wrote, "one wonders how, or when, it will be otherwise."[27] Alex Haley, who published his best-selling *Roots: The Saga of an American Family* in 1976, in raw theory might have chosen to present that family as Irish, since the bloodline on his father's side ran back to Erin rather than the Gambia. But as Hollinger pointed out, Haley's choice had actually been a Hobson's choice, an unreal one.[28] One drop of African blood (or thereabouts) had, through most of American history, been enough to fix one's identity as black; and 25 percent Native American blood had sufficed to make one an Indian. But this did not work in reverse. One drop of German blood, or one or more Irish ancestors, had never been accredited in any comparable way.

Certainly some measure of despair, and a large measure of frustration, were and still are warranted. "Haley's choice" will become a real one at about the same time when descendants of British and European immigrants cease to feel gut-level amazement that a second- or third-generation Asian American speaks unaccented English; and one may indeed wonder just when that time will come. Nonetheless, with the incidence of interracial marriage mounting almost as rapidly as that of interfaith marriage—black-white liaisons were 300 percent more common in 1990 than they had been in 1970—Alex Haley's America is becoming something just a bit closer to Tiger Woods's America.[29] Woods, a celebrated golf champion, is only one of the more prominent among the millions of Americans who were finally, in the census of 2000, permitted to record themselves as multiracial. (Almost three million exercised that option.)

This does not mean that Professor Kallen was dead wrong in his famous observation that the progeny of immigrants (or forced immigrants, or original inhabitants) "cannot change their grandfathers." It does mean that more Americans are now choosing among a number of biological and other communities when they construct their personal identity and seek to construct one for their children and descendants. It does mean, I think, that the question "Whose America?" is increasingly being answered as the words, though not the deeds, of America's founders demanded.

Notes

INTRODUCTION

1. Stephen J. Stein, "Something Old, Something New, Something Borrowed, Something Left to Do: Choosing a Textbook for Religion in America," *Religion and American Culture*, 3 (Summer 1993), 226.
2. The broadening-down imagery so often used in this connection probably appeared first in Alfred Tennyson's poem "You Ask Me Why" (1842). The classic work, however, is Herbert Butterfield's *The Whig Interpretation of History* (London, 1931).
3. Thomas Tweed, who does not subscribe to this view, found it strongly represented among the historians of American religion who gathered in the early 1990s to explore ways of reconsidering standard approaches and accounts in the field. Tweed, *Retelling*, 5.
4. Stein, "Something Old," 226.
5. Ahlstrom, *Religious History*, 12.
6. Hugh McLeod, *Secularisation in Western Europe, 1848–1914* (New York: St. Martin's, 2000), 17–28 and passim; Noll, *History*, 131, 260–61.
7. Herbert Butterfield, *Christianity and History* (London: G. Bell and Sons, 1950), 92. See also John Higham, "Beyond Consensus: The Historian as Moral Critic," *American Historical Review*, 67 (April 1962), 609–25.
8. See Glazer, *Multiculturalists*.
9. See Marty, *One and Many*.
10. See especially Hollinger, *Postethnic America*.

1. "HERE ARE NO DISPUTES"

1. Crèvecoeur, *Letters*, 49.
2. Ibid., 54–56.
3. William Cobbett, *A Year's Residence in the United States of America* [1819] (Carbondale: Southern Illinois University Press, 1964), 235, 229.
4. Fredrika Bremer, *Homes of the New World: Impressions of America* (2 vols., New York: Harper and Brothers, 1853) 2: 624; Lord Carlisle (G. W. F. Howard, 7th earl), *Travels in America. The Poetry of Pope: Two Lectures . . .* (New York: G. P. Putnam, 1851), 77.
5. Schaff, *America*, 91–95; Frances Trollope, *The Domestic Manners of the Americans* [1832] (New York: Alfred A. Knopf, 1949), 108.

6. Hannah Adams, *A Dictionary of All Religions and Religious Denominations* (Atlanta: Scholars Press, 1992), 132.

7. Baird, *Religion in America*, 318.

8. Ibid., 283, 129–30.

9. Ibid., 318; Leo Ribuffo, "Religious Prejudice and Nativism," in Lippy and Williams, *Encyclopedia*, 1529.

10. Baird, *Religion in America*, 296.

11. Billington, *Protestant Crusade*, 220.

12. National Lord's Day Convention, *Abstract of the Proceedings* [etc.]. Baltimore: Evangelical Lutheran Church, 1845.

13. See, for example, Tocqueville, *Democracy*, vol. 2, book 2, chapter 13 ("Why the Americans Are So Restless"); and vol. 1, chapter 15 ("Unlimited Power of the Majority").

14. Hughes, "Decline," esp. 88, 99; and "Catholic Chapter," esp. 110, 121.

15. Noll, *History*, 62, 80; reader's report for this book.

16. Kallen, *Culture and Democracy*, 63.

17. Gaustad and Barlow, *New Historical Atlas*, 7–8; Hudson, *American Protestantism*, 18–29.

18. Butler, *Becoming America*, 185–92.

19. Although Butler (*Becoming America*, 295) thinks that Charles O. Paullin (*Atlas of the Historical Geography of the United States* [Washington, D.C.: Carnegie Institution, 1932]) overestimated the total number of religious congregations in the revolutionary period, Paullin is still the best source for the approximate numerical relation of these groups in 1780; see 49–50 and plate 82. The numbers are more scattered in the Gaustad-Barlow *Atlas* of 2001, but see 8–9, 37. Gaustad and Barlow's comparative figures for eighteenth-century Quakers involve a serious error that, according to Barlow (correspondence of February 6, 2001), will be corrected in later editions; the numbers given are for monthly meetings (about eighty in 1780) instead of for congregations (about three hundred). For the Shakers, see Robert S. Fogarty, *Dictionary of American Communal and Utopian History* (Westport, Conn.: Greenwood, 1980), 173–75.

20. Nelson, *Lutherans*, 41–43.

21. The delegates in the Matteson painting are identified in "Key to 'The First Prayer in Congress,'" a document (no. 115816) held by the Essex Institute in Salem, Massachusetts. For Hopkins, see *The National Cyclopedia of American Biography* (New York: James T. White, 1909), 10: 13–14.

22. Jones, *American Immigration*, 94.

23. Gaustad, *Historical Atlas*, 41–42.

24. Takaki, *Different Mirror*, 192–204.

25. See also Miller, *Unwelcome Immigrant*, passim.

26. A vigorous debate about the 1790 figures has tended to lower the estimate of Irish-heritage population but not much altered estimates relating to Germans. See Thomas L. Purvis, "The European Ancestry of the United States Population, 1790,"

William and Mary Quarterly, 41 (January 1984), 84. For the 1850 proportions, see Gaustad and Barlow, *Historical Atlas*, 61.

27. Gaustad, *Historical Atlas*, 43; Nelson, 204–6.

28. Baird's figures are reported and elaborated in Marsden, *Religion and American Culture*, 87. See also Gaustad, *Historical Atlas*, 110.

29. *Statistisches Jahrbuch 2001 für die Bundesrepublik Deutschland* (Wiesbaden: Statistisches Bundesamt, 2001), 65; Office for National Statistics, *Britain 2000: The Official Yearbook of the United Kingdom* (London: Stationer's Office, 1999), 115.

30. *The Correspondence of Emerson and Carlyle*, ed. Joseph Slater (New York: Columbia University Press, 1964) 283; Ahlstrom, *Religious History*, 491.

31. Emerson, "New England Reformers," 591.

32. Ibid., 591–92.

33. In Lippy and Williams, *Encyclopedia*, 1534.

2. JUST BEHAVE YOURSELF

1. G. M. Young, *Last Essays* (London: Rupert Hart-Davis, 1950), 9. I first heard something close to this quotation in the early 1950s, in the Oxford lectures of the social historian Asa Briggs (now Lord Briggs). Briggs informs me that Young offered this, his favorite admonition, in a number of forms, oral and written. Correspondence, December 21, 2000.

2. See Marty, *Nation of Behavers*, 32–39 et passim.

3. Baird, *Religion in America*, 318; Richard E. Bennett, *Mormons at the Missouri, 1846–52* (Norman: University of Oklahoma Press, 1987), 103; Schaff, *America*, 96, 97.

4. Hutchison, *Transcendentalist Ministers*, 117–21; Commager, "Kneeland," 32, 41, and 29–41 passim.

5. Baird, *Religion in America*, 111. For an extended treatment of the alleged "infidelity of the Tom Paine school," see Marty, *Infidel*, chapter 1.

6. Vale, *Thomas Paine*, 5, 122; Sparks, *Ethan Allen*, 220–25.

7. Marty, *Infidel*, 45.

8. Ibid., 41. See also on the Baptist John Leland, ibid.

9. Harold A. Larrabee, "The Trumpeter of Doomsday," *American Heritage* 15 (April 1964), 96–97.

10. Ibid., 97; Scharnhorst, "Millerites," 27–28.

11. Dagobert Runes, "Transcendentalism," in Runes, ed., *Dictionary of Philosophy* (Totowa, N.J.: Littlefield, Adams, 1962); Norton, *Infidelity*.

12. A. B. Dod, "Transcendentalism," in Andrews Norton, *Two Articles*, 11.

13. Quoted in Gura and Myerson, *American Transcendentalism*, 30–31.

14. In Ralph Waldo Emerson, *Collected Poems and Translations*, ed. Harold Bloom and Paul Kanel (New York: Library of America, 1994). Subsequent citations are to this edition.

15. Walter Hamilton, ed., *Parodies of the Works of English and American Authors* (6 vols., New

York: Johnson Reprint, 1967), 5: 246; Walter Jerrold and James Leonard, eds., *A Century of Parody and Imitation* (London: Oxford University Press, 1913), 355.

16. Thomas Carlyle, *Past and Present* [1843] (London: Chapman and Hall, 1893), 253.

17. Clarke is quoted in James Elliott Cabot, *A Memoir of Ralph Waldo Emerson* (2 vols., Cambridge, Mass.: Riverside, 1887), 1: 249; for Peabody: Bruce A. Ronda, *Elizabeth Palmer Peabody: A Reformer on Her Own Terms* (Cambridge: Harvard University Press, 1999), 261; Emerson, "The Transcendentalist," 207. I am much indebted to Joel Myerson for pointing me, in the cases of the Clarke and Peabody quotations, to sources that I had "known long since but lost awhile."

18. Emerson, "The Transcendentalist," 199, 203; Miller, *Cranch*.

19. Emerson, "Nature," 10, 38.

20. Emerson, "The Transcendentalist," 208–9.

21. Bushnell, *Nurture*, passim; Nevin, *Anxious Bench*, 51.

22. Quoted in Nevin, *Anxious Bench*, 53.

23. Bratt, "Anti-Revivalism," 7–8.

24. See, for example, Jane Hunter, *The Gospel of Gentility: American Women Missionaries in Turn-of-the-Century China* (New Haven: Yale University Press, 1984).

25. Kanter, *Commitment and Community*, 105.

26. Baird, *Religion in America*, 42–43; see also 270–72.

27. Leo Ribuffo, in Lippy and Williams, *Encyclopedia*, 1534. See also Billington, *Protestant Crusade*, chapter 16 et passim.

28. Billington, *Protestant Crusade*, 361. For a more recent, highly detailed and informative, analysis of this literature, see Franchot, *Roads to Rome*.

29. Ibid., 412–15. See also John R. Mulkern, *The Know-Nothing Party in Massachusetts: The Rise and Fall of a People's Movement* (Boston: Northeastern University Press, 1990).

30. Hughes, "Catholic Chapter," 111.

31. Hughes, "Decline," 99.

32. O'Dea, *Mormons*, 246.

33. Baird, *Religion in America*, 285.

34. O'Dea, *Mormons*, 46–7; Shipps, *Mormonism*, 158.

35. O'Dea, *Mormons*, 111–18.

36. This and the other Mormon verses in this chapter are transcribed from Duncan B. M. Emrich, ed., "Songs of the Mormons and Songs of the West," sound recording, Archive of American Folk Song, L30 (Washington, D.C.: Music Division, Library of Congress, n.d.). On Mormon self-deprecating humor, see Thomas E. Cheney, ed., *Mormon Songs from the Rocky Mountains: A Compilation of Mormon Folksong* (Austin: American Folklore Society, 1968), 16 et passim.

37. Barlow, *Mormons and the Bible*, 144–5 and chapter 4 passim.

38. Stokes, *Church and State*, 2: 275–80; O'Dea, *Mormons*, 111.

39. Gordon B. Hinckley, interview with Michael Paulson, *Boston Globe*, September 2, 2000, B2.

40. Potter, *People of Plenty*, 93 and Chapter 5 passim.

3. MARCHING TO ZION

1. Tocqueville, *Democracy*, 1: 303, 2: 6.
2. Andrew Reed and James Matheson, *A Narrative of [a] Visit to the American Churches* (2 vols., New York: Harper, 1835), 2: 191; John Henry Newman, "The American Church," *British Critic and Quarterly Theological Review*, 26 (October 1839): 327.
3. Tocqueville, *Democracy*, 2: 22.
4. On hegemonic structures see Antonio Gramsci, *Selections from the Prison Notebooks*, ed. Quinton Hoare and Geoffrey Nowell Smith (New York: International Publishers, 1971), especially 12, 55–60.
5. Albanese, *America*, 249.
6. Norman, *Conscience of the State*, 9–19.
7. *Webster's New World Dictionary* (New York: World, 1970); Albanese, *America*, 248.
8. Schaff, *America*, 94. For a later influential assessment by a European of Calvinist influences in American culture, see André Siegfried, *America Comes of Age* (New York: Harcourt, Brace, 1927), chapter 3.
9. Schaff, *America*, 93–95.
10. Ibid., 85.
11. Cotton Mather, *Magnalia Christi Americana* [1702], ed. Kenneth B. Murdock (Cambridge: Harvard University Press, 1977), 144. This assertion, already widely repeated by Mather's time, supposedly originated with John Robinson, the pastor who preached a farewell sermon to the Pilgrims before they sailed from Holland in 1620.
12. Charles Hodge, "Inspiration," *Biblical Repertory and Princeton Review*, 29 (1857), 663.
13. George M. Marsden, "Everyone One's Own Interpreter? The Bible, Science, and Authority in Mid-Nineteenth Century America," in Nathan O. Hatch and Mark A. Noll, eds., *The Bible in America: Essays in Cultural History* (New York: Oxford University Press, 1982), 91.
14. Quoted in George M. Marsden, *The Evangelical Mind and the New School Presbyterian Experience* (New Haven: Yale University Press, 1980), 170–71.
15. Bernard A. Weisberger, *They Gathered at the River: The Story of the Great Revivalists and Their Impact upon Religion in America* (Boston: Little, Brown, 1958), 88. For a more extended and nuanced treatment of Finney's representativeness in evangelical America, see Hambrick-Stowe, *Finney*.
16. Weisberger, *They Gathered*, 101.
17. Charles G. Finney, "Sinners Bound to Change Their Own Hearts," *Sermons on Various Subjects* (New York: S. W. Benedict, 1834), 20.
18. Ibid., 28.
19. Clark, "Ten Nights," 16–17.
20. Available, with jacket notes by Richard Jackson, on the recorded *Angels' Visits, and Other Vocal Gems of Victorian America*, New World Records no. 220.
21. For an excellent discussion of the forms of American optimism and their encroachment upon the value systems of "outsiders," see Tweed, *Encounter*, xxiii–xxiv, 10–11,

and chapter 6 ("Optimism and Activism") passim. The degree to which "chosenness" was or (mostly) was not a distinctively American self-estimate is examined in Hutchison and Lehmann, *Many Are Chosen*.

22. *Brighten the Corner*, New World Records no. 224.

23. Tuveson, *Redeemer Nation*; Jonathan Edwards, *The Works of Jonathan Edwards*, vol. 4, ed. C. C. Goen (New Haven: Yale University Press, 1972), 353; Strong, *Our Country*, 216–17, 218.

24. Luker, *Black and White*, 268–75 et passim; Meyer, "Cultural Decline."

25. Robert E. Speer, *South American Problems* (New York: Student Volunteer Movement, 1912), 225 and chapter 8 passim.

26. They were also contested within the mainstream. See Hanley, *Christian Commonwealth*.

27. The temperance issue, especially as it became more and more a dispute about prohibition, was perhaps the most divisive one (along with revivalism) in Lutheran and Catholic settings. See Philip Gleason, *The Conservative Reformers: German-American Catholics and the Social Order* (Notre Dame: University of Notre Dame Press, 1968), 37–39; Nelson, *Lutherans*, 140–41, 356, 418; Maria Erling, "Creating an Urban Piety: New England's Swedish Immigrants and Their Religious Culture from 1880 to 1915" (Ph.D. diss., Harvard University, 1995), chapter 6 ("'Pulling Back the Curtain': Temperance and Swedish Culture").

28. Max Lerner, *America as a Civilization* (New York: Simon and Schuster, 1957), 62.

29. Clarence C. Goen, *Broken Churches, Broken Nation: Denominational Schisms and the Coming of the American Civil War* (Macon, Ga.: Mercer University Press, 1985).

30. Quoted in Stokes, *Church and State*, 3: 585.

31. Ibid., 584–85.

32. Ibid., 585.

33. Ibid., 586.

34. Ibid., 587–88.

35. Ibid., 588–89, 591.

36. Ibid., 592.

37. Quoted in Hudson, *Great Tradition*, 65.

38. See, for example, Clifford S. Griffin, *Their Brothers' Keepers: Moral Stewardship in the United States, 1800–1865* (New Brunswick: Rutgers University Press, 1960).

4. "REPENTANCE FOR OUR SOCIAL SINS"

1. Luker, *Black and White*; White, *Liberty and Justice*.

2. Rauschenbusch, *Christianity*, 332 and chapter 6 passim.

3. Thomas N. Huxley, *Evolution and Ethics* (London: Macmillan, 1893).

4. Sumner, *Social Classes*, 168–69; Sumner, "Absurd Effort," 97, 105, 106.

5. Sumner, *Social Classes*, 157–58.

6. Andrew Carnegie, *The Gospel of Wealth, and Other Timely Essays* [1900] (New York: Doubleday, Doran, 1933), 16.

7. Horatio Alger, Jr., *Ragged Dick; or, Street Life in New York with the Boot-Blacks* [1868] (Philadelphia: Henry T. Coates, 1895), 283–84.

8. Ibid., 283–87.

9. Ibid., 291–93.

10. Ibid., 279–80.

11. Ibid., 280.

12. Daniel W. Bjork, *The Victorian Flight: Russell Conwell and the Crisis of American Individualism* (Washington: University Press of America, 1979), 38.

13. Russell Conwell, "Acres of Diamonds," as excerpted in Harry R. Warfel et al., eds., *The American Mind: Selections from the Literature of the United States* (2d ed., 2 vols., New York: American Book Company, 1963), 2: 1086.

14. Ibid., 2: 1086–87. The testimonials I cite are not at this location. I obtained them when writing a lecture on Conwell in the 1960s, and am now unable to find them in the several editions available to me. Agnes Burr's biography of Conwell, however, has an entire chapter of and about such testimonials. The Reynoldsville one is there, as is one from a former prisoner who heard Conwell's lecture and eventually advanced (?) to a sixteen-year career as a member of the United States Congress! Agnes R. Burr, *Russell H. Conwell and His Work* (Philadelphia: John C. Winston, 1917), chapter 31.

15. Conwell, "Acres," 1087.

16. Henry W. Bowden, ed., *Dictionary of American Religious Biography* (Westport, Conn.: Greenwood, 1977).

17. Rodeheaver can be heard singing this (and hearing him is an experience) on the record called *Brighten the Corner*, New World Records no. 224.

18. John P. Ferré, *A Social Gospel for Millions: The Religious Bestsellers of Charles Sheldon, Charles Gordon, and Harold Bell Wright* (Bowling Green, Ohio: Bowling Green State University Popular Press, 1988), 8, 9, 40.

19. Ibid., 16.

20. Charles M. Sheldon, *In His Steps: "What Would Jesus Do?"* [1897] (New York: H. M. Caldwell, 1899), 11.

21. Ibid., 268.

22. For a convincing set of illustrations for this point, see Jonathan A. Dorn, " 'Our Best Gospel Appliances': Institutional Churches and the Emergence of Social Christianity in the South End of Boston, 1880–1920" (Ph.D. diss., Harvard University, 1994).

23. Jane Addams, *Twenty Years at Hull House, with Autobiographical Notes* (New York: Macmillan, 1910), 246; Jane Addams, *Newer Ideals of Peace* (New York: Macmillan, 1907), 18, 49; Jane Addams, *Democracy and Social Ethics* (New York: Macmillan, 1902), 32, 68–70, 32–70 passim.

24. Performed on *The Hand That Holds the Bread*, New World Records no. 267.

25. Ibid.

26. Washington Gladden, *Working People and Their Employers* (Boston: Lockwood, Brooks, 1876), 165.

27. Gladden, *The Labor Question* (Boston: Pilgrim, 1911).

28. Rauschenbusch, *Crisis*, 343–422.

29. Ibid., 396.

30. Ibid., 349, 349–56 passim.

31. Ibid., 362–63, 386.

32. Walter Rauschenbusch, *Dare We Be Christians?* (Boston: Pilgrim, 1914), 35–37.

33. Quoted in Dores R. Sharpe, *Walter Rauschenbusch* (New York: Macmillan, 1942), 233.

34. Hopkins, *Social Gospel*, 291.

35. Ibid., 316–17; H. Shelton Smith, Robert T. Handy, and Lefferts A. Loetscher, eds., *American Christianity: An Historical Interpretation with Representative Documents* (2 vols, New York: Scribner's, 1963), 2: 395.

36. May, *Industrial America*, 231.

37. Sharpe, *Rauschenbusch*, 413; May, *Industrial America*, 230.

38. Sharpe, *Rauschenbusch*, 413–14.

5. IN (PARTWAY) FROM THE MARGINS

1. Quoted in Seager, *Parliament*, 58.

2. Quoted in Seager, *Dawn of Pluralism*, 79.

3. Shaw, *Pioneer*; Moses, *Crummell*.

4. Fosdick, *Living*, 66.

5. Theodore T. Munger, *The Freedom of Faith* (Boston: Houghton, Mifflin, 1904), 32.

6. Fiske is quoted in Lyman Abbott, *Reminiscences* (Boston: Houghton Mifflin, 1915), 460.

7. Parker, *Transient and Permanent*, 12.

8. Parker, "Some Account of My Ministry," in *Two Sermons Preached Before the Twenty Eighth Congregational Society* (Boston: Benjamin Mussey, 1853), 14–15.

9. The literature is remarkably extensive, but see especially Clarke, *Ten Great Religions*.

10. Hofstadter, *Social Darwinism*, 171.

11. Dewey, *Darwinism*, 8–9.

12. William Jewett Tucker, *My Generation*, as excerpted in Hutchison, *Protestant Thought*, 19.

13. On this point see Paul Jerome Croce, *Science and Religion in the Era of William James*, vol. 1, *Eclipse of Certainty* (Chapel Hill: University of North Carolina Press, 1995).

14. Meyer, *Modernity*, 245.

15. David Einhorn, *Inaugural Sermon* [1855] (Baltimore, 1909), 7, 11.

16. Meyer, *Modernity*, 269–70. For a dissent from the more ebullient claims about the extent of Pittsburgh's (and Reform's) influence, see Jonathan Sarna, "New Light on the Pittsburgh Platform," *American Jewish History* 76 (March 1987), 367–68 and 358–68 passim.

17. Central Conference, *Pittsburgh*, 8, 17, 24–25.

18. Ibid., 33.

19. Ibid., 24–25.

20. Quoted in W. Gunther Plaut, *The Growth of Reform Judaism: American and European Sources Until 1948* (New York: World Union for Progressive Judaism, 1965), 9.

21. Quoted in Meyer, *Modernity*, 293.

22. *Jewish Chronicle*, July 12, 1912.

23. Ibid.

24. England, *Works*, 7: 32.

25. John Lancaster Spalding, *An Address, Delivered at the Laying of the Cornerstone of the Catholic University* (Washington: B. Cremer, 1888), 13, 21, 16, 13–14.

26. Ibid., 12–13.

27. Ibid., 7.

28. John Ireland, *The Church and Modern Society: Lectures and Addresses* (New York: D. H. McBride, 1903), 107, 108.

29. Ibid., 113, 115.

30. Ibid., 123, 127–28, 130.

31. Samuel Worcester, *Paul on Mars Hill: Or a Christian Survey of the Pagan World* (Andover, Mass.: Flagg and Gould, 1815), 26.

32. Adams, *Dictionary of All Religions*; see McDermott, *Edwards Confronts the Gods*.

33. Gordon, *The Gospel for Humanity*, as excerpted in Hutchison, ed., *Protestant Thought*, 99–100, 103.

34. Ibid., 103.

35. Seager, *World's Parliament*, 50.

36. Robert A. Schneider, "Voice of Many Waters: Church Federation in the Twentieth Century," in Hutchison, *Between the Times*, 103; Jordan, *Evangelical Alliance*; Hill, *World Their Household*; Robert, *Women in Mission*.

6. SURVIVING A WHILE LONGER

1. Strong, *Our Country*, 200 and chapter 14 passim.

2. See, on this point, Lears, *No Place of Grace*. Lears dates the change from 1880.

3. William Graham Sumner, *The Conquest of the United States by Spain* (Boston: D. Estes, 1899), 24–25.

4. P. Meyer, "Cultural Decline," 399, 404, et passim.

5. Josiah Strong, *Expansion Under New World-Conditions* (New York: Baker and Taylor, 1900), 99–100.

6. Leander E. Keck, *The Church Confident* (Nashville: Abingdon, 1993), 71–74.

7. Moses N. Moore, *Orishatukeh Faduma: Liberal Theology and Evangelical Pan-Africanism, 1857–1946* (Lanham, Md.: Scarecrow, 1996), 2–3, 11–12.

8. Hutchison, *Modernist Impulse*, 3–4, 113–15.

9. Ibid., 116.

10. Ahlstrom, *Religious History*, 581. But cf. Jonathan D. Sarna, *A Great Awakening: The Transformation That Shaped Twentieth Century American Judaism and Its Implications for Today* (New York: Council for Initiatives in Jewish Education, 1995).

11. Ellis, *Documents*, 2: 517.

12. Marsden, *Fundamentalism*, 187.

13. Dwight L. Moody, "The Inspiration of the Bible," in *Moody's Latest Sermons* (Chicago: Rhodes and McClure, 1896), 712–13.

14. Charles Hodge, *What Is Darwinism?* (New York: Scribner, Armstrong, 1874), 177.

15. Princeton Theological Seminary, *Proceedings Connected with the Semi-centennial Commemoration of the Professorship of Rev. Charles Hodge . . . April 24, 1872* (New York: A. D. F. Randolph, [1872?]), 52.

16. Thomas Nichols, in *Presbyterian and Reformed Review*, 5 (October 1894), 738.

17. Benjamin B. Warfield, "False Religions and the True" [1903], in *Biblical and Theological Studies* (Philadelphia: Presbyterian and Reformed Publishing, 1952), 565–66, 577.

18. Moody, "Inspiration," 712.

19. George S. Patton, in *Presbyterian and Reformed Review*, 8 (July 1897), 540.

20. Benjamin Warfield, in *Presbyterian and Reformed Review*, 5 (January 1894), 188.

21. Marsden, *Religion and American Culture*, 182–83.

22. Machen, *Christianity and Liberalism*, 2.

23. Ibid., 6, 7, 8.

24. Fosdick, "Shall the Fundamentalists Win?" 172, 181.

25. Philip Gibbs, quoted in Fussell, *Great War*, 8.

26. Ibid., 21–22; Walter Lippman, *Essays in the Public Philosophy* (Boston: Little, Brown, 1955), 10.

27. Fussell, *Great War*, 21.

28. Niebuhr, "What the War Did," 1161.

29. Theodore Dreiser, *An American Tragedy* [1925] (Cleveland: World, 1948), 526–33, 866–71.

30. F. O. Matthiessen, *Theodore Dreiser* (New York: Sloane, 1951), 204; Dreiser, *Tragedy*, 728; F. Scott Fitzgerald, *The Great Gatsby* [1925] (Cambridge: Cambridge University Press, 1991), 141.

31. Matthiessen, *Dreiser*, 210.

32. This was John Chamberlain's plaint in *Farewell to Reform: The Rise, Life, and Decay of the Progressive Mind in America* (New York: John Day, 1932).

33. Bruce Barton, *The Man Nobody Knows: A Discovery of the Real Jesus* (Indianapolis: Bobbs-Merrill, 1925), unpaginated preface.

34. Ibid., 23, 26, 37, 129–30, 143, 125, 177.

35. Winfred Garrison, in *Christian Century*, 42 (July 16, 1925), 927.

36. Fox, *Niebuhr*, 88–89.

37. Reinhold Niebuhr, "The Reverend Doctor Silke," *Christian Century*, 43 (March 11, 1926), 316–17.

38. Ibid., 316.

39. Ibid., 318.

40. Hutchison, *Modernist Impulse*, 206–23, 251–54.

41. Reinhold Niebuhr, *Does Civilization Need Religion?* (New York: Macmillan, 1927), 234.

42. Halford Luccock, "With No Apologies to Barth," *Christian Century*, 56 (August 9, 1939), 972.

43. Ibid.

44. Cyril Connolly, "Comment," in *Horizon*, 20 (December 1949), 362.

45. Fox, *Niebuhr*, 160.

46. H. Richard Niebuhr, Translator's Preface to Paul Tillich, *The Religious Situation* [*Die Religiöse Lage der Gegenwart*, 1926] (New York: Henry Holt, 1932), 9–10.

47. Tillich, *Religious Situation*, 52, 50, 41–53 passim.

48. Reinhold Niebuhr, *Reflections on the End of an Era* (New York: Scribner's, 1934), 170.

49. Tillich, *Religious Situation*, 217–18 et passim.

50. Ibid., 191–219. See also, Tillich, *The Protestant Era*, trans. and ed. James Luther Adams (Chicago: University of Chicago Press, 1948), chapter 14.

51. Ahlstrom, *Religious History*, 941.

52. Niebuhr, *Moral Man*, 49. Cf. Rauschenbusch, *Theology for the Social Gospel*, chapters 8, 9, 11.

53. Norman Thomas, in *The World Tomorrow*, 15 (December 14, 1932), 566.

54. Shirley Jackson Case, in *Journal of Religion*, 13 (July 1933), 360–61.

55. Handy, *Christian America*, chapter 7.

56. "A Protestant Message," *Newsweek* (May 2, 1955), 90; "Parnassus, Coast to Coast," *Time* (June 11, 1956), 67; Arthur M. Schlesinger, Jr., "Reinhold Niebuhr's Rôle in American Political Thought and Life," in *Reinhold Niebuhr: His Religious, Social, and Political Thought*, ed. Charles W. Kegley and Robert W. Bretall (New York: Macmillan, 1956), 150.

57. Fox, *Niebuhr*, 152–53, 196.

58. See Hutchison, *Between the Times*, 6–13.

7. "DON'T CHANGE YOUR NAME"

1. Shelley Berman, "Father and Son," in *Outside Shelley Berman*, Verve recording, MGUS 6107 (1959).

2. Alfred Lord Tennyson, "Locksley Hall," lines 128–29, 178.

3. Michael O. Riley, *Oz and Beyond: The Fantasy World of L. Frank Baum* ([Lawrence]: University Press of Kansas, 1997), 57–58; Suzanne Rahn, *The Wizard of Oz: Shaping an Imaginary World* (New York: Twayne, 1998), 43–51.

4. Quoted in Rydell, *All the World's a Fair*, 48.

5. See, e.g., Thomas A. Woods, "Museums and the Public," *Journal of American History*, 82 (December 1995), 1111–15.

6. Richard H. Seager found a report of the "cannibalism" sign in the diary of his grandfather, Schuyler Fiske Seager IV. Correspondence with author, June 13, 2001.

7. Constance McLaughlin Green, *Washington: Capital City, 1879-1950* (Princeton: Princeton University Press, 1963), 38–39.

8. Quoted in Rydell, *All the World's a Fair*, 65.

9. Ibid., 57.

10. *Official Views of the World's Columbian Exposition* (Chicago: Chicago Photo-gravure, 1893), 327.

11. Reproduced and performed on *The Hand That Holds the Bread*, New World Records, 267.

12. Barrows, *World's Parliament*, vii.

13. Ibid., 171.

14. Ibid., 170–71.

15. Stanton, *Woman's Bible*. See also Kern, *Mrs. Stanton's Bible*, chapter 2.

16. Du Bois, "Christ in Georgia," 70–74.

17. William Seraile, *Voice of Dissent: Theophilus Gould Steward (1843–1924) and Black America* (Brooklyn: Carlson, 1991), 91-92.

18. Ibid., 72.

19. Steward, *End of the World*, 71, 63, 68–71.

20. Ibid., 72.

21. Ibid., 74, 83, 123, 124.

22. Here I am indebted to Michael Elliott of Emory University, who in March 2000 presented a paper at the Charles Warren Center, Harvard, called "Culture, Race, and Narrative: Reading Franz Boas." This is the first chapter in a forthcoming book on "Culture and Narrative in the Age of Realism."

23. [Franz Boas for] United States Immigration Commission, *Changes in Bodily Form of Descendants of Immigrants* (Washington, D.C.: Government Printing Office, 1910).

24. Franz Boas, "The Occurrence of Similar Inventions in Areas Widely Apart," *Science*, 9 (May 20, 1887), 485.

25. Grant, *Great Race*, 11–12.

26. Zangwill, *Melting Pot*; Ralph Waldo Emerson, *Journals* (10 vols., Boston: Houghton Mifflin, 1911), 7: 116; Herman Melville, *Redburn, His First Voyage* (Harmondsworth, England: Penguin, 1976), 239, 238.

27. Zangwill, *Melting Pot*, 33.

28. Ibid., 184–85.

29. Quoted in Maurice Wohlgelernter, *Israel Zangwill: A Study* (New York: Columbia University Press, 1964), 176.

30. Ibid., 184.

31. Zangwill, Afterword [for 1914 and later editions], 203–4.

32. Novak, *Rise*.

33. Sarah Schmidt, "Horace M. Kallen and the 'Americanization' of Zionism: In Memoriam," *American Jewish Archives*, 28 (April 1976), 59; Milton R. Konvitz, "Horace M. Kallen (1882–1974): Philosopher of the Hebraic-American Idea," *American Jewish Year Book* 75 (1974–75), 55.

34. Kallen, "Democracy *versus* the Melting Pot" [1915], rpt. in *Culture and Democracy*, 116.

35. Ibid., 116–17.

36. Franklin D. Roosevelt, "Extemporaneous Remarks Before the Daughters of the American Revolution, Washington, D.C., April 21, 1938," in *The Public Papers and Ad-*

dresses of Franklin D. Roosevelt (13 vols., New York: Random House, 1938–[c. 1950]) 7: 259; Theodore Roosevelt, "Americanism: An Address Delivered Before the Knights of Columbus, Carnegie Hall . . . October 12, 1915." (New York[?]: n.p., 1915[?]), 6; Kallen, Culture, 97–98.

37. Melville, Redburn, 239.

38. Kallen, Culture, 114–15.

39. Bourne, quoted by Stephen J. Whitfield in Introduction to Kallen, Culture and Democracy (New Brunswick, N.J.: Transaction, 1998), xxv; Dewey, quoted ibid., xxvii.

40. Quoted ibid., xxxviii.

8. PROTESTANT-CATHOLIC-JEW

1. Benny Kraut, "A Wary Collaboration: Jews, Catholics, and the Protestant Goodwill Movement," in Hutchison, Between the Times, 193-230.

2. Hutchison, Errand, chapter 6.

3. Toward Brotherhood: Annual Report 1942 of the President of the National Conference of Christians and Jews (New York: NCCJ, 1942), 19.

4. Silk, Spiritual Politics, chapter 2.

5. "Four Chaplains," Time, December 11, 1944.

6. The Eisenhower quotation appears in the New York Times, December 23, 1952. The "down deep" quip originated, as far as I know, with Ernest S. Griffith, a staunch Methodist best known as the founder of what was then called the Legislative Reference Service. (Conversation with the author, 1960.)

7. William Lee Miller, "Piety Along the Potomac," Reporter, August 17, 1954; Herberg, Protestant-Catholic-Jew, chapter 4 and 283.

8. Deborah Pierce, I Prayed Myself Slim (New York: Citadel, 1960).

9. This appeared in the February through May issues and was reprinted as a brochure: James Agee et al., Religion and the Intellectuals: A Symposium (New York: Partisan Review, 1950).

10. Gaustad and Barlow, New Historical Atlas, 349; Herberg, Protestant-Catholic-Jew, 14; Ahlstrom, Religious History, 953.

11. William G. McLoughlin, Modern Revivalism: Charles Grandison Finney to Billy Graham (New York: Ronald, 1959), 482–502.

12. The quotations are from "Will Herberg: A Tribute," National Review, 29 (August 5, 1977), 880–86; "movable seminar": Donald G. Jones, "Herberg as Teacher," 886; "for a time, a sociologist": Nathan Glazer, "Herberg as Sociologist," 881.

13. See, in particular, Ruby Jo Reeves Kennedy, "Single or Triple Melting Pot? Intermarriage Trends in New Haven, 1870–1940," American Journal of Sociology, 49 (January 1944).

14. Marcus Hansen, The Problem of the Third Generation Immigrant (Rock Island, Ill.: Augustana Historical Society, 1938), 9–10.

15. Novak, Rise, 291.

16. Glazer and Moynihan, *Melting Pot*, v, 311.

17. Tom Lehrer, "National Brotherhood Week," *That Was the Year That Was*, recorded in July 1965 (at the Hungry I in San Francisco) for Reprise Records, R6179.

18. Oscar Hammerstein II (lyricist), *South Pacific: A Musical Play*, New York: Random House, 1949.

19. Steven R. Weisman, "Paul Blanshard, Writer and Critic of Catholic Church, Is Dead at 87," *New York Times*, January 30, 1980.

20. Blanshard, *American Freedom*, 5, 6, 4.

21. Ibid., 303, 306.

22. W. E. Garrison, in *Christian Century*, 66 (June 8, 1949), 709.

23. John Courtney Murray, in *Catholic World*, 169 (June 1949), 233.

24. A. S. Foley, in *Commonweal*, 50 (June 17, 1949), 250; *Social Forces*, 28 (December 1949), 226.

25. England, *Works*, 7: 32.

26. Quoted in *Newsweek* (January 25, 1960), 86.

27. McWilliams, *Mask for Privilege*, xii, 224, et passim. See also Baltzell, *Protestant Establishment*.

28. George R. Stewart, *American Ways of Life* (Garden City, N.Y.: Doubleday, 1954), 23, 28.

29. Herberg, *Protestant-Catholic-Jew*, 33.

30. Ibid., 94 and 88–95 passim.

31. Allan Temko, "The Air Academy Chapel: A Critical Appraisal," *Architectural Forum*, 117 (December 1962), 75.

32. The Education as Transformation Project, *Creating Multi-Faith Spaces on College and University Campuses* (Wellesley, Mass.: Education as Transformation Project, 2000).

33. I am informed by Professor David G. Wilkins, the noted art historian at the University of Pittsburgh, that the chapel at that institution provided another precedent. From the start (1939) its main sanctuary was available for use by others besides Protestant Christians. Conversations, August 2002, with Wilkins and with members of the University of Pittsburgh chaplaincy.

34. For the lengthy and complex decision-making process, and the disputes that divided even the architects at Skidmore, Owings, and Merrill, see Sheri Olson, "Lauded and Maligned: The Cadet Chapel," in *Modernism at Mid-Century: The Architecture of the United States Air Force Academy*, ed. Robert Bruegmann (Chicago: University of Chicago Press, 1994), 157–68. The equally extensive, often vitriolic, exchanges in the broader architectural and political communities are sampled in two issues of *Architectural Record*, those of August 1955 and December 1957.

35. "Four Chaplains," *Time* (February 12, 1951), 19.

36. Silk, *Spiritual Politics*, 51.

37. Ibid., 50.

38. Lehrer, "Brotherhood Week."

39. Baldwin, Terkel interviews, 5.

40. Ibid.

41. Ibid., 4.

42. Ibid., 5–6.

43. Baldwin, *Native Son*, 6–7.

44. Ibid., 7.

45. Baldwin, *Nobody Knows My Name* and *No Name in the Street*.

9. WHOSE AMERICA IS IT ANYWAY?

1. Peter Baker, "With Outburst at Fairfax Forum, Race Initiative Finally Hits a Nerve," *Washington Post* (December 18, 1997).

2. Ronan Hoffman, "Yes! Conversion and the Mission of the Church," in *The Conciliar-Evangelical Debate: The Crucial Documents, 1964–1976,* ed. Donald McGavran (South Pasadena, Calif.: William Carey, 1977), 82.

3. Norman Goodall, ed., *The Uppsala Report 1968: Report of the Fourth Assembly of the World Council of Churches* (Geneva: World Council of Churches, 1968), xvii; Hutchison, *Errand,* 180–86.

4. Diana Eck, in *New Religious America,* 2–3, subscribes to the conventional turn-of-the-century estimate of "about six million." For a review and sharp critique of the studies that have produced such figures, see Tom W. Smith, of the National Opinion Research Center in Chicago, *Estimating the Muslim Population in the United States* (New York: American Jewish Committee, 2001). Smith concludes (10) that the "best available estimates" warrant a count of between two and three million.

5. Pete Seeger, *Pete Seeger Singalong in Sanders Theater, Harvard, January 11, 1980,* Folkways Records FXM 36055.

6. Berger, "Crisis," 22.

7. Peter Marshall and David Manuel, *The Light and the Glory* (Old Tappan, N.J.: Revell, 1977), 17.

8. Ibid., 16, 358, 276, 351, 344–45.

9. See, for example, the review in *Christian Century,* 94 (November 2, 1977), 1012.

10. Falwell, *Listen, America!* 261.

11. Noll, Hatch, and Marsden, *Search,* 22, 19, 72, 73.

12. Ibid., 24, 23; Joseph M. McShane, in *America,* 150 (March 24, 1984), 225.

13. Marsden, *Religion and American Culture,* 43; Marsden and Longfield, *Secularization.*

14. United Church of Christ, *New Century Hymnal* (Cleveland: Pilgrim, 1995).

15. Richard L. Christensen, ed., *How Shall We Sing the Lord's Song? An Assessment of the New Century Hymnal* (Centerville, Mass.: Confessing Christ, 1997).

16. Berger, "Crisis," 18.

17. Mary Douglas, "The Effects of Modernization on Religious Change," in Douglas and Tipton, *Religion and America,* 29.

18. William R. Hutchison, "Past Imperfect: History and the Prospect for Liberalism," part 2, *Christian Century* (January 15, 1986), 43.

19. Richard L. Berke, "Unhumbled, Buchanan Backs Bush," *New York Times,* August 18, 1992.

20. Marsden, *Religion and American Culture*, 277.

21. Bellah, *Broken Covenant*.

22. Glazer, *Multiculturalists*, 14.

23. See especially Amos 9, verses 7–9: "Are ye not as the children of the Ethiopians unto me, O children of Israel? . . . For lo, I will command, and I will sift the house of Israel among all the nations, like as grain is sifted in a sieve." For a critique of common notions about the biblical basis for ideas of national chosenness, see Paul Mendes-Flohr, "In Pursuit of Normalcy: Zionism's Ambivalence Toward Israel's Election," in Hutchison and Lehman, *Many Are Chosen*, 211–16.

24. Robert E. Speer was typical in distinguishing this from a "false imperialism which is abhorrent to Christianity." Quoted in Hutchison, *Errand*, 91.

25. Waters, *Ethnic Options*.

26. Hollinger, *Postethnic America*, 116.

27. Glazer, *Multiculturalists*, 160.

28. Hollinger, *Postethnic America*, 20.

29. Rise in interracial marriage: U.S. Census Bureau, *Statistical Abstract of the United States: 1991* (Washington, D.C.: National Technical Information Service, 1991), table 53.

Bibliography

Adams, Hannah. *A Dictionary of All Religions and Religious Denominations: Jewish, Heathen, Mahometan, Christian, Ancient, and Modern.* 4th ed. [1817], ed. Thomas A. Tweed. Atlanta: Scholars Press, 1992.

Ahlstrom, Sydney E. *A Religious History of the American People.* New Haven: Yale University Press, 1972.

Albanese, Catherine L. *America: Religions and Religion.* Belmont, Calif.: Wadsworth, 1981.

Appleby, R. Scott. *"Church and Age Unite": The Modernist Impulse in American Catholicism.* Notre Dame: University of Notre Dame Press, 1992.

Baird, Robert. *Religion in America.* New York: Harper and Brothers, 1844.

Baldwin, James. Interview with Studs Terkel, July 1961. In *Conversations with James Baldwin,* ed. Fred L. Standley and Louis H. Pratt. Jackson: University Press of Mississippi, 1989, 3–23.

———. *Nobody Knows My Name: More Notes of a Native Son.* New York: Dial, 1961.

———. *No Name in the Street.* New York: Dial, 1972.

Baltzell, E. Digby. *The Protestant Establishment: Aristocracy and Caste in America.* New York: Random House, 1964.

Barlow, Philip L. *Mormons and the Bible: The Place of the Latter-day Saints in American Religion.* New York: Oxford University Press, 1991.

Barrows, John Henry, ed. *The World's Parliament of Religions.* 2 vols. Chicago: Parliament, 1893.

Bellah, Robert N. *The Broken Covenant: American Civil Religion in Time of Trial.* New York: Seabury, 1975.

Berger, Peter L. "From the Crisis of Religion to the Crisis of Secularity." In Douglas and Tipton, *Religion and America,* 14–24.

Billington, Ray Allen. *The Protestant Crusade, 1800–1860: A Study of the Origins of American Nativism.* New York: Rinehart, 1938.

Blanshard, Paul. *American Freedom and Catholic Power.* Boston: Beacon, 1949.

Bratt, James D. "Anti-Revivalism in Antebellum America: A Typology." Paper delivered at spring meeting of American Society of Church History, March 20, 2001.

Bushnell, Horace. *Barbarism the First Danger: A Discourse for Home Missions.* New York: American Home Missionary Society, 1847.

———. *Views of Christian Nurture and of Subjects Adjacent Thereto.* Hartford: Edwin Hunt, 1847.

Butler, Jon. *Awash in a Sea of Faith: Christianizing the American People*. Cambridge: Harvard University Press, 1990.

———. *Becoming America: The Revolution Before 1776*. Cambridge: Harvard University Press, 2000.

Carpenter, Joel A. *Revive Us Again: The Reawakening of American Fundamentalism*. New York: Oxford University Press, 1997.

Clark, William M. "Ten Nights in a Barroom," *American Heritage*, 15 (June 1964), 14–17.

Clarke, James Freeman. *Ten Great Religions: An Essay in Comparative Theology*. Boston: Osgood, 1871.

Commager, Henry Steele. "The Blasphemy of Abner Kneeland." *New England Quarterly*, 8 (March 1935), 29–41.

Crèvecoeur, J. Hector St. John. *Letters from an American Farmer*. [1782]. Gloucester, Mass.: Peter Smith, 1968.

Dewey, John. *The Influence of Darwin on Philosophy and Other Essays in Contemporary Thought*. New York: Henry Holt, 1910.

Doan, Ruth Alden. *The Miller Heresy, Millennialism, and American Culture*. Philadelphia: Temple University Press, 1987.

Douglas, Mary, and Stephen M. Tipton, eds. *Religion and America: Spiritual Life in a Secular Age*. Boston: Beacon, 1982.

Du Bois, William E. B. "Jesus Christ in Georgia." *The Crisis*, 3 (November 1911), 70–74.

Eck, Diana L. *A New Religious America: How a "Christian Country" Has Now Become the World's Most Religiously Diverse Nation*. San Francisco: Harper San Francisco, 2001.

Ellis, John Tracy, ed. *Documents of American Catholic History*. 2 vols. Milwaukee: Bruce, 1956.

Emerson, Ralph Waldo. "New England Reformers," "The Transcendentalist," and "Nature." In *Essays and Lectures*, ed. Joel Porte. New York: Library of America, 1983.

England, John. *Works of the Rt Rev. John England*. 7 vols. Cleveland: Arthur H. Clarke, 1908.

Falwell, Jerry. *Listen, America!* Garden City, N.Y.: Doubleday, 1980.

Fosdick, Harry Emerson. *The Living of These Days: An Autobiography*. New York: Harper and Row, 1956.

———. "Shall the Fundamentalists Win?" In Hutchison, *American Protestant Thought*, 170–82.

Fox, Richard W. *Reinhold Niebuhr: A Biography*. New York: Pantheon, 1985.

Franchot, Jenny. *Roads to Rome: The Antebellum Protestant Encounter with Catholicism*. Berkeley: University of California Press, 1994.

Fussell, Paul. *The Great War and Modern Memory*. New York: Oxford University Press, 1975.

Gaustad, Edwin S. *Historical Atlas of Religion in America*. New York: Harper and Row, 1962.

Gaustad, Edwin S., and Philip L. Barlow. *New Historical Atlas of Religion in America*. New York: Oxford University Press, 2001.

Glazer, Nathan. *We Are All Multiculturalists Now*. Cambridge: Harvard University Press, 1997.

Glazer, Nathan, and Daniel Patrick Moynihan. *Beyond the Melting Pot*. Cambridge: MIT Press and Harvard University Press, 1963.

Grant, Madison. *The Passing of the Great Race, or, The Racial Basis of European History.* Rev. ed. New York: Scribner's, 1918.

Gura, Philip F., and Joel Myerson, eds. *Critical Essays on American Transcendentalism.* Boston: G. K. Hall, 1982.

Hambrick-Stowe, Charles E. *Charles G. Finney and the Spirit of American Evangelicalism.* Grand Rapids, Mich.: Eerdmans, 1996.

Handy, Robert T. *A Christian America: Protestant Hopes and Historical Realities.* New York: Oxford University Press, 1971.

Hanley, Mark Y. *Beyond a Christian Commonwealth: The Protestant Quarrel with the American Republic, 1830–1860.* Chapel Hill: University of North Carolina Press, 1994.

Hansen, Klaus J. *Mormonism and the American Experience.* Chicago: University of Chicago Press, 1981.

Hart, D. G. *Defending the Faith: J. Gresham Machen and the Crisis of Conservative Protestantism in America.* Baltimore: Johns Hopkins University Press, 1994.

Herberg, Will. *Protestant-Catholic-Jew: An Essay in American Religious Sociology.* Garden City, N.Y.: Doubleday, 1955.

Hill, Patricia R. *The World Their Household: The American Woman's Mission Movement and Cultural Transformation, 1870–1920.* Ann Arbor: University of Michigan Press, 1985.

Hofstadter, Richard. *Social Darwinism in American Thought.* Philadelphia: University of Pennsylvania Press, 1944.

Hollinger, David A. *Postethnic America: Beyond Multiculturalism.* New York: Basic, 1995.

———. *Science, Jews, and Secular Culture: Studies in Mid-Twentieth-Century American Intellectual History.* Princeton: Princeton University Press, 1996.

Hopkins, Charles Howard. *The Rise of the Social Gospel in American Protestantism, 1865–1915.* New Haven: Yale University Press, 1940.

Hudson, Winthrop S. *The Great Tradition of the American Churches.* New York: Harper and Brothers, 1953.

Hughes, John. "The Decline of Protestantism, and Its Cause" [1850] and "The Catholic Chapter in the History of the United States" [1852]. In *Complete Works of the Most Rev. John Hughes.* Vol. 2, ed. Lawrence Kehoe. New York: Lawrence Kehoe, 1866.

Hutchison, William R. *American Protestant Thought in the Liberal Era.* [1968]. Lanham, Md.: University Press of America, 1985.

———. *Errand to the World: American Protestant Thought and Foreign Missions.* Chicago: University of Chicago Press, 1987.

———. *The Modernist Impulse in American Protestantism.* Cambridge: Harvard University Press, 1976.

———. *The Transcendentalist Ministers: Church Reform in the New England Renaissance.* New Haven: Yale University Press, 1959.

———, ed. *Between the Times: The Travail of the Protestant Establishment in America, 1900–1960.* Cambridge: Cambridge University Press, 1989.

Hutchison, William R., and Hartmut Lehmann, eds. *Many Are Chosen: Divine Election and Western Nationalism.* Minneapolis: Fortress, 1994. Reissued Cambridge: Harvard University Press, 2002.

Jones, Maldwyn A. *American Immigration.* Chicago: University of Chicago Press, 1960.

Jordan, Philip D. *The Evangelical Alliance for the United States of America, 1847–1900*. New York: E. Mellen, 1982.

Kallen, Horace M. *Culture and Democracy in the United States*. New York: Boni and Liveright, 1924.

Kanter, Rosabeth Moss. *Commitment and Community: Communes and Utopia in Sociological Perspective*. Cambridge: Harvard University Press, 1972.

Kern, Kathi. *Mrs. Stanton's Bible*. Ithaca: Cornell University Press, 2001.

Lears, T. J. Jackson. *No Place of Grace: Antimodernism and the Transformation of American Culture 1880–1920*. New York: Pantheon, 1981.

Lippy, Charles H. *Pluralism Comes of Age: American Religious Culture in the Twentieth Century*. Armonk, N.Y.: M. E. Sharpe, 2000.

Lippy, Charles, and Peter Williams. *Encyclopedia of the American Religious Experience*. 3 vols. New York: Scribner's, 1988.

Luker, Ralph E. *The Social Gospel in Black and White*. Chapel Hill: University of North Carolina Press, 1991.

Machen, J. Gresham. *Christianity and Liberalism*. New York: Macmillan, 1923.

Marsden, George M. *Fundamentalism and American Culture: The Shaping of Twentieth Century Evangelicalism, 1870–1925*. New York: Oxford University Press, 1980.

———. *Religion and American Culture*. San Diego: Harcourt Brace Jovanovich, 1990.

Marsden, George M., and Bradley J. Longfield, eds. *The Secularization of the Academy*. New York: Oxford University Press, 1992.

Marty, Martin E., "American Religious History in the Eighties: A Decade of Achievement." *Church History*, 62 (September 1993), 335–77.

———. *The Infidel: Freethought and American Religion*. Cleveland: Meridian, 1961.

———. *Modern American Religion*. Vol. 3, *Under God, Indivisible, 1941–1960*. Chicago: University of Chicago Press, 1996.

———. *A Nation of Behavers*. Chicago: University of Chicago Press, 1976.

———. *The One and the Many: America's Struggle for the Common Good*. Cambridge: Harvard University Press, 1997.

Massa, Mark S. *Catholics and American Culture: Fulton Sheen, Dorothy Day, and the Notre Dame Football Team*. New York: Crossroad, 1999.

May, Henry F. *Protestant Churches and Industrial America*. New York: Harper and Row, 1949.

McDermott, Gerald R. *Jonathan Edwards Confronts the Gods: Christian Theology, Enlightenment Religion, and Non-Christian Faiths*. New York: Oxford University Press, 2000.

McWilliams, Carey. *A Mask for Privilege: Anti-Semitism in America*. Boston: Little, Brown, 1948.

Meyer, Michael A. *Response to Modernity: A History of the Reform Movement in Judaism*. New York: Oxford University Press, 1988.

Meyer, Paul R. "The Fear of Cultural Decline: Josiah Strong's Thought About Reform and Expansion." *Church History*, 42 (September 1973), 396–405.

Miller, F. DeWolfe. *Christopher Pearse Cranch and His Caricatures of New England Transcendentalism*. Cambridge: Harvard University Press, 1951.

Miller, Stuart Creighton. *The Unwelcome Immigrant: The American Image of the Chinese, 1785–1882*. Berkeley: University of California Press, 1969.

Moses, Wilson Jeremiah. *Alexander Crummell: A Study of Civilization and Discontent*. Oxford: Oxford University Press, 1989.

Nelson, E. Clifford, ed. *The Lutherans in North America*. Philadelphia: Fortress, 1975.

Nevin, John W. *The Anxious Bench*. Chambersburg, Pa.: Offices of the *Weekly Messenger*, 1843.

Niebuhr, Reinhold. "What the War Did to My Mind," *Christian Century*, 45 (September 27, 1928), 1161–63.

Noll, Mark A. *A History of Christianity in the United States and Canada*. Grand Rapids, Mich.: Eerdmans, 1992.

Noll, Mark A., Nathan O. Hatch, and George M. Marsden. *The Search for Christian America*. Westchester, Ill.: Crossway, 1983.

Norman, Edward. *The Conscience of the State in North America*. Cambridge: Cambridge University Press, 1968.

Norton, Andrews. *A Discourse on the Latest Form of Infidelity*. Cambridge, Mass.: John Owen, 1839.

———. *Two Articles from the Princeton Review, Concerning the Transcendental Philosophy*. Cambridge, Mass.: J. Owen, 1840.

Norton, Bettina A. *Prints at the Essex Institute*. Salem, Mass.: Essex Institute, 1978.

Novak, Michael. *The Rise of the Unmeltable Ethnics: Politics and Culture in the Seventies*. New York: Macmillan, 1972.

Numbers, Ronald L., and Jonathan M. Butler, eds. *The Disappointed: Millerism and Millenarianism in the Nineteenth Century*. Knoxville: University of Tennessee Press, 1993.

O'Dea, Thomas F. *The Mormons*. Chicago: University of Chicago Press, 1957.

Parker, Theodore. *A Discourse on the Transient and Permanent in Christianity . . . May 19, 1841*. Boston: Freeman and Bolles, 1841.

Porterfield, Amanda. *The Transformation of American Religion: The Story of a Late-Twentieth-Century Awakening*. New York: Oxford University Press, 2001.

Potter, David M. *People of Plenty: Economic Abundance and the American Character*. Chicago: University of Chicago Press, 1954.

Rauschenbusch, Walter. *Christianity and the Social Crisis*. [1907]. New York: Harper and Row, 1964.

———. *A Theology for the Social Gospel*. New York: Macmillan, 1917.

Robert, Dana L. *American Women in Mission: A Social History of Their Thought and Practice*. Macon, Ga.: Mercer University Press, 1996.

Rydell, Robert W. *All the World's a Fair: Visions of Empire at American International Expositions, 1876–1916*. Chicago: University of Chicago Press, 1984.

———. "The World's Columbian Exposition of 1893: Racist Underpinnings of a Utopian Artifact." *Journal of American Culture*, 1 (Summer 1978), 253–75.

Sarna, Jonathan D. *Minority Faiths and the American Protestant Mainstream*. Urbana: University of Illinois Press, 1998.

Schaff, Philip. *America: A Sketch of Its Political, Social, and Religious Character*. [1854]. Cambridge: Harvard University Press, 1961.

Scharnhorst, Gary. "Images of the Millerites in American Literature." *American Quarterly*, 32 (Spring 1980): 19–36.

Schlesinger, Arthur M., Jr. *The Disuniting of America: Reflections on a Multicultural Society.* Rev. edn. New York: Norton, 1998.

Seager, Richard H. *The World's Parliament of Religions: The East/West Encounter, Chicago, 1893.* Bloomington: Indiana University Press, 1995.

———, ed. *The Dawn of Religious Pluralism: Voices from the World's Parliament of Religions, 1893.* La Salle, Ill.: Open Court, 1993.

Shaw, Anna Howard. *The Story of a Pioneer.* New York: Harper and Brothers, 1915.

Shipps, Jan. *Mormonism: The Story of a New Religious Tradition.* Urbana: University of Illinois Press, 1985.

Silk, Mark. *Spiritual Politics: Religion and America Since World War II.* New York: Simon and Schuster, 1988.

Songs of the Mormons and Songs of the West. Library of Congress, Archives of American Folk Song, AAFS L30.

Sparks, Jared. *Memoir of Colonel Ethan Allen.* [Bound with Daniel Chipman, *Memoir of Colonel Seth Warner.*] Middlebury, Vt.: L. W. Clark, 1848.

Stanton, Elizabeth Cady. *The Woman's Bible.* 2 vols. New York: European, 1895–98.

Steward, Theophilus Gould. *The End of the World; or, Clearing the Way for the Fullness of the Gentiles.* Philadelphia: A.M.E. Church Book Rooms, 1888.

Stokes, Anson Phelps. *Church and State in the United States.* 3 vols. New York: Harper and Brothers, 1950.

Strong, Josiah. *Our Country: Its Possible Future and Its Present Crisis* [1885], ed. Jurgen Herbst. Cambridge: Harvard University Press, 1963.

Sumner, William Graham. "The Absurd Effort to Make the World Over." In *The Essays of William Graham Sumner,* ed. Albert G. Keller and Maurice Davie, 91–106. 2 vols. New Haven: Yale University Press, 1934.

———. *What Social Classes Owe to Each Other.* New York: Harper and Brothers, 1883.

Takaki, Ronald. *A Different Mirror: A History of Multicultural America.* Boston: Little, Brown, 1993.

Tocqueville, Alexis de. *Democracy in America.* [1835–40]. 2 vols. New York: Alfred A. Knopf, 1945.

Tuveson, Ernest Lee. *Redeemer Nation: The Idea of America's Millennial Role.* Chicago: University of Chicago Press, 1968.

Tweed, Thomas A. *The American Encounter with Buddhism, 1844–1912: Victorian Culture and the Limits of Dissent.* Bloomington: Indiana University Press, 1992.

———, ed. *Retelling U.S. Religious History.* Berkeley: University of California Press, 1997.

Vale, G[ilbert]. *The Life of Thomas Paine.* New York: Beacon, 1841.

Waters, Mary C. *Ethnic Options: Choosing Identities in America.* Berkeley: University of California Press, 1990.

Wells, Robert V. *Revolutions in Americans' Lives: A Demographic Perspective on the History of Americans, Their Families, and Their Society.* Westport, Conn.: Greenwood, 1982.

White, Ronald C., Jr. *Liberty and Justice for All: Racial Reform and the Social Gospel, 1877–1925.* San Francisco: Harper and Row, 1990.

Wolfe, Alan. *One Nation After All.* New York: Viking, 1998.

Zangwill, Israel. *The Melting Pot: Drama in Four Acts.* [1909]. New York: Macmillan, 1932.

Index